MCTS 70-680
Rapid Review:

Configuring Windows 7

Orin Thomas

Published with the authorization of Microsoft Corporation by:
O'Reilly Media, Inc.
1005 Gravenstein Highway North
Sebastopol, California 95472

ISBN: 978-0-7356-5729-8

1 2 3 4 5 6 7 8 9 LSI 7 6 5 4 3 2

Printed and bound in the United States of America.

Microsoft Press books are available through booksellers and distributors worldwide. If you need support related to this book, email Microsoft Press Book Support at *mspinput@microsoft.com*. Please tell us what you think of this book at *http://www.microsoft.com/learning/booksurvey*.

Acquistions and Developmental Editor: Ken Jones

Production Editor: Kristen Borg

Composition: Dessin Designs

Technical Reviewer: Zachary Niemann

Copyeditor: Nancy Sixsmith

Proofreader: Teresa Horton

Indexer: Angela Howard

Cover Design: Best & Company Design

Cover Composition: Karen Montgomery

Contents at a Glance

Contents

What do you think of this book? We want to hear from you!

Microsoft is interested in hearing your feedback so we can continually improve our
books and learning resources for you. To participate in a brief online survey, please visit:

microsoft.com/learning/booksurvey

What do you think of this book? We want to hear from you!

Microsoft is interested in hearing your feedback so we can continually improve our
books and learning resources for you. To participate in a brief online survey, please visit:

microsoft.com/learning/booksurvey

Chapter 4   **Configuring Network Connectivity**   **65**

Introduction

This *Rapid Review* is designed to help you assess—and complete—your readiness for MCTS Exam 70-680: Windows 7, Configuring. The *Rapid Review* series is intended for exam candidates who already have a solid grasp on the exam objectives through a combination of experience, skills, and study and could use a concise review guide to help with the final stages of preparation.

The 70-680 exam is aimed at professionals who have at least one year of experience supporting desktop operating systems in organizational environments. Although this experience focuses on the Windows 7 operating system, you might have real-world experience with other Windows client operating systems, such as Windows Vista and Windows XP that you can build on and apply. Most candidates who take this exam work in an environment where Windows 7 either has been deployed or is about to be deployed. It is important to note that you should have real world experience with Windows 7 prior to taking the 70-680 exam and that having practical knowledge is a key component to achieving a passing mark.

This book will review every concept described in the following exam objective domains:

- Installing, Upgrading, and Migrating to Windows 7
- Deploying Windows 7
- Configuring Hardware and Applications
- Configuring Network Connectivity
- Configuring Access to Resources
- Configuring Mobile Computing
- Monitoring and Maintaining Systems that Run Windows 7
- Configuring Backup and Recovery Options

This is a Rapid Review and not a comprehensive exam prep or skills training resource such as the Microsoft Press *Self-Paced Training Kit*. The book covers every exam objective for the 70-680 exam as presented in the objective domain. The exam team does not give anyone access to the exam questions and regularly adds new questions to the exam, which makes complete coverage a real challenge. The coverage in this book is as complete as possible based on the information available. This book should be an excellent supplement to your existing independent study and real-world experience with the product.

If you encounter a topic in this book that you do not feel completely comfortable with, you can visit the links described in the text, in addition to researching the topic further using Microsoft TechNet, as well as consulting support forums. If you review a topic and find that you don't understand it, you should consider consulting books such as the *Windows® 7 Resource Kit* and the *MCTS Self-Paced Training Kit (Exam 70-680): Configuring Windows® 7* from Microsoft Press. You can also purchase practice tests, or use the one available with the Training Kit, to determine if you need further study on particular topics.

NOTE The *MCTS Self-Paced Training Kit (Exam 70-680): Configuring Windows® 7* provides comprehensive coverage of each 70-680 exam objective, along with exercises, review questions, and practice tests. The Training Kit also includes a discount voucher for the exam.

Microsoft Certified Professional Program

Microsoft certifications provide the best method for proving your command of current Microsoft products and technologies. The exams and corresponding certifications are developed to validate your mastery of critical competencies as you design and develop, or implement and support, solutions with Microsoft products and technologies. Computer professionals who become Microsoft certified are recognized as experts and are sought after industry-wide. Certification brings a variety of benefits to the individual and to employers and organizations.

> **MORE INFO** For a full list of Microsoft certifications, go to *www.microsoft.com/ learning/mcp/default.asp*.

Acknowledgments

I'd like to thank my good mate Ken Jones at O'Reilly for his support in getting the Rapid Review series off the ground. It's always a pleasure to work with Ken, and I'm forever thankful for the opportunities that he presents me with as an author.

I'd also like to thank Zachary Niemann, the technical reviewer; Kristen Borg, the production editor; Dan Fauxsmith, the production manager; and Nancy Sixsmith, the copy editor. Without your assistance and professionalism, the book wouldn't have come together as well as it has!

As always I'd like to thank my wife Oksana and son Rooslan for their patience with me during the writing process.

I'd also like to thank you, the reader, for picking up this book. If you have any questions about anything and you want to get in touch with me, you can find me on Twitter: *http://twitter.com/OrinThomas*.

Support & Feedback

The following sections provide information on errata, book support, feedback, and contact information.

Errata

We've made every effort to ensure the accuracy of this book and its companion content. Any errors that have been reported since this book was published are listed on our Microsoft Press site at oreilly.com:

http://go.microsoft.com/FWLink/?Linkid=242588

If you find an error that is not already listed, you can report it to us through the same page.

If you need additional support, email Microsoft Press Book Support at *mspinput@ microsoft.com*.

Please note that product support for Microsoft software is not offered through the addresses above.

We Want to Hear from You

At Microsoft Press, your satisfaction is our top priority, and your feedback our most valuable asset. Please tell us what you think of this book at:

http://www.microsoft.com/learning/booksurvey

The survey is short, and we read every one of your comments and ideas. Thanks in advance for your input!

Stay in Touch

Let's keep the conversation going! We're on Twitter: *http://twitter.com/Microsoft-Press*

CHAPTER 1

Installing, Upgrading, and Migrating to Windows 7

Approximately 14 percent of the 70-680 exam focuses on the topic of installing, upgrading, and migrating to Microsoft Windows 7. That means that you need to have a good grasp of how to perform a clean installation, how to upgrade to Windows 7 from previous editions of the Windows client operating system, and how to migrate user profiles and data to Windows 7 from previous versions of Windows.

This chapter covers the following objectives:

- Objective 1.1: Perform a clean installation
- Objective 1.2: Upgrade to Windows 7 from previous versions of Windows
- Objective 1.3: Migrate user profiles

Objective 1.1: Perform a clean installation

This objective requires you to demonstrate that you know how to determine whether a particular hardware profile is appropriate for the Windows 7 operating system, how to perform a traditional and dual-boot installation, the different methods that you can use to deploy Windows 7, and the steps that you should take to prepare each installation source.

Exam need to know

- Identifying hardware requirements
  For example: How to determine whether computer hardware meets the minimum requirement for the deployment of Windows 7.
- Setting up as the sole operating system
  For example: How to deploy Windows 7 as the only operating system on a computer.

- Setting up as dual boot

  For example: How to configure Windows 7 to dual boot with Windows Vista.

- Installation methods

  For example: Choose when to use a PXE-based or media-based installation.

- Boot from the source of installation

  For example: How to determine when to use bootable media to install Windows 7.

- Preparing the installation source USB, CD, Network share, WDS

  For example: How to configure a USB installation source.

Identifying hardware requirements

You need to know the minimum hardware requirements for the 32-bit and 64-bit versions of Windows 7.

True or False? The minimum amount of disk space required for Windows 7 Enterprise edition (x64) is 16 GB.

Answer: *False.* The hardware requirements for the 32-bit (x86) editions of Windows 7 differ from the hardware requirements of the 64-bit (x64) edition of Windows 7. Windows 7 has the following hardware requirements:

- 1 GHz or faster 32-bit or 64-bit processor, depending on whether you are installing the x86 or x64 version of an edition.

- 1 GB RAM (for 32-bit editions) or 2 GB RAM (for 64-bit editions). The 32-bit editions do not support more than 4 GB of RAM.

- 16 GB available hard disk space (32-bit) or 20 GB (64-bit)

- Device that supports DirectX9 Graphics with a WDDM 1.0 or higher compatible graphics adapter.

Although these are the listed minimum hardware requirements, in some cases it might be possible to actually install Windows 7 on computers that don't reach these specifications.

> **EXAM TIP** When considering answering an exam question, use an answer based on the published documentation rather than what you might have been able to accomplish shoehorning Windows 7 onto a computer in the real world.

True or False? Windows 7 Home Premium edition will support a system configuration where there are two separate physical processors, each with eight cores.

Answer: *False.* The number of processors supported by Windows 7 depends on the edition of Windows 7. For example:

- Windows 7 Professional, Enterprise, and Ultimate allow for two physical processors.

- Windows Starter, Home Basic, and Home Premium recognize only a single processor.

A single processor can have multiple cores with dual-core, quad-core, and 8-core processors common on desktop and mobile configurations. Windows 7 SP1 supports the following:

- The 32-bit versions of Windows 7 can support up to 32 processor cores.
- The 64-bit versions of Windows 7 Enterprise and Ultimate edition support up to 256 processor cores.

MORE INFO To learn more about the hardware requirements of Windows 7, consult the following webpage: *http://windows.microsoft.com/en-US/windows7/products/ system-requirements.*

EXAM TIP Understand the difference between processors and cores.

Setting up as the sole operating system

You need to know what steps to take to perform a fresh installation of Windows 7 as the sole operating system on a computer.

True or False? You can install a bootable version of the Windows 7 operating system on a removable USB disk drive.

Answer: *False.* You can install Windows 7 on a local hard disk drive as long as there is enough space on the volume. You can't install the Windows 7 operating system on a removable USB disk drive. When setting up Windows 7 as the sole operating system on a computer that has no existing operating system, you have several options:

- Install Windows 7 on a computer that does not have an operating system installed.
- Upgrade a previous version of Windows to Windows 7. This topic is covered later in the chapter.
- Install Windows 7 in a multiboot configuration. This topic is also covered later in this chapter.

Installing Windows 7 on a computer that does not have an existing operating system requires some form of bootable media. You can use a DVD-ROM with the Windows 7 installation media installed, a specially prepared USB storage device, or a PXE boot to deploy Windows 7.

EXAM TIP You can also use the WinPE environment in advanced deployment scenarios.

To install Windows 7, perform the following steps:

1. Power on the computer. The computer boots to the Install Windows screen.
2. On the Please Read The License Terms page, review the license terms and choose I Accept The License Terms. Click Next.
3. On the Which Type Of Installation Do You Want? page, click Custom. You use Custom for all installations except upgrades.

4. On the Where Do You Want To Install Windows? page, you can choose an existing partition that has unallocated space. You can also choose to partition and format a disk by clicking New or Drive Options (Advanced) if there is an existing partition scheme. You don't need to choose to format and partition the hard disk and can allow the Windows 7 installation routine to perform this task for you by choosing an existing partition with unallocated space as long as it meets the minimum size requirements. If a computer has a special type of disk drive that is not recognized, you can click Load Driver to load the hard disk drive's driver. This process is necessary only if the hard disk drive is not recognized by the installation routine.

5. Once you have selected the location, installation begins. The computer reboots, and you need to specify a user name and a computer name. The specified user name will be the default administrative account for the computer. You are asked to provide a password for this default administrative account and to provide a password hint.

6. With a traditional installation, you are given the option to provide a product key and to automatically activate Windows 7 when an Internet connection is detected. It is possible to click Skip to bypass entering the product key and activation.

7. You choose what the update settings the computer will use. You learn more about updates in Chapter 7, "Monitoring and Maintaining Systems that Run Windows 7."

8. You choose the time and date settings.

9. You choose the computer's current network location. You learn more about network locations in Chapter 4, "Configuring Network Connectivity."

MORE INFO To learn more about installing Windows 7 as the sole operating system on a computer, consult the following webpage: *http://windows.microsoft.com/en-US/windows7/Installing-and-reinstalling-Windows-7.*

EXAM TIP Remember that if a computer has an existing operating system, you have the option of upgrading the existing installation or installing in a dual-boot configuration. Both these options are covered later in this chapter.

True or False? Windows 7 Professional edition supports VHD boot.

Answer: *False.* It is possible to install Windows 7 on a Virtual Hard Disk (VHD) file stored on an NTFS-formatted volume if the VHD is configured with an appropriate amount of free space. This type of deployment is known as native VHD boot. Windows 7 Enterprise and Windows 7 Ultimate support native VHD boot. Native VHD boot involves configuring a VHD file as a boot volume and installing all the operating system volume files within the VHD, as opposed to on the formatted hard disk drive, which is the case with traditional single operating system deployments. You learn more about native VHD boot in Chapter 2, "Deploying Windows 7."

MORE INFO To learn more about VHD native boot, consult the following webpage: *http://technet.microsoft.com/en-us/library/gg318048(WS.10).aspx.*

Setting up as dual boot

You need to know the conditions under which you can configure Windows 7 to dual boot, also known as multiboot, with one or more operating systems.

True or False? You need to have more than one partition if you are going to dual boot Windows 7 Home Premium edition with Windows XP.

Answer: *True*. It is possible to configure a computer dual boot as long as you have enough free disk space to create an appropriately sized second partition or if such a partition already exists. You can also install Windows 7 in dual-boot configuration by installing Windows 7 on a separate disk drive. You usually configure Windows 7 to dual boot by installing Windows 7 on a separate partition (although it's possible to use a single partition with VHD boot, an advanced scenario you learn about in Chapter 2). When configuring Windows 7 to dual boot with Windows XP or Windows Vista, you must ensure that the older operating system is installed prior to the installation of Windows 7. You can't use the built-in operating system tools to install Windows 7 first and then install Windows XP in a dual-boot configuration.

EXAM TIP Unless a VHD boot is mentioned, dual boot means multiple partitions.

True or False? You must choose the Custom installation type when installing Windows 7 in dual-boot configuration.

Answer: *True*. To install Windows 7 in dual-boot configuration, perform the following general steps:

1. Ensure that the original operating system is completely backed up.
2. Insert the Windows 7 installation media. Setup either launches automatically or you can run setup.exe to trigger installation. In most cases, you do not boot from the installation media when configuring a dual-boot installation. An exception to this rule is when you are configuring multiboot with VHD files.
3. On the Install Windows menu, click Install Now.
4. On the Get Important Updates For Installation page, choose to retrieve updates. On the Please Read The License Terms page, accept the license terms.
5. On the What Type Of Installation Do You Want? page, choose Custom.
6. On the Where Do You Want To Install Windows? page, choose a partition or disk different from the one on which the original operating system is present.

You can configure Windows 7 to dual boot with another installation of Windows 7. When dual booting between installations of Windows 7, it doesn't matter which Windows 7 edition or version you install first.

MORE INFO To learn more about booting Windows 7 in multiboot configurations, consult the following webpage: *http://windows.microsoft.com/en-US/windows7/Install-more-than-one-operating-system-multiboot.*

EXAM TIP Remember that older versions of Windows must be installed before you install Windows 7.

Installation methods

You need to know different ways to deploy the Windows 7 operating system when performing a clean installation.

True or False? You can install Windows 7 using a CD-ROM as an installation source.

Answer: *False.* You can perform a fresh install of Windows 7 when one of the following locations is configured to host the Windows 7 installation files:

- **DVD-ROM** This can be a DVD-ROM manufactured by Microsoft or a DVD-ROM that you create from a disk image file in ISO format.
- **USB Installation Media** A specially prepared bootable USB disk that holds the Windows 7 installation files.
- **Network Share** A network share can hold the Windows 7 installation files. You can connect to this network share when booted from Windows PE.
- **PXE Boot** In this scenario you perform a PXE boot using a wired network card. You can't PXE boot using a wireless network adapter. In PXE boot scenarios, the Windows 7 installation image is deployed from a machine running Windows Server 2008, Windows Server 2008 R2, Windows Server 2003 with Service Pack 2, or Windows Server 2003 R2 with Windows Deployment Services (WDS) installed. System Center Configuration Manager 2012 leverages WDS for operating system deployment.

You can't directly install Windows 7 from CD-ROM as a single CD-ROM does not have the capacity to hold the Windows 7 installation files. You can boot from a CD-ROM that is configured with WinPE and then connect to an installation source. You can install Windows 7 from an ISO image if you are installing Windows 7 as a virtual machine hosted on Hyper-V, but this scenario is not directly addressed by the 70-680 exam. You can also buy a copy of Windows 7 from Microsoft online and perform an installation after downloading an installer file to your computer, but this is an upgrade scenario addressed later in this chapter.

EXAM TIP When considering the best deployment method, take into account the computer hardware.

Boot from the source of installation

You need to know which deployment methods allow you to boot from the installation media and which require you to be running an existing operating system.

True or False? You can install Windows 7 directly from an external USB CD-ROM drive.

Answer: *False.* You can perform a clean installation of Windows 7 by booting off the installation media and installing the operating system. You can install Windows 7 in the following ways using this technique:

- **Boot from DVD-ROM**   Requires the computer to have a DVD-ROM drive or an external DVD-ROM drive attached. The installation files are on the DVD, which can be a retail copy of Windows 7 or a DVD created from a Windows 7 ISO file. You can boot from an externally attached DVD-ROM drive that is connected from a USB port to install Windows 7. You can also boot from a DVD-ROM or CD-ROM that is configured as a WinPE disk, but you can't perform a direct installation in this manner and have to make a remote connection to the installation files.
- **Boot from USB flash drive**   Requires the computer to have a USB port and an appropriate USB flash device prepared with the Windows 7 installation files. It is also possible to boot from a USB drive configured as a WinPE disk.
- **PXE**   Requires a PXE boot server to be present on the network. You must use a wired network connection to PXE boot a computer; it is not possible to PXE boot off a wireless network using Windows Deployment Services.

To boot from the installation source might require you to modify the computer's BIOS. Not all computer BIOSs are configured to boot the computer off USBs, DVDs, or network adapters. You might need to restart your computer for the new BIOS settings to take effect.

MORE INFO   To learn more about booting Windows 7 from the installation media, consult the following document: *http://windows.microsoft.com/en-US/windows7/Start-your-computer-from-a-Windows-7-installation-disc-or-USB-flash-drive.*

EXAM TIP   A PXE boot requires a PXE-compliant network adapter.

Preparing the installation source: USB, CD, network share, WDS

You need to know what steps to take to prepare certain installation source types so that they can be used to deploy the Windows 7 operating system. Even though the objective mentions CD, you can't directly install Windows 7 using CD-ROMs—only DVD-ROMs.

True or False? You can use third-party, DVD-authoring software to burn Windows 7 installation images to DVD-ROM**.**

Answer: *True*. Windows 7 installation media is commercially available on DVD-ROM. This media requires no preparation and can be used immediately. If your organization has a volume licensing agreement with Microsoft or if you have an MSDN or TechNet subscription, you can obtain disk image files in ISO format that you can burn to DVD-ROM by using the Burn Disc Image option in Windows 7 and Windows Server 2008 R2 or a third-party DVD-authoring utility.

EXAM TIP   You can also use custom images with DVD-ROM, though these are usually deployed using other methods.

True or False? When preparing a USB storage device to function as Windows 7 installation media, you format it using the NTFS file system.

Answer: *False.* A USB storage device needs to be approximately 4 GB in size or larger to function as installation media for Windows 7. Preparing the USB storage device will wipe all data from that device. To prepare a USB storage device to function as Windows 7 installation media, perform the following steps:

1. Connect a USB storage device to a computer running Windows 7, Windows Vista, Windows Server 2008, or Windows Server 2008 R2.
2. Open an elevated command prompt and type **diskpart**.
3. At the DISKPART> prompt, type **list disk**. Identify the number that represents the USB storage device. Type **select disk X** to select this storage device (X is the device number)
4. Type the following commands:

```
clean
create partition primary
format fs=fat32 quick
active
exit
```

5. Copy all the files located on the Windows 7 installation media across to the USB storage device.

True or False? You must boot using a WinPE disk or USB storage device to perform a clean installation of Windows 7 on a computer that does not have an existing operating system.

Answer: *True.* Preparing a network share to host the installation files is a matter of copying the contents of the Windows 7 installation media to a share that will be accessible to the computers on which you want to install Windows 7. If you are upgrading a computer to Windows 7 or configuring a multiboot deployment, you access this network location from within Windows. If you are performing a clean installation, you boot using a WinPE disk or USB storage device and then map a network drive. The installation media includes the Win PE environment. The account that you use to map the network drive must have read access to the shared folder that hosts the Windows 7 installation files.

> **EXAM TIP** Remember when you need to use a WinPE disk or USB storage device.

True or False? You can install the WDS role on computers running Windows 7 Enterprise edition.

Answer: *False.* WDS is a role that you can install on computers running the Windows Server 2008, Windows Server 2008 R2, Windows Server 2003 Service Pack 2, and Windows Server 2003 R2 operating systems. You can configure WDS to deploy

Windows 7 through PXE boot. This requires that the computer has a PXE-capable network adapter that can connect to a wired network. If the computer's wired network adapter is not PXE-compliant, it might be possible to boot off of a WDS discover image, a special form of bootable image that contains extra network drivers and allows for the detection of WDS servers.

To prepare the WDS server, you must install the WDS role and then populate the WDS server with Windows image files. Windows image files are stored in .WIM format. The Windows 7 installation media contains the file install.wim. You can use this file with WDS to deploy Windows 7. An advantage of using WDS on Windows Server 2008 and Windows Server 2008 R2 to deploy Windows 7 is that it uses multicast transmissions to deploy the operating system, meaning that one WDS server can be used to simultaneously deploy many copies of Windows 7. You learn more about managing .WIM files in Chapter 2.

MORE INFO To learn more about WDS, consult the following webpage: *http://tech-net.microsoft.com/en-us/library/dd744343(WS.10).aspx.*

EXAM TIP Remember that to use WDS you need to be able to perform a PXE boot or boot off a discover image.

Can you answer these questions?

You can find the answers to these questions at the end of the chapter.

1. What is the maximum number of physical processors supported by Windows 7 Enterprise (x64)?

2. What steps must you take to prepare a computer running Windows XP so it can be configured to dual boot with the Windows 7 operating system?

3. You have placed the Windows 7 installation files on a network share. You want to boot a computer that doesn't have an existing operating system and use the files on the network share to install Windows 7. What method should you use to boot the computer?

4. In what format are the Windows image files that you use to populate WDS with Windows 7 installation images?

Objective 1.2: Upgrade to Windows 7 from previous versions of Windows

This objective requires you to demonstrate that you know the conditions under which it is possible to upgrade from Windows Vista to Windows 7, from Windows XP to Windows 7, and when it is possible to upgrade one edition of Windows 7 to another edition.

Exam need to know

- Upgrading from Windows Vista

  For example: How to know which versions of Windows 7 you can upgrade to on a computer running the x86 version of Windows Vista Business edition.

- Migrating from Windows XP

  For example: How to know which steps to take to migrate from Windows XP to Windows 7.

- Upgrading from one edition of Windows 7 to another edition of Windows 7

  For example: How to know how to use Windows Anytime Upgrade to upgrade from one edition of Windows 7 to another.

Upgrading from Windows Vista

You need to know the conditions under which you can upgrade a computer running Windows Vista to Windows 7.

True or False? You can upgrade from Windows Vista Business (x64) to Windows 7 Enterprise (x64).

Answer: *True.* It is only possible to perform upgrades from specific editions of Windows Vista to specific editions of Windows 7. You can upgrade Windows Vista to Windows 7 under the following conditions:

- You can only upgrade to a version of Windows 7 that has the same processor. You can upgrade from an x86 version of Windows Vista to an x86 version of Windows 7 and from an x64 version of Windows Vista to an x64 version of Windows 7. You can't upgrade from an x86 version of Windows Vista to an x64 version of Windows 7 or from an x64 version of Windows Vista to an x86 version of Windows 7.

- You can't upgrade from one language version to another (for example, from a Russian version of Windows Vista to an English version of Windows 7).

- You can upgrade from Windows Vista Home Basic to the Home Basic, Home Premium, and Ultimate editions of Windows 7.

- You can upgrade from Windows Vista Home Premium to the Home Premium and Ultimate editions of Windows 7.

- You can upgrade from Windows Vista Business to the Professional, Enterprise, and Ultimate editions of Windows 7.

- You can upgrade from Windows Vista Enterprise to the Enterprise edition of Windows 7.

- You can upgrade from Windows Vista Ultimate to the Ultimate edition of Windows 7.

MORE INFO To learn more about supported upgrade paths, consult the following TechNet document: *http://technet.microsoft.com/en-us/library/dd772579(WS.10).aspx.*

EXAM TIP Remember to not only keep track of edition but also architecture when answering upgrade questions.

True or False? Upgrading from Windows Vista to Windows 7 will retain applications and data.

Answer: *True*. Upgrading from Windows Vista to Windows 7 has the benefit of retaining applications and data without having to perform a complex migration process using a tool such as the User State Migration Tool (USMT). Prior to upgrading, you should run the Windows 7 Upgrade Advisor. This is an application you can download from Microsoft's website that can check to determine whether there are any known compatibility issues with applications or hardware. A similar check is performed when you run the actual upgrade to Windows 7.

> **MORE INFO** To learn more about the Windows 7 Upgrade Advisor, consult the following document: *http://windows.microsoft.com/en-US/windows/downloads/upgrade-advisor.*

True or False? You choose Custom on the What Type Of Installation Do You Want? page when upgrading a computer from Windows Vista to Windows 7.

Answer: *False*. You launch an upgrade to Windows 7 from Windows Vista by running setup.exe from the location in which the installation files are present. You need to be a member of the local Administrators group on the computer running Windows Vista to successfully perform an upgrade. Inserting the DVD installation media into the DVD-ROM drive or connecting the USB installation media will also launch a screen from which you can begin the upgrade. When performing an upgrade to Windows 7, ensure that you choose the Upgrade installation option rather than the Custom installation option. You choose the Custom installation option only in dual-boot scenarios. Prior to starting the upgrade, ensure that the following conditions are met:

- You have upgraded Windows Vista to Service Pack 1 or later.
- The volume on which Windows Vista is installed has at least 10 GB of free disk space.

You can roll back a failed upgrade at any point in the process up until you perform a successful logon to the Windows 7 operating system.

> **MORE INFO** To learn more about Windows 7 upgrade paths, consult the following webpage: *http://technet.microsoft.com/en-us/library/dd772579(WS.10).aspx.*

> **EXAM TIP** Remember that Windows Vista needs at least Service Pack 1 to be upgraded to Windows 7.

Migrating from Windows XP

You need to know which steps to take to configure a computer running Windows XP so that Windows 7 is the sole operating system.

True or False? You can directly upgrade a computer running Windows XP to Windows 7.

Answer: *False*. It is not possible to upgrade directly from Windows XP to Windows 7. You can perform a migration in which you replace the Windows XP operating system with the Windows 7 operating system. If you have an extra disk or can create a separate partition with an appropriate amount of disk space, you can configure the computer to dual boot.

EXAM TIP You can upgrade directly from Windows XP to Windows Vista and then from Windows Vista to Windows 7.

Prior to beginning the migration process, make a complete backup of the computer running Windows XP. Use the Windows 7 Upgrade Advisor to determine whether existing devices and applications will function with Windows 7. Even though you'll be installing a separate operating system, the migration process assumes that you will be reinstalling the same applications that were running on the computer running Windows XP on the computer running Windows 7. Use Windows Easy Transfer to save important files and settings if performing a small number of migrations. Use the USMT if you need to perform a large number of migrations. You'll learn more about migrating data later in this chapter.

True or False? You choose Upgrade on the What Type Of Installation Do You Want? page when migrating a computer from Windows XP to Windows 7.

Answer: *False*. To transition a computer running Windows XP as its sole operating system to Windows 7 as its sole operating system, perform the following steps:

1. If you are migrating to an x86 version of Windows 7, log on to Windows XP with an account that has local administrative rights and perform one of the following steps:
   - If you have purchased Windows 7 from Microsoft's online store and downloaded the installation file, double-click that file to trigger Windows 7 Setup.
   - If you have a specially prepared USB storage device that hosts the Windows 7 installation files, connect this device to the computer. This should trigger Windows 7 Setup. If it does not, open setup.exe directly from the device.
   - If you have a Windows 7 installation DVD-ROM, place it in the DVD-ROM drive. This should trigger Windows 7 Setup. If it does not, open setup.exe directly from the device.
2. On the Install Windows page, click Install Now.
3. Proceed through the Get Important Updates For Installation page and the Please Read The License Terms page.
4. On the Which Type Of Installation Do You Want? page, choose Custom.
5. Choose the disk partition that hosts the Windows XP installation.
6. In the Windows.old dialog box, click OK.
7. Continue the installation as normal.

If you want to install the x64 version of Windows 7, boot from the installation media and then follow steps 2 to 7.

MORE INFO To learn more about migrating from Windows XP to Windows 7, consult the following webpage: *http://windows.microsoft.com/en-US/windows7/help/ upgrading-from-windows-xp-to-windows-7*.

EXAM TIP Remember that you can't directly upgrade from Windows XP to Windows 7.

Upgrading from one edition of Windows 7 to another edition of Windows 7

You need to know the possible upgrade paths available using Windows Anytime Upgrade.

True or False? You can use Windows Anytime Upgrade to upgrade from Windows 7 Professional to Windows 7 Enterprise.

Answer: *False.* You can use Windows Anytime Upgrade to upgrade from certain editions of Windows 7 to editions with more features. Windows Anytime Upgrade involves running the application and entering the new edition's license key if you have one available or going online to purchase a key. You can't use Windows Anytime Upgrade to do the following:

- Upgrade from an x86 edition to an x64 edition.
- Upgrade from an x64 edition to an x86 edition.
- Upgrade to or from Windows 7 Enterprise.

You can use Windows Anytime Upgrade to perform the following edition upgrades:

- Windows 7 Home Basic to Home Premium, Professional, and Ultimate editions
- Windows 7 Home Premium to Professional and Ultimate editions
- Windows 7 Professional to Ultimate editions
- Starter to Home Premium, Professional, and Ultimate editions

MORE INFO To learn more about Windows 7 upgrade paths, consult the following webpage: *http://technet.microsoft.com/en-us/library/dd772579(WS.10).aspx*.

EXAM TIP Remember which editions of Windows 7 it is possible to upgrade to and from using Windows Anytime Upgrade.

Can you answer these questions?

You can find the answers to these questions at the end of the chapter.

1. You want to upgrade your organization's computers from Windows Vista to Windows 7. What prerequisites should the computers running Windows Vista meet before you attempt the upgrade?

2. Your organization has Windows Vista Enterprise (x64) deployed. To which versions and editions of Windows 7 can you upgrade?

3. You have a computer running the x64 version of Windows 7 Home Premium. Which editions of Windows 7 can you upgrade to using Windows Anytime Upgrade?

4. Which tool should you use to determine whether any hardware or applications installed on a computer running Windows Vista have compatibility problems with Windows 7?

Objective 1.3: Migrate user profiles

This objective requires you to demonstrate that you know which tools to use to migrate user profile data from one computer to another from a previous version of Windows to Windows 7, and the situations in which you would perform a side-by-side versus wipe-and-load migration.

Exam need to know

- Side-by-side vs. wipe and load

  For example: How to determine when it is appropriate to use a side-by-side or wipe-and-load migration.

- Migrating from one machine to another

  For example: How to migrate from Windows 7 on one computer to Windows 7 on another.

- Migrating from previous versions of Windows

  For example: How to migrate profile data from Windows XP to Windows 7.

Side-by-side vs. wipe and load

You need to know the difference between these two migration types, and what factors dictate that you use one migration type over another.

True or False? A side-by-side migration is appropriate if your organization's computers had 512 MB of RAM and 10 GB hard disk drives and could not be upgraded.

Answer: *True.* When replacing a user's computer and the original computer has profile data locally stored, you need to perform a side-by-side migration. A side-by-side migration involves shifting user profile data from one computer to another computer. Side-by-side migrations can use removable storage or a network location to host exported profile data. You use side-by-side migrations in desktop replacement scenarios. Desktop replacement scenarios are common when an organization is transitioning to Windows 7 and its current hardware does not support the operating system.

> **EXAM TIP** When considering whether desktop replacement is necessary, look at the hardware specifications listed in the question.

True or False? A wipe-and-load migration is appropriate in your organization if you currently have desktop computers that have the 64-bit version of Windows XP installed, 100 GB of free space on the hard disk drives, and 8 GB of RAM.

Answer: *True.* A wipe-and-load migration involves removing the current operating system and replacing it with Windows 7. Wipe-and-load migrations can use removable storage, a network location, or a locally fixed disk if a hard-link migration store is used with USMT. Wipe-and-load migrations are suitable when your organization's computers can run Windows 7 current hardware. Wipe-and-load migrations require that you have a location to store profile data, either on an external drive, a network share, or using a hard-link migration. You might choose to perform a wipe-and-load migration rather than an upgrade when Windows Vista is the original operating system if you want to migrate from an x86 version of Windows Vista to an x64 version of Windows 7.

> **MORE INFO** To learn more about Windows 7 upgrade and migration, consult the following webpage: *http://technet.microsoft.com/en-us/library/dd446674(WS.10).aspx.*

Migrating from one machine to another

You need to know how to perform a side-by-side migration and can choose the appropriate tool to perform this migration given a specific set of conditions.

True or False? You can use Windows Easy Transfer to migrate data from computers running Windows XP (x64) to Windows 7 (x64).

Answer: *True.* Windows Easy Transfer is a tool included with Windows 7. You can download Windows Easy Transfer for computers running the 32-bit or 64-bit versions of Windows XP and Windows Vista. You use Windows Easy Transfer on the source computer in a side-by-side migration to collect all migrated data. You use Windows Easy Transfer on the destination computer to restore that data. You can use Windows Easy Transfer to transfer local user accounts, documents, music, pictures, email, bookmarks, and digital certificates from the source computer to the destination computer. When using Windows Easy Transfer for side-by-side migration, you can leverage the following methods of transferring profile data:

- **Easy Transfer Cable** A special cable that has USB connectors. Connect one end to the source computer, and the other end to the destination. Both computers are powered on during migration.
- **Network** You run Windows Easy Transfer on both computers connected to the same LAN. Profile data is transferred across the network from one computer to the other.
- **External Hard Disk or USB Flash Drive** You can also specify an internal hard disk drive or a network location with this method. Migration data is stored in the specified location, and you import it using Windows Easy Transfer on the destination computer. This is the only Windows Easy Transfer method that you can use to perform a wipe-and-load migration.

You can't use Windows Easy Transfer to transfer files from a 64-bit version of Windows to a 32-bit version of Windows.

MORE INFO   To learn more about Windows Easy Transfer, consult the following TechNet document: *http://windows.microsoft.com/en-us/windows7/Transfer-files-and-settings-from-another-computer.*

True or False? You can use the hard-link migration store when migrating profile data from one machine to another.

Answer: *False.* When using USMT to transfer data from one computer to another, you create a migration store that stores the migrated data. You can use a network share or a locally attached storage device when using USMT. You can't use the hard-link migration store when migrating from one computer to another. The hard-link migration store stores data on a fixed hard drive in wipe-and-load migrations.

EXAM TIP   If you have a choice of migration stores, determine why one of the choices is inappropriate given the scenario.

True or False? When using USMT in side-by-side migrations, you run the ScanState tool on the destination computer.

Answer: *False.* USMT consists of two tools: ScanState and LoadState. ScanState is run on the source computer, and LoadState is run on the destination computer. USMT allows you to automate the process of migrating user profile data from one computer to another. USMT uses migration rules, stored in XML format, to specify which of the following are migrated:

- User accounts
- User files
- Operating-system settings
- Application settings

You can use USMT with WDS and System Center Configuration Manager 2012 to fully automate the process of migrating user profiles.

USMT 4.0 ships with the following sample scripts:

- **MigApp.XML**   Contains sample rules to migrate application settings.
- **MigDocs.XML**   Used with the MigXMLHelper.GenerateDocPatterns helper function. User documents can be automatically located without the necessity of authoring complex migration .XML files.
- **MigUser.XML**   Sample rules that gather everything in a user's profile and scan local fixed drives for files with commonly extensions. The properties of this sample script are covered in more detail later in the chapter.

MORE INFO   To learn more about USMT and the items it can migrate, consult the following webpage: *http://technet.microsoft.com/en-us/library/dd560792(WS.10).aspx.*

True or False? You must have local administrator privileges on the source computer to run the ScanState tool.

Answer: *True.* You must run the ScanState tool on the source computer using local administrator privileges. If you boot the source computer using the WinPE environment, you have local administrator access to the source computer.

A migration report provides you with information about what USMT will migrate prior to performing the actual migration. For example, to create a migration report, named genMig.xml, in the c:\Migration folder, run the following command:

```
Scanstate.exe /genmigxml:"C:\Migration\genMig.xml"
```

By default, the ScanState tool will create a compressed migration store. To use ScanState with the migdocs.xml and migapp.xml files to create a migration store on the file server \\Migration\\mystore using a detailed log file named scan.log, use the following command:

```
Scanstate.exe \\migration\mystore /i:migdocs.xml /i:migapp.xml /v:13
/l:scan.log
```

To use a hard-link migration store named c:\HD-LNK, use this command:

```
Scanstate.exe /hardlink /nocompress c:\HD-LINK /i:migdocs.xml /i:migapp.xml
/v:13 /l:scan.log
```

> **EXAM TIP**   Hard-link migration stores are the most efficient way of using disk space.

If you are using a network share or if you are concerned about the security of the migration store, you can encrypt the migration store data using the /encrypt /key:"mykey" switch with the ScanState tool. When using the encryption option, you must use the /decrypt /key:"mykey" options with the LoadState tool.

> **MORE INFO**   To learn more about scanstate.exe, consult the following TechNet document: *http://technet.microsoft.com/en-us/library/dd560781(WS.10).aspx.*

True or False? You should install all applications that you exported data from on the source computer on the destination computer prior to running the LoadState tool.

Answer: *True.* You use LoadState to restore data exported using the ScanState tool. You run the LoadState with local administrator permissions on the destination computer. For example, to restore all data from the \\migration\mystore network store when you used the migapp.xml and miguser.xml configuration files, execute the following command:

```
loadstate \\migration\mystore /i:migapp.xml /i:miguser.xml
```

> **MORE INFO**   To learn more about loadstate.exe, consult the following TechNet document: *http://technet.microsoft.com/en-us/library/dd560804(WS.10).aspx.*

True or False? You can boot into the WinPE environment and use ScanState to capture profile data without booting into the original operating system.

Answer: *True*. Offline migration allows you to use the ScanState component of USMT when booted from the WinPE environment to gather settings and files from a Windows XP, Windows Vista, or Windows 7 installation. You can also use offline migration to gather files and settings from the Windows.old directory created during an upgrade from a previous version of Windows if you are booted into Windows 7. You must use ScanState with the /offline option to extract data when not booted in to the source operating system.

> **MORE INFO** To learn more about offline migration, consult the following TechNet document: *http://technet.microsoft.com/en-us/library/dd560758(WS.10).aspx.*

Migrating from previous versions of Windows

You need to know what steps to take when migrating from Windows XP or Windows Vista to Windows 7.

True or False? You can use a hard-link migration store with Windows Easy Transfer.

Answer: *False*. You should consider the following strategies when migrating data from previous versions of Windows to Windows 7:

- If you need to perform a side-by-side migration of a small number of computers, you should consider Windows Easy Transfer when both computers are connected to the same LAN.

- You should use Windows Easy Transfer and an external hard disk drive or network location if you need to perform a wipe-and-load migration of a small number of computers. You can't use hard-link migration stores with Windows Easy Transfer.

- You should use USMT when performing side-by-side or wipe-and-load migrations of large numbers of computers because you can automate the migration process.

- You should use hard-link migration store in wipe-and-load scenarios when you want to minimize the amount of storage used to host migrated data.

- You should use ScanState to encrypt migrated data when stored on accessible network locations.

> **MORE INFO** To learn more about migrating from previous versions of Windows, consult the following webpage: *http://technet.microsoft.com/en-us/library/dd446674(WS.10).aspx.*

> **EXAM TIP** Spend time investigating and remembering the ScanState and LoadState syntax. If possible, perform a hard-link migration using the following Step-By-Step guide: *http://technet.microsoft.com/en-us/library/dd883247(WS.10).aspx*

Can you answer these questions?

You can find the answers to these questions at the end of the chapter.

1. What three methods can you use to migrate profile data using Windows Easy Transfer?

2. You need to migrate local user profile data from two computers running Windows Vista to two new computers running Windows 7. You don't have local administrator access on the computers running Windows Vista. What steps can you take to accomplish this task?

3. You have 50 computers that have Windows Vista Enterprise (x86) installed, on which you want to deploy Windows 7 Enterprise (x64). You do not want to use removable storage or a network folder to store migration data. What migration store option should you choose?

4. You have five computers running Windows XP Professional (x64) that you want to replace with Netbook computers running Windows 7 Professional (x86). Which tools can you use to migrate profile data with a minimum of effort?

Answers

This section contains the answers to the "Can you answer these questions?" sections in this chapter.

Objective 1.1: Perform a clean installation

1. Windows 7 Enterprise edition supports a maximum of two physical processors.

2. You need to create a partition or add an extra disk that has enough space to host the Windows 7 operating system. You need to run setup from within Windows rather than running it when booted off the Windows installation media.

3. You need to boot off a WinPE disk, which includes the Windows 7 installation media, or a USB storage device. You then can make a connection to the network share and can then install Windows 7.

4. Images are in .WIM format.

Objective 1.2: Upgrade to Windows 7 from previous versions of Windows

1. You should ensure that the computers running Windows Vista have at least Windows Vista Service Pack 1 installed and have at least 10 GB of free space on the operating system volume.

2. You can only upgrade from Windows Vista Enterprise (x64) to Windows 7 Enterprise (x64).

3. You can use Windows Anytime Upgrade to upgrade to the x64 versions of Professional and Ultimate.

4. You can use the Windows 7 Upgrade Advisor to determine whether there are known hardware-, driver-, or application-compatibility issues.

Objective 1.3: Migrate user profiles

1. You can use the Windows Easy Transfer Cable, Network, or External Hard Disk/USB Flash Drive method of transferring profile data using Windows Easy Transfer.

2. Boot using WinPE and use ScanState to perform an offline migration.

3. You should use a hard-link migration store with USMT to support this migration.

4. You can use USMT to migrate profile data. You can't use Windows Easy Transfer to transfer profile data from a 64-bit version of Windows to a 32-bit version of Windows.

CHAPTER 2

Deploying Windows 7

A pproximately 13 percent of the 70-680 exam focuses on the topic of deploying Microsoft Windows 7. That means that you need to have a good grasp of how to capture a Windows 7 system image, prepare a Windows 7 system image for deployment, and actually deploy the image to computers. This topic also involves deploying and managing Virtual Hard Disks (VHDs) as a system image replacement.

This chapter covers the following objectives:

- Objective 2.1: Capture a system image
- Objective 2.2: Prepare a system image for deployment
- Objective 2.3: Deploy a system image
- Objective 2.4: Configure a VHD

Objective 2.1: Capture a system image

This objective requires you to demonstrate that you know what steps you need to take and what tools you need to have available to capture a Windows 7 operating system image in Windows Imaging (WIM) format. You also need to know how to extend that knowledge to being able to automate the process of image capture by configuring automated image capture with WDS.

Exam need to know

- Preparing system for capture
  For example: How to use sysprep.exe to prepare an image.
- Manual capture
  For example: What steps should you take and what tools are required for image capture?
- Creating a WIM file
  For example: How to create a WIM file by performing a system image capture.
- Automated capture
  For example: How to configure WDS to automate image capture.

Preparing system for capture

You need to know what utilities to use to ready a Windows 7 deployment for capture.

True or False? You use Sysprep with the /audit option if you need to perform additional image customization before image capture.

Answer: *True*. Preparing a Windows 7 image for capture involves deploying Windows 7; installing all necessary applications, drivers, and updates on the computer; and then running sysprep.exe.

You can use sysprep.exe to do the following:

- **Remove system-specific information from Windows**   Sysprep.exe can remove all deployment-specific information from a Windows image including the computer security identifier (SID) and computer name. You accomplish this by using sysprep.exe with the /generalize option.

- **Configure Windows to boot to Audit mode**   With Audit mode, you can install third-party device drivers and applications. You can also check the computer's functionality before you perform image capture. You can't use settings chosen in the Out-Of-Box-Experience (OOBE) Wizard to be applied, but you accomplish this by using sysprep.exe with the /audit option.

- **Configure Windows to boot to Out-Of-Box-Experience (OOBE)**   Windows boots to the Windows Welcome the next time the computer restarts. You accomplish this using sysprep.exe with the /oobe option.

- **Reset Windows Product Activation**   Sysprep can reset Windows Product Activation up to three times. You can bypass resetting activation using the SkipRearm setting. Microsoft recommends that you use the SkipRearm setting if you need to run sysprep.exe multiple times on a computer.

You cannot use the /oobe and /audit options together. To configure a computer to remove all system-specific information, to shut down, and to start in OOBE mode when next booted, use the following command:

```
Sysprep.exe /oobe /generalize /shutdown
```

> **MORE INFO**   To learn more about sysprep.exe, consult the following webpage: *http://technet.microsoft.com/en-us/library/dd799240(WS.10).aspx.*

> **EXAM TIP**   Remember the difference between OOBE and Audit mode.

Manual capture

You need to know what steps are involved in manually capturing a reference deployment of Windows 7 as a system image.

True or False? You boot into the Windows Recovery Environment (WinRE) to perform manual image capture.

Answer: *False*. Manual capture involves manually booting the reference computer into the Windows Preinstallation Environment (WinPE), in which the Windows AIK tool ImageX.exe is available. With WinPE, you can access network resources, so once you complete the capture of the operating system image, you can copy that image to an available network location.

MORE INFO To learn more about manual image capture, consult the following web-page: *http://technet.microsoft.com/en-us/library/dd349348(WS.10).aspx#BKMK_4.*

Creating a WIM file

You need to know what tools to use to create a WIM file of a Windows 7 reference deployment.

True or False? After booting into WinPE, you use dism.exe to capture an installation to WIM format.

Answer: *False*. ImageX.exe is a component of the Windows Automated Installation Kit (AIK). You use ImageX.exe to capture the Windows 7 reference deployment to a WIM file. You do this by performing the following steps:

1. Boot the computer off a specially prepared WinPE image that includes the ImageX.exe tool. You can configure a bootable USB storage device with WinPE and also use it to store the captured WIM image.

2. Use the ImageX.exe tool to capture the image. For example, if you want to capture an image named d:\win7.wim of volume C: of the reference com-puter in which ImageX.exe is located at the root of D: on the WinPE volume, use this command:

```
D:\imagex.exe /capture C: d:\win7.wim "Win7 Deployment" /compress
fast /verify
```

MORE INFO To learn more about capturing images using ImageX.exe, consult the following webpage: *http://technet.microsoft.com/en-us/library/dd744298(WS.10).aspx.*

Automated capture

You need to know how to configure WDS to automate the capture process.

True or False? You configure the file WDSCapture.inf to automate the Image Cap-ture Wizard in WDS.

Answer: *True*. When automated capture is configured correctly, you can PXE boot a reference computer and have the image capture perform automatically. Automatic image capture uses an answer file named WDSCapture.inf to automate the WDS's Image Capture Wizard. To automate the Image Capture Wizard, perform the follow-ing steps:

1. Create a WDSCapture.inf file. This file is a text file that contains informa-
    tion about which volumes should be captured, image names, destination
    locations, and whether the captured image should be uploaded to the WDS
    server or copied to a network share.
2. Create a capture image. This is usually the boot.wim file from the Windows
    Server 2008 R2 product DVD.
3. Modify the boot image using dism.exe so that the WDSCapture.inf file that
    you created is stored as the Windows\Systemr32\wdscapture.inf
4. Add this capture image to the WDS server.

MORE INFO   To learn more about automating the capture process, consult the following webpage: *http://technet.microsoft.com/en-us/library/cc771321(WS.10).aspx.*

Can you answer these questions?

You can find the answers to these questions at the end of the chapter.

1. Which sysprep.exe option would you use to so that you can add additional
    third-party drivers and applications?
2. Which utility do you use to capture a reference deployment as a WIM file?
3. What environment should you boot into when performing a manual image
    capture?
4. Which file should you configure and add to a capture image to automate the
    WDS Image Capture Wizard?

Objective 2.2: Prepare a system image for deployment

This objective requires you to demonstrate that you know how to add an application
to a system image, add a device driver to a system image, include important software updates into a system image, and automate important post-installation tasks.

Exam need to know

- Inserting an application into a system image
  For example: How to use Deployment Image Servicing and Management
  (DISM) to inject an application into an image.
- Inserting a driver into a system image
  For example: How to add new device drivers to an offline image using DISM.
- Inserting an update into a system image
  For example: How to add software updates to an offline image using DISM.
- Configuring tasks to run after deployment
  For example: How to configure Windows 7 to automatically join a domain
  after image deployment.

Inserting an application into a system image

You need to know how to add an application to an existing WIM image.

True or False? You must mount a WIM image before you make modifications such as adding packages and drivers.

Answer: *True*. Before you can modify a WIM image using dism.exe, you need to copy the WIM file to a file system that allows you to make changes and then mount the image using the /Mount-Wim option. For example, to mount the fourth image index of the WIM image c:\images\win7.wim in the c:\mount directory, use the following command:

```
Dism.exe /mount-wim /wimfile:c:\images\win7.wim /index:4 /mountdir:c:\mount
```

When you have completed image modification, you must commit the changes. If you dismount the image without committing changes, the changes you made are lost. To commit current changes and dismount the image that you mounted in the c:\mount directory, use this command:

```
Dism.exe /unmount-wim /MountDir:c:\mount /commit
```

To discard any changes that you made to the WIM image, use the following command:

```
Dism.exe /unmount-wim /MountDir:c:\mount /discard
```

> **MORE INFO** To learn more about using DISM to mount, commit, and unmount images, consult the following TechNet document: *http://technet.microsoft.com/en-us/library/dd744382(WS.10).aspx*.

True or False? You use DISM to insert an application into a system image.

Answer: *True*. You can use Dism.exe to add and remove packages from a mounted WIM image. You can use Dism.exe to add a single package in .cab format, a folder containing an expanded .cab file, or a folder containing multiple .cab files. Once the WIM image is mounted, you add packages using Dism.exe with the /Add-Package option. For example, to add the package application.cab stored in the c:\packages directory to the mounted image c:\mount, use the following command:

```
Dism.exe /image:c:\mount /Add-Package /PackagePath:C:\packages\application.cab
```

To verify which packages have been added to the image, use the /Get-Packages option. For example, to check which packages have been installed on the mounted image c:\mount, use the following command:

```
Dism.exe /image:c:\mount /Get-Packages
```

You can remove packages using the /Remove-Package option, either by specifying the package name, which you can determine by using the /Get-Packages option, or by specifying the original package location. For example, to remove the package c:\packages\application.cab use the following command:

```
Dism.exe /image:c:\mount /Remove-Package /PackagePath:c:\packages\
application.cab
```

MORE INFO To learn more about adding applications to images, consult the following webpage: *http://technet.microsoft.com/en-us/library/dd744311(WS.10).aspx.*

Inserting a driver into a system image

You need to know what steps you need to take to add a device driver to a mounted WIM image.

True or False? You can use Dism.exe to recursively add all drivers in a particular folder to a mounted WIM image.

Answer: *True.* You can use the Dism.exe utility to add individual drivers in .inf format or all drivers in a specific folder and its subfolders recursively to a mounted WIM image. For example, to add all drivers under the c:\drivers folder recursively to the WIM image mounted in folder c:\mount, use the following command:

```
Dism.exe /image:c:\mount /Add-Driver /driver:c:\drivers /recurse
```

You can use the /ForceUnsigned option with the /Add-Driver option to force the installation of unsigned drivers to computers running the x64 version of the Windows 7 operating system. For example, to add the driver c:\drivers\unsigned.inf to the image mounted in the c:\mount folder, use this command:

```
Dism.exe /image:c:\mount /Add-Driver /driver:c:\drivers\unsigned.inf /
ForceUnsigned
```

To verify that the driver has been added to the mounted image, run this command:

```
Dism.exe /image:c:\mount /Get-Drivers
```

You can remove drivers using the /Remove-Driver option, but you must specify each driver that you want to remove. For example, to remove the driver graphicscard.inf from the WIM image mounted in the c:\mount folder, use the following command:

```
Dism.exe /image:c:\mount /Remove-Driver /driver:graphicscard.inf
```

You can't remove default drivers from an image using Dism.exe.

MORE INFO To learn more about inserting drivers into images, consult the following webpage: *http://technet.microsoft.com/en-us/library/dd799258(WS.10).aspx.*

Inserting an update into a system image

You need to know what tools to use to insert a software update into a mounted system image using Dism.exe.

True or False? You can insert updates that are in .msu format into mounted WIM images using the Dism.exe tool.

Answer: *True.* You can use the /Add-Package option to the Dism.exe utility to add updates in .msu format to a mounted WIM image. For example, to add the update c:\updates\kb12345.msu to the WIM image mounted in folder c:\mount, use the following command:

```
Dism.exe /image:c:\mount /Add-Package /PackagePath:c:\updates\kb12345.msu
```

Unlike application packages in .cab format, you can't remove updates in .msu format that you've added to a WIM image using Dism.exe.

Configuring tasks to run after deployment

You need to know how to use Dism.exe to apply an answer file to an operating system image.

True or False? You can apply an answer file created using Windows System Image Manager to a WIM file using DISM.

Answer: *True.* Answer files allow you to automate post-deployment tasks such as domain join. You can use DISM to apply an answer file to an image. Although you can create your own answer files in any text editor, Microsoft recommends that you use Windows System Image Manager (SIM) to create your answer file. Windows SIM is part of the Windows AIK. You should use Windows SIM to validate your answer file if you create it manually.

You can use the /Apply-Unattend option. For example, to apply the answer file c:\answerfile\unattend.xml to the WIM image mounted as c:\mount, use the following command:

```
Dism.exe /image:c:\mount /Apply-Unattend:c:\answerfile\unattend.xml
```

You can't use other servicing commands in the same command that you use to apply the unattend.xml answer file to the mounted WIM image.

Can you answer these questions?

You can find the answers to these questions at the end of the chapter.

1. Which command would you use to mount the third image index of the image c:\WIM\win7ent.wim in the c:\imgmount directory?

2. Which command would you use to add the package d:\install\program.cab to the WIM image mounted as e:\imgmount?

3. You have extracted 10 device drivers to the directory f:\stage. You want to add these drivers to the WIM image mounted as d:\mount. Which command would you use to accomplish this goal?

4. You have created an unattended installation file named c:\dev\unattend.xml. You want to add this to the WIM image win7.wim, which is mounted in the f:\mount directory. What command would you use to add this unattended installation file to the mounted WIM image?

Objective 2.3: Deploy a system image

This objective requires you to demonstrate that you know how to deploy a specially prepared system image through manual, Lite-Touch, and Zero-Touch Deployment strategies.

Exam need to know

- Manually deploying a customized image

  For example: How to deploy Windows 7 using ImageX.exe.

- Automated deployment methods

  For example: How to describe the difference been Lite-Touch and Zero-Touch Deployment.

Manually deploying a customized image

You need to know what steps to take to manually deploy a customized Windows 7 image.

True or False? You use DISM to apply the Windows 7 image in WIM format to a prepared volume when manually deploying a custom image.

Answer: *False.* Manual image deployment involves using command-line utilities to apply a customized WIM file to a specially prepared volume on a computer and then configuring the boot configuration data (BCD) store to support booting the deployed operating system. Manual image deployment requires direct intervention at all steps, from booting, to partitioning disks, to applying the image, and then configuring the computer to boot.

To manually deploy an image, perform the following steps:

1. Boot off the WinPE media that includes the ImageX.exe tool.

2. From the WinPE command prompt, use the DiskPart utility to format and create the partitions that you will use to deploy the image. For example, to create a 50-MB system partition and then use the remainder of the disk to create a volume to host the Windows 7 image, perform the following steps:

```
DiskPart
Select disk
clean
create partition primary size=500
select partition 1
format fs=ntfs label="system"
assign letter=S
active
create partition primary
select partition 2
format fs=ntfs label="Windows 7"
assign letter=C
exit
```

3. Transfer the WIM file from the location where it is stored to the local hard disk drive.

4. Apply the image to the volume using ImageX.exe. For example, if ImageX.exe is in the root directory of your WinPE D: volume, and the WIM file, named win7ult.wim, is located in the root of volume C:, use the following command to apply the image:

```
D:\imagex.exe /apply c:\win7ult.wim 1 c:\
```

5. Use BCDboot to initialize the BCD store and copy the appropriate files to the system partition using the following command:

```
C:\windows\system32\bcdboot c:\windows
```

MORE INFO To learn more about manually deploying operating system images, consult the following webpage: *http://technet.microsoft.com/en-us/library/dd349348(WS.10).aspx.*

EXAM TIP Remember that you use ImageX.exe to capture and deploy images and that you use DISM to service images.

Automated deployment methods

You need to know when it is appropriate to use WDS, Microsoft Deployment Toolkit (MDT), and System Center Configuration Manager to deploy Windows 7 to computers in your organization.

True or False? You can use WDS without an answer file to deploy Windows 7 images.

Answer: *True.* A simple method of automating the deployment of a Windows 7 image is by using WDS and an answer file. When configured, a prepared operating system image is streamed to a PXE client, with additional configuration, such as domain join, configured through the answer file. You can use WDS without an answer file, though this will require substantially more interaction on the part of the IT professional.

> **MORE INFO** To learn more about deploying Windows 7 using WDS, consult the following webpage: *http://technet.microsoft.com/en-us/magazine/gg293118.aspx.*

True or False? Lite-Touch, High-Volume deployments leverage the MDT.

Answer: *True.* A Lite-Touch deployment strategy is one that requires a small amount of interaction for deployment to successfully occur. High-Volume deployment refers to large-scale operating system deployments. Lite-Touch, High-Volume deployment uses MDT. MDT is a Microsoft solution accelerator that provides a framework for the deployment of Windows operating systems. You use MDT in a Lite-Touch, High-Volume deployment strategy to handle application, device driver, and update installation with Windows images. MDT 2010 supports thin and thick images.

- **Thin image** A Windows operating system image that is deployed with minimal customization. Applications, device drivers, and updates are installed after image deployment.

- **Thick image** A Windows image that is deployed with applications, device drivers, and updates already installed.

> **EXAM TIP** You can remember the difference between thick and thin images by remembering that a thick image will be larger because it will include applications, device drivers, and updates that the thin image does not include.

Lite Touch, High-Volume deployment strategies use the following components:

- Microsoft Assessment and Planning Toolkit
- Volume-licensed (VL) media provided by Microsoft
- MDT 2010
- User State Migration Tool (USMT)
- Application Compatibility Toolkit (ACT)
- Windows Automated Installation Kit (AIK)

- File server distribution share
- Either media that allows clients to boot to start deployment, such as WinPE, or a server configured with the WDS role.

EXAM TIP The current revision of the 70-680 exam deals with MDT 2010. A future revision of the 70-680 exam will deal with MDT 2012. You can learn about the current version of MDT on the Microsoft Deployment Toolkit (MDT) website at the following address: *http://technet.microsoft.com/en-us/solutionaccelerators/dd407791.aspx*

True or False? Task sequences are sets of instructions for installing and configuring Windows, drivers, and applications.

Answer: *True.* Setting up your organization's environment to support a Lite-Touch, High-Volume deployment involves the following general steps:

1. Use the Microsoft Assessment and Planning Toolkit to assess your organization's readiness for Windows 7 (optional).

2. Use Application Compatibility Toolkit to determine the compatibility of your organization's applications. (optional)

3. Configure WDS on Windows Server 2008 R2 (optional) and configure a file server as the distribution shared resource.

4. Install MDT 2010 on the file server. Install additional components including USMT.

5. Create a distribution share on the file server. This share will host operating systems, application installers, device driver files, and operating system and application updates.

6. Use MDT 2010 to create a task sequence for each different operating system configuration that you want to deploy. A task sequence is a list of instructions for installing and configuring Windows 7, drivers, and applications

7. Use MDT 2010 to create a deployment point. Deployment points determine how clients connect to files used in the distribution shared resource. Updating a deployment point creates special WinPE images that you can use with client computers to initiate deployment. You can deploy this WinPE image to clients by using either removable media or WDS.

8. Boot client computers using the WinPE image. Connect to the distribution shared resource. Select one of the preconfigured task sequences to install a specific Windows configuration.

MORE INFO To learn more about Lite-Touch, High-Volume deployment, consult the following webpage: *http://technet.microsoft.com/en-us/library/dd919179(WS.10).aspx*.

True or False? The Zero-Touch, High-Volume deployment strategy requires a System Center Operations Manager 2012 and System Center Orchestrator 2012 deployment.

Answer: *False.* Zero-Touch, High-Volume deployment strategies are almost completely automated and require little interaction from IT professionals other than powering on the client computers that are the target of the deployment. The Zero-Touch, High-Volume deployment strategy leverages both MDT 2010 and System Center Configuration Manager 2007 R2. A Zero-Touch, High-Volume deployment strategy leverages the automation potential of System Center Configuration Manager 2007 R2 to build and capture reference images.

EXAM TIP Future revisions of the 70-680 exam are likely to mention MDT 2012 and System Center Configuration Manager 2012.

A Zero-Touch, High-Volume deployment strategy requires that you have the following components:

- Microsoft Assessment and Planning Toolkit
- Volume-licensed (VL) media
- MDT 2010
- USMT
- Application Compatibility Toolkit
- Windows AIK
- System Center Configuration Manager 2007 R2

True or False? You must configure MDT 2010 integration with System Center Configuration Manager 2007 R2 to use a Zero-Touch, High-Volume deployment strategy.

Answer: *True.* A Zero-Touch, High-Volume deployment strategy involves performing the following steps:

1. Use the Microsoft Assessment and Planning Toolkit to verify your organization's readiness for the deployment of Windows 7 (optional).
2. Use the Application Compatibility Toolkit to determine application compatibility status (optional).
3. Ensure that System Center Configuration Manager and Active Directory Domain Services are properly deployed and configured.
4. Install MDT 2010 and configure the Configuration Manager 2007 R2 integration.
5. Create a custom reference image using Configuration Manager 2007 R2 to deploy Windows 7 to a reference computer, deploy applications and drivers to the reference computer, Sysprep, and then capture the custom image.

MORE INFO To learn more about Zero-Touch, High-Volume deployments, consult the following webpage: *http://technet.microsoft.com/en-us/library/dd919178(WS.10).aspx.*

EXAM TIP Remember that Zero-Touch deployment requires System Center Configuration Manager.

Can you answer these questions?

You can find the answers to these questions at the end of the chapter.

1. Which tool do you use to create and validate answer files for Windows 7 deployments?
2. Which tool do you use to apply an image file in WIM format to an NTFS-formatted volume?
3. Which tool can you use to create task sequences when leveraging the Lite Touch, High-Volume deployment strategy?
4. Which infrastructure component is required to support a Zero-Touch, High-Volume deployment strategy that isn't to support a Lite-Touch, High-Volume deployment strategy?

Objective 2.4: Configure a VHD

This objective requires you to demonstrate that you know how to manage operating systems' images in the VHD image format. This includes the steps you need to take to create, mount, deploy, and update, operating system images in this format. You also need to know how to add applications and drivers to operating system images in this format.

Exam need to know

- Creating, deploying, booting, mounting, and updating VHDs
  For example: How to create a VHD image.
- Offline updates
  For example: How to add updates to a VHD image.
- Offline servicing
  For example: How to add a package to a VHD image.

Creating, deploying, booting, mounting, and updating VHDs

You need to know what steps you need to take to create VHD files, how to deploy VHD files, how to mount them, and what steps to take to update those files.

True or False? You can create VHD files using the Dism.exe command-line utility.

Answer: *False.* You can create a VHD using the Disk Management snap-in and the DiskPart command-line utility. To create a VHD using the Disk Management snap-in, perform the following general steps:

1. Open the Disk Management snap-in and click Create VHD on the Action menu.
2. Specify the following properties of the VHD:
   - **Location**   Where you want the VHD file to be placed. If you create a fixed VHD, this location must have enough space to store the VHD file.

- **Virtual Hard Disk Size**   Size of the fixed VHD or the maximum size of the dynamically expanding VHD.
- **Virtual Hard Disk Format**   Fixed or dynamically expanding. Maximum size of a dynamically expanding VHD is 2040 GB.

Once the VHD is created, you need to initialize it. After the VHD is initialized, you can manage it as if it were a normal disk: creating volumes, formatting those volumes, and creating drive letters.

You create VHDs from the command line using the DiskPart command-line utility. You need to perform this task from an elevated command prompt. For example, to create an expandable VHD file named Win7Ult.vhd in the c:\VHD folder that can grow to 50 GB in size, issue the following commands:

```
DiskPart
Create vdisk file=c:\VHD\win7Ult.vhd maximum=50000 type=expandable
```

To view current virtual disks from within DiskPart, use the list vdisk command. To manipulate a VHD within DiskPart, you must select and then attach the disk. You can do this with the following commands:

```
DiskPart
Select vdisk file=c:\vhd\win7ult.vhd
Attach vdisk
```

Once the disk is attached, you can create partitions and format those partitions. For example, to create a partition inside the attached VHD that is 30 GB in size, use the DiskPart command:

```
Create partition primary size=30000
```

To format the newly created partition with the NTFS file system, use the following DiskPart command:

```
Format fs=ntfs label=Win7 quick
```

To assign the VHD as a drive letter, use the assign letter=X DiskPart command. For example, to assign the currently selected VHD file to drive V:, use this command:

```
Assign letter=v
```

> **MORE INFO**   To learn more about creating virtual hard disks, consult the following webpage: *http://technet.microsoft.com/en-us/library/gg318052(WS.10).aspx.*

True or False? You can use the ImageX command-line tool to apply a Windows image to a VHD.

Answer: *True.* After you have created a VHD, created a partition within that VHD, formatted that partition, and assigned the VHD to a particular drive letter, you can make a VHD bootable by applying a .WIM image to the VHD. You can use the ImageX command-line tool from the Windows AIK to apply a .WIM image. You can also use the Install-WindowsImage.ps1 PowerShell script that can be downloaded from the Microsoft website.

Use ImageX.exe /info <path to .WIM> to determine the index identifier of the edition of Windows 7 that you wish to apply to the VHD file. Once you have determined the number, use the following syntax to apply the image to the VHD volume: imagex /apply <path to .wim> <image_index> <VHD path>. For example, if the WIM file is located at d:\sources\install.wim, you've mounted the VHD at V: and the index number of the version of Windows 7 you wanted to install is 4, you would use this command:

```
Imagex.exe /apply d:\sources\install.wim 4 v:\
```

You can make a VHD bootable using the bcdedit.exe command. For example, to make the newly configured VHD c:\vhd\win7.vhd bootable, perform the following steps:

1. Ensure that the VHD is detached.

2. From an elevated command prompt, type the following:

   ```
   Bcdedit /copy {default} /D "VHD Boot"
   ```

3. A GUID will be output. You will use this GUID in the next two commands.

   ```
   Bcdedit /set {GUID} device vhd=[c:]\vhd\win7.vhd
   Bcdedit /set {GUID} osdevice vhd=[c:]\vhd\win7.vhd
   ```

MORE INFO To learn more about creating bootable virtual hard disks, consult the following webpage: *http://technet.microsoft.com/en-us/library/gg318049(WS.10).aspx.*

True or False? You can deploy prepared bootable VHDs to computers without operating systems using WDS.

Answer: *True.* You can deploy bootable VHDs to computers using the following methods:

- Boot using the WinPE environment and copy the bootable VHD file across from a network share to a prepared local volume. It will then be necessary to manually configure the boot configuration using bcdedit.exe

- Use WDS on Windows Server 2008 R2. You can add bootable VHD files to WDS using the WDSUtil command-line utility, but not using the WDS GUI. This allows you to automate the deployment of VHD files instead of having to deploy them manually.

MORE INFO To learn more about deploying virtual hard disks, consult the following webpage: *http://technet.microsoft.com/en-us/library/gg318050(WS.10).aspx.*

True or False? You must attach a VHD before you can service the VHD.

Answer: *True.* To service a VHD using the DISM tool, you need to attach the VHD file. This is done by assigning it to a volume. For example, to assign a VHD named win7ult.vhd, which is located in the c:\vhd folder to volume V: in preparation for servicing, issue the following commands from an elevated command prompt:

```
Diskpart
Select vdisk file=c:\vhd\win7ult.vhd
Attach vdisk
Assign letter=v
exit
```

Be careful when servicing VHD images because you can't discard changes in the manner that you can when managing WIM files. You should make a copy of the VHD prior to making modifications to the VHD. You'll find out more about servicing VHD images later in this chapter. You detach a VHD once you have completed servicing it. For example, to detach the VHD win7ult.vhd in the c:\vhd directory, use the following commands from an elevated command prompt:

```
Diskpart
Select vdisk file=c:\vhd\win7ult.vhd
Detach vdisk
exit
```

> **MORE INFO**   To learn more about servicing VHD images, consult the following web-page: *http://technet.microsoft.com/en-us/library/dd799267(WS.10).aspx.*

> **EXAM TIP**   Remember that only the Enterprise and Ultimate editions of Windows 7 can use native-VHD boot.

Offline updates

You need to know how to apply software updates to a VHD file without booting the operating system hosted in the VHD.

True or False? You can apply software update files in .msu format to a VHD image.

Answer: *True.* You can add update files in .msu format to VHD images in a way that is similar to adding an update file to a WIM image. You can add a package in .msu format to an image using the /Add-Package option. For example, to add the update c:\updates\kb12345.msu to the VHD image mounted on volume V:, use this command:

```
Dism.exe /image:V:\ /Add-Package /PackagePath:C:\updates\kb12345.msu
```

You can verify which packages have been installed within an image by using the /Get-Packages option. For example, to view which packages have been added to the VHD mounted on volume V:, use this command:

```
Dism.exe /image:V:\ /Get-Packages
```

> **MORE INFO**   To learn more about updating VHD files, consult the following web-page: *http://technet.microsoft.com/en-us/library/dd799267(WS.10).aspx.*

Offline servicing

You need to know how to add drivers to VHD images when the operating system that the VHD hosts is not powered on.

True or False? You use ImageX.exe to add drivers to a VHD file.

Answer: *False*. You can add drivers to a VHD image in much the same way that you add drivers to a WIM image. To add drivers to a VHD image, perform the following steps:

1. Use DiskPart or the Disk Management Console to mount the VHD that you want to service.

2. Use DISM to add drivers to the VHD using the /Add-Driver option. For example, to add the driver c:\drivers\driver.inf to the VHD that you've mounted as volume V:issue this command:

    ```
    Dism.exe /image:V:\ /Add-Driver /driver:C:\drivers\driver.inf
    ```

True or False? You can use ImageX.exe to list which drivers have been added to a VHD file.

Answer: *False*. You can verify that the driver has been added to the VHD by using the /Get-Driver option of the Dism.exe command. For example, to check which drivers have been added to the VHD mounted as V:, issue this command:

```
Dism.exe /image:V:\ /Get-Drivers
```

Once you have finished adding drivers, you can dismount the VHD using either DiskPart or Disk Management.

> **MORE INFO**   To learn more about adding drivers to VHD files, consult the following webpage: *http://technet.microsoft.com/en-us/library/gg318053(WS.10).aspx*.

> **EXAM TIP**   Remember that you can use DISM to add drivers to both WIM and VHD files.

Can you answer these questions?

You can find the answers to these questions at the end of the chapter.

1. What string of commands would you use from an elevated command prompt to create a 30-GB dynamically expanding VHD named Win7 in the c:\VHD directory, create a 25-GB partition within that VHD, and then format that newly created partition with the NTFS file system and the volume label Win7VHD?

2. What commands would you use from an elevated deployment tools command prompt on a computer running Windows 7 to apply the fourth indexed operating system in the Windows image d:\sources\install.wim to the VHD mounted on volume V:?

3. What method can you use to centralize the deployment of bootable VHDs to PXE clients?

4. You have a driver named graphicscard.inf located in the c:\stage directory. You have mounted a VHD that you want to service as volume V:. What command would you use to add this driver to this VHD?

Answers

This section contains the answers to the "Can you answer these questions?" sections in this chapter.

Objective 2.1: Capture a system image

1. Use Sysprep with Audit mode so that you can add additional drivers and applications.

2. You use ImageX.exe.

3. You boot into the WinPE environment when performing a manual image capture.

4. You configure WDSCapture.inf to automate the Image Capture Wizard in WDS.

Objective 2.2: Prepare a system image for deployment

1. dism.exe /mount-wim /wimfile:c:\WIM\win7ent.wim /index:3 /mountdir:c:\ imgmount

2. dism.exe /image:e:\imgmount /Add-Package /PackagePath:d:\install\ program.cab

3. dism.exe /image:d:\mount /Add-Driver /driver:f:\stage /recurse

4. dism.exe /image:f:\mount /Apply-Unattend:c:\dev\unattend.xml

Objective 2.3: Deploy a system image

1. You use the Windows SIM to create and validate answer files.

2. You use ImageX.exe to apply an image file in WIM format to an NTFS-formatted volume.

3. You use Microsoft Deployment Toolkit 2010 to create task sequences when leveraging the Lite-Touch, High-Volume deployment strategy.

4. You need to use System Center Configuration Manager 2007 R2 to support a Zero-Touch, High-Volume deployment strategy.

Objective 2.4: Configure a VHD

1. Use the following code to accomplish your goal:

```
DiskPart
Create vdisk file=c:\VHD\win7.vhd maximum=30000 type=expandable
Select vdisk file=c:\VHD\win7.vhd
Attach vdisk
Create partition primary size=25000
Format fs=ntfs label=Win7VHD quick
Assign letter=v
```

2. Imagex.exe /apply d:\sources\install.wim 4 v:\

3. You can use WDS to centralize the deployment of VHDs to PXE clients.

4. Dism.exe /image:V:\ /Add-Driver /driver:C:\stage\graphicscard.inf

CHAPTER 3

Configuring Hardware and Applications

A pproximately 14 percent of the 70-680 exam focuses on the topic of configuring hardware and applications. That means that you need to have a good
grasp of how to configure devices, manage application compatibility, configure
application restrictions, and manage Internet Explorer.

This chapter covers the following objectives:

- Objective 3.1: Configure devices
- Objective 3.2: Configure application compatibility
- Objective 3.3: Configure application restrictions
- Objective 3.4: Configure Internet Explorer

Objective 3.1: Configure devices

This objective requires you to demonstrate that you know how to manage applications and devices. You'll need to know how to update, disable, and uninstall
drivers. You'll also need to know how to deal with signed drivers, how to resolve
conflicts between drivers, and how to deal with a problematic device driver.

Exam need to know

- Updating, disabling, and uninstalling drivers

  For example: How to uninstall a driver from Windows 7.

- Signed drivers

  For example: How to know which versions of Windows 7 require digitally
  signed drivers.

- Configuring driver settings

  For example: How to configure a device to use a different interrupt request
  (IRQ).

- Resolving problem device driver

  For example: How to determine when to roll back and when to remove a
  problematic device driver.

- Conflicts between drivers

  For example: How to resolve a resource conflict between two device drivers.

Updating, disabling, and uninstalling drivers

You need to know what steps to take to update a specific driver, disable a specific driver, and uninstall a driver.

True or False? A user who is a member of the power users local group on a computer running Windows 7 can manually update the device driver for any device.

Answer: *False.* Updating or changing a device driver requires that the user attempting the task be a member of the local Administrators group if the driver is not already in the drivers store. A standard user can install a driver under the following conditions:

- The driver package is signed using a certificate present in the Trusted Publishers certificate store.

- The device setup class for the driver is listed in the Allow Limited Users To Install Drivers For These Device Classes policy.

> **MORE INFO** To learn more about updating or changing device drivers, consult the following webpage: *http://technet.microsoft.com/en-us/library/cc730965.aspx.*

When a new device is detected, Windows 7 will examine the driver store to determine whether an applicable device driver is staged there. If no applicable device driver is found, Windows will check the following locations:

- All folders specified in the DevicePath registry setting
- Windows Update hosted on the Microsoft website
- Any specific file path entered by the user

When an applicable device driver is found, Windows copies it to the driver store. Once the driver is staged in this location, it will be installed. You can add folders to the DevicePath setting by editing the HKEY_LOCAL_MACHINE\Software\Microsoft\Windows\Current Version\DevicePath registry item, separating each location with a semicolon. Ensure that %systemroot%\inf is one of the folders listed in this location.

To block Windows 7 from checking Windows Update for updated drivers, configure the Computer Configuration\Administrative Templates\System Internet Communication Management\Internet Communication Settings\Turn Off Windows Update Device Driver Searching policy. Set this policy to Enabled to prevent Windows from checking Windows Update. Set this policy to Disabled or Not Configured to have Windows check Windows Update for device drivers.

> **MORE INFO** To learn more about changing the folders that Windows 7 examines when looking for device drivers, consult the following webpage: *http://technet.microsoft.com/en-us/library/cc753716.aspx.*

True or False? You can use pnputil.exe from a standard command prompt to stage device drivers in the driver store.

Answer: *False*. Staging a driver places it in the driver store, ensuring that it will automatically be installed when a compatible device is detected without requiring that a user with local administrator privileges provide permission. Staging is useful in operating system deployment scenarios to ensure that all necessary drivers are part of the image. An administrator can stage a driver in the driver store using the pnputil.exe command-line utility from an elevated command prompt. A standard user can stage a driver only if the driver is signed and the device class is listed in the Allow Non-Administrators To Install Drivers For These Device Classes policy.

True or False? You must remove a driver from the driver store before you attempt to uninstall a device.

Answer: *False*. To uninstall a device, a user needs to be a member of the local Administrators group or the device setup class, and the driver must be listed in the Allow Non-Administrators To Install Drivers For These Device Classes policy. To uninstall a device using Device Manager, perform the following steps:

1. Right-click the device that you want to remove in Device Manager and then click Uninstall. You can also view the device's properties and click Uninstall on the Drivers tab of the device properties.

2. On the Confirm Device Removal page, you can choose the Delete The Driver Software For This Device option if you want to remove the device driver package from the driver store.

3. Once the process is complete, remove the device from the computer.

> **MORE INFO** To learn more about uninstalling a device, consult the following webpage: *http://technet.microsoft.com/en-us/library/cc725782.aspx.*

True or False? You can remove a device driver from the driver store using the pnputil.exe command-line utility**.**

Answer: *True*. Removing a staged device driver package from the driver store will not uninstall any currently operational devices that use those drivers. When you remove a package, only the driver package is deleted. If a new device that uses this driver is connected to the computer, Windows needs to locate the driver files because they will no longer be located in the driver store.

To remove a driver from the driver store, perform the following steps:

1. Open an elevated command prompt and run the pnpuntil.exe –e command.

2. Determine the name of the driver. It will be in the format OEM#.inf, where # is a unique number.

3. To remove the driver from the driver store, type the command **pnputil.exe –d OEM#.inf**, where OEM#.inf is the name of the device driver that you want to remove. If the computer reports that the driver package is in use, you can uninstall the device or force removal of the package by using the –f option with the pnputil.exe command.

MORE INFO To learn more about removing device drivers, consult the following webpage: *http://technet.microsoft.com/en-us/library/cc730875.aspx*.

EXAM TIP Remember that removing a driver package from the driver store does not uninstall any currently operational devices that use that driver.

Signed drivers

You need to know the situations under which a device driver must be signed.

True or False? You can install digitally signed drivers only on computers running x64 versions of Windows 7.

Answer: *True*. You can install only device drivers that are signed by a trusted certification authority (CA) on computers running 64-bit versions of Windows 7. An organization that wants to digitally sign driver packages needs to use the MakeCert, Signability, and SignTool tools in the Windows Driver Kit (WDK). An organization can use these tools to sign unsigned drivers or replace the digital signatures of other publishers with their own digital signature. When using drivers that are signed by an organizational CA, it is necessary to ensure that the organization's CA is trusted by the computer running Windows 7. An exception to this is kernel-mode drivers. Kernel-mode drivers for 64-bit versions of Windows 7 must be signed by a CA that has an approved CA in its trust chain; they cannot be signed by organizational CAs.

MORE INFO To learn more about driver singing in Windows 7, consult the following webpage: *http://technet.microsoft.com/en-us/library/dd919200(WS.10).aspx*.

EXAM TIP Remember that drivers for 64-bit versions of Windows 7 must be signed.

Configuring driver settings

You need to know how to configure driver settings using Device Manager.

True or False? You can configure which hardware resources are used by some devices using Device Manager.

Answer: *True*. Each system resource that a device uses must be unique to that device. Plug and Play (PnP) devices manage this process automatically. It is also possible to perform this task manually using Device Manager. Resources used by devices include the following:

- Interrupt request (IRQ) line numbers
- Direct Memory Access (DMA) channels
- Input/output (I/O) port addresses
- Memory address ranges

Windows can't automatically configure the resource settings for a non-PnP device. You might need to use a special setup utility to configure resource allocation for these devices. To configure the resources for a device, alter the settings on the Resource tab of the Device's properties in Device Manager.

MORE INFO To learn more about understanding device configuration, consult the following webpage: *http://technet.microsoft.com/en-us/library/cc753282.aspx.*

Resolving problem device driver

You need to know when you must remove a device driver and when you can roll back a device driver.

True or False? Members of the power users local group can roll back device drivers.

Answer: *False.* If a newly installed driver is functioning in a problematic way, you can use Device Manager to roll the driver back to a previous, hopefully better functioning, version. By default, the account used to perform this task needs to be a member of the local Administrators group. A normal user can also perform this task if the driver is for a device class that is listed in the Allow Limited Users To Install Drivers For These Device Classes policy. The Roll Back Driver button is available only if a previous version of the current device driver was installed on the computer.

If a driver is not functioning properly, and you have access to a previous version of the driver software that you believe will run properly, you can remove the current driver, ensuring that you also delete it from the driver store. Once the newer non-functioning driver has been completely removed, you can install the earlier version of the driver. Removing the newer driver is necessary only if the earlier version of the driver was not installed.

MORE INFO To learn more about rolling back device drivers, consult the following webpage: *http://technet.microsoft.com/en-us/library/cc732648.aspx.*

EXAM TIP Remember that you can roll back a driver only if a previous version of the driver was installed on the computer.

True or False? You can use Driver Verifier to stress-test drivers to determine if they become faulty when subject to resource pressure.

Answer: *True.* You can use Driver Verifier to troubleshoot driver issues. You can use Driver Verifier to stress-test a system to determine whether a driver exhibits faulty behavior in situations such as when a system has low resources. Driver Verifier is included with Windows 7 and you launch it using the verifier.exe command.

MORE INFO To learn more about Driver Verifier, consult the following webpage: *http://support.microsoft.com/kb/244617.*

Conflicts between drivers

You need to know what steps you can take to resolve conflicts between device drivers, such as attempting to upgrade drivers to newer versions or resolving resource conflicts.

True or False? You can use Device Manager to determine which devices are in conflict with one another.

Answer: *True*. Although rare, it is possible that two different devices or device drivers, when installed on the same computer running Windows 7, might conflict rendering both devices nonfunctional. You can pursue the following strategies in an attempt to resolve this conflict:

- Use Device Manager to determine which two devices are in conflict with each other. Disable each device in turn to verify that you have correctly identified which devices are conflicting.

- Attempt to update the device driver software for each device. Updated drivers might resolve the conflict issue.

- If possible, determine whether the problem is caused by a resource conflict. It might be possible to manually reconfigure one of the devices so that the conflict no longer occurs.

- If you cannot resolve the conflict, you might need to replace one of the conflicting devices with one that is more compatible with your configuration.

True or False? You can use msinfo32.exe to view resource conflicts on a computer running Windows 7.

Answer: *True*. The msinfo32.exe utility can be used to view the memory, I/O, and IRQ resources assigned to every device connected to the computer. The Hardware Resources\Conflicts/Sharing node will display where resources are being shared and where they are in conflict.

> **MORE INFO** To learn more about msinfo32.exe, consult the following webpage: *http://support.microsoft.com/kb/300887.*

> **EXAM TIP** Attempt to update drivers as a first step in resolving driver conflicts.

Can you answer these questions?

You can find the answers to these questions at the end of the chapter.

1. Under what conditions can a user who is not a member of the local Administrators group roll back a device driver?

2. You have just installed a new device on a computer running Windows 7. You download and install version 2.2 of the device driver on the computer, but find that the device behaves erratically. After checking technical support forums, you discover that you can solve the problem by using version 2.1 of

the device driver, which you can also download from the vendor's website. What steps should you take to ensure that version 2.1 of this device driver is used instead of version 2.2?

3. Which tools can you use to view resource conflicts?

4. Which tool can you use to stress-test a driver to determine whether it functions problematically in low-resource scenarios?

Objective 3.2: Configure application compatibility

Some of the main things blocking organizations from adopting Windows 7 are application-compatibility issues. Some applications that run perfectly well on Windows XP can't function when you attempt to run them on Windows 7. This objective requires you to demonstrate that you know how to set a compatibility mode, implement shims, and resolve compatibility issues with Internet Explorer.

Exam need to know

- Setting compatibility mode

  For example: How to configure Windows 7 to run a program using the Windows XP (SP3) compatibility settings.

- Implementing shims

  For example: How to deploy custom shims to computers running Windows 7.

- Compatibility issues with Internet Explorer

  For example: How to test webpages for compatibility with Internet Explorer on Windows 7.

Setting compatibility mode

You need to know which options there are for running programs that are not compatible with Windows 7.

True or False? There is a Windows Me compatibility mode.

Answer: *True.* Compatibility modes partially replicate the operating system environment of previous versions of Windows. You can configure a program to run using a compatibility mode by editing the settings on the Compatibility tab of the program's properties dialog box. Although some aspects of the operating system environment are reproduced, a program that functioned on a computer running Windows XP (SP 2) might not fully function when the Windows XP (SP 2) compatibility mode is selected, and you might have to take other steps to get it to function.

Windows 7 SP 1 supports the following compatibility modes:

- Windows 95
- Windows 98/Me
- Windows NT 4.0 (SP 5)

- Windows 2000
- Windows XP (SP 2)
- Windows XP (SP 3)
- Windows Server 2003 (SP 1)
- Windows Server 2008 (SP 1)
- Windows Vista
- Windows Vista (SP 1)
- Windows Vista (SP 2)
- Windows 7

Additional compatibility options that you can configure include the following:

- **Run In 256 Colors**   Use this option with applications that can run only with a limited color palette.

- **Run In 640 x 480 Screen Resolution**   Use this option with applications that cannot display in resolutions above 640x480.

- **Disable Visual Themes**   Helps with applications that have display problems with visual themes.

- **Disable Desktop Composition**   Disables certain features of the Aero user interface while the application is running.

- **Disable Display Scaling On High DPI Settings**   Disables automatic resizing of applications if large-scale fonts cause problems with the application appearance.

True or False? Users who are members of the local Administrators group can run the Program Compatibility Assistant manually.

Answer: *False*. The Program Compatibility Assistant detects when you execute programs known to have compatibility issues with Windows 7. It notifies you of the problem and provides information about a fix for when you next execute the program. The Program Compatibility Assistant can resolve User Account Control (UAC) conflicts or automatically configure the program to run in one of the compatibility modes listed earlier in this chapter. The Program Compatibility Assistant runs automatically when it detects the execution of an application for which it has compatibility problem-resolution information. The Program Compatibility Assistant cannot be run manually.

> **MORE INFO**   To learn more about the Program Compatibility Assistant, consult the following webpage: *http://windows.microsoft.com/en-US/windows7/Program-Compatibility-Assistant-frequently-asked-questions.*

True or False? Applications installed in Windows XP mode can be launched from the Windows 7 Start menu.

Answer: *True*. Windows XP mode runs a virtualized copy of Windows XP (SP 3) on a computer running Windows 7 Professional, Enterprise, or Ultimate. From the user's perspective, Windows XP can be opened as a separate window that functions as a full version of Windows XP. Users can interact with the virtual operating system in the same manner as they interact with the host operating system. If you install a program in the Windows XP mode operating system, the program will be installed in the virtual operating system and will also be available directly from the Start menu on Windows 7. If organizations can't get compatibility modes to work or can't use the Application Compatibility Toolkit to make incompatible programs function, Windows XP mode is likely to work as a last resort. Windows XP mode is a last resort because the virtual Windows XP operating system still needs to be managed and updated, and deploying Windows XP mode increases the number of operating system instances that the IT department needs to manage.

> **MORE INFO** To learn more about Windows XP mode, consult the following webpage: *http://windows.microsoft.com/en-US/windows7/install-and-use-windows-xp-mode-in-windows-7.*

Implementing shims

You need to know when to use and deploy shims as an application compatibility solution.

True or False? You can use shims to make Windows XP device drivers compatible with Windows 7.

Answer: *False*. Shims function as a translation layer redirecting API calls from programs that have compatibility problems with Windows 7 to the shim. The shim code then translates those incompatible API calls into API calls understood by Windows 7. Shims run as user-mode code inside a user-mode application process. It is not possible to use shims to resolve compatibility issues with device driver or other kernel-mode code such as some older anti-malware applications.

> **MORE INFO** To learn more about shims, consult the following webpage: *http://technet.microsoft.com/en-us/library/dd837644(WS.10).aspx.*

True or False? You can deploy a custom shim database as a part of operating system deployment.

Answer: *True*. Windows 7 uses a shim database when attempting to load applications. A shim database is already included with Windows 7. This database contains shims for many popular applications, and this database is updated through Windows Update. If your organization has unique incompatible applications that would not be present in the Microsoft shim database, you can deploy a custom shim database to the Windows 7 client that will host shims that allow your organization's unique incompatible applications to run. You can create and manage custom shims and custom shim databases using the Compatibility Administrator, which is a part of the Application Compatibility Toolkit.

MORE INFO To learn more about deploying shim databases, consult the following webpage: *http://technet.microsoft.com/en-us/library/dd837647(WS.10).aspx.*

Compatibility issues with Internet Explorer

You need to know how to use Internet Explorer Compatibility View and the Internet Explorer Compatibility Test Tool (IECTT).

True or False? You can use Compatibility View to emulate the characteristics of third-party browsers.

Answer: *False*. With Compatibility View, Internet Explorer can emulate the way that previous versions of Internet Explorer displayed webpages. Compatibility View does not emulate the characteristics of third-party browsers. When upgrading to Windows 7, you need to ensure that web applications used by people in your organization are compatible with either Internet Explorer 8, which shipped with the operating system, or the current version of Internet Explorer. In some cases, you'll either have to use Compatibility View to display the web application if it doesn't work in more modern versions of Internet Explorer or use a solution such as Windows XP mode, so that the application can be accessed by the browser running on the virtual machine. You'll learn more about managing Compatibility View later in this chapter.

MORE INFO To learn more about Compatibility View, consult the following webpage: *http://windows.microsoft.com/en-US/windows7/How-to-use-Compatibility-View-in-Internet-Explorer-9.*

True or False? You can use the IECTT to automate the testing of internal websites to determine whether they are compatible with Internet Explorer.

Answer: *True*. The IECTT is a tool that you can run to view web-based compatibility issues in real time. With the IECTT, you can automate the process of testing the compatibility of existing web applications to see how well they would work with Internet Explorer on Windows 7.

MORE INFO To learn more about the IECTT, consult the following webpage: *http://technet.microsoft.com/en-us/library/cc721989(WS.10).aspx.*

Can you answer these questions?

You can find the answers to these questions at the end of the chapter.

1. You have three custom applications that are incompatible with Windows 7. You need to ensure that these applications can run but want to minimize the number of operating systems to which you need to apply software updates every month. Which solution should you implement to meet your goals?

2. You have one application that runs fine on Windows XP with SP 3, but cannot be run on Windows 7 using a compatibility mode. This application is used by three people. What solutions could you use to ensure that these applications can run on the computers of these three users?

3. Which editions of Windows 7 support Windows XP mode?

4. Which tool can you use to automatically check websites on the intranet to determine whether they might have compatibility issues with Internet Explorer?

Objective 3.3: Configure application restrictions

This objective requires you to demonstrate that you know how to use Software Restriction Policies and Application Control Policies, also known as AppLocker Policies, to control the execution of applications and scripts on computers running Windows 7.

Exam need to know

- Setting Software Restriction Policies

  For example: How to configure Windows 7 Professional edition to run all applications written by a specific vendor.

- Setting Application Control Policies

  For example: How to configure Windows 7 to block the execution of all applications written by a particular vendor.

- Setting through Group Policy or Local Security Policy

  For example: How to determine which tool to use to configure AppLocker on a stand-alone computer running Windows 7.

Setting Software Restriction Policies

You need to know the different types of Software Restriction Policies' rules and their order of precedence.

True or False? You can use Software Restriction Policies to block the execution of applications on computers running Windows 7 Professional.

Answer: *True.* Software Restriction Policies allow you to block the execution of applications on computers running Windows 7, Windows Vista, and Windows XP. Software Restriction Policies are the predecessors to AppLocker Policies. Besides working with previous versions of Windows, you can use Software Restriction Policies to control the execution of applications on editions of Windows 7 that don't support AppLocker. Software Restriction Policies use the following settings:

- **Unrestricted** The application can be executed.
- **Disallowed** The application is blocked from executing.

True or False? Certificate rules override path rules.

Answer: *True*. Software Restriction Policies are applied in a specific order, with more explicit rules overriding general rules. The order, with specific hash rules overriding all other rule types, is as follows:

1. Hash rules
2. Certificate rules
3. Path rules
4. Zone rules
5. Default rules

When two rules conflict for the same program, the more specific rule takes precedence. For example, a certificate rule that sets a particular application to Unrestricted will override a path rule that sets a particular application to Disallowed. With AppLocker rules, covered later in this chapter, any block rule overrides allow rules.

True or False? You can use a default rule to block all applications except those allowed by explicit Software Restriction Policies.

Answer: *True*. Default rules apply when no other Software Restriction Policy matches an application. Only one default rule can be enforced using Software Restriction Policies. There are three default rules:

- **Disallowed**   Users cannot execute an application that isn't specifically allowed by another Software Restriction Policy.
- **Basic User**   Users can execute any applications that do not require administrative rights. Users can execute applications that require administrative rights as long as there is a specific Software Restriction Policy that allows the application.
- **Unrestricted**   Users can execute any application not explicitly blocked by an existing Software Restriction Policy.

True or False? You can configure Software Restriction Policies so that they are enforced for all users except local administrators.

Answer: *True*. With the Enforcement Properties Policy, you can configure the following settings:

- Whether Software Restriction Policies apply to all software files except DLLs or to all files including DLLs
- Whether Software Restriction Policies apply to all users or to all users except those who have accounts that are members of the local Administrators group
- Whether certificate rules are enforced or ignored

True or False? You can configure new executable file types through policy.

Answer: *True*. The Designated File Types Policy specifies which file extensions are treated as executable and which are therefore subject to Software Restriction Policies. You can modify the list of designated file types to include or exempt some executable file types, although some, such as .com, .exe, and .vbs, cannot be modified.

True or False? Certificate rules cover all applications digitally signed by the same vendor.

Answer: *True.* The difference between the Software Restriction Policy rules is as follows:

- **Path Rules**   You can specify a file, folder, or registry key as the target of a Software Restriction Policy. You can use wildcards with path rules. Path rules are specific, so if someone moves an executable to another location, the path rule no longer applies to that executable.

- **Hash Rules**   Hash rules use a cryptographic hash to identify a file. The file is identifiable even if it changes name and location. Applying a software update to a file means that the cryptographic hash needs to be recalculated.

- **Certificate Rules**   Identify files based on software publisher's certificate. Multiple applications from a single publisher can be covered by a single rule. Certificate rules still apply even when you apply software updates to files because these updates will be from the vendor, and the updated file will still be signed by the same publisher. Certificate rules can't be used to differentiate between different applications supplied by the same vendor. A certificate rule will allow all applications published by a vendor.

- **Network Zone Rule**   This rule applies to Windows Installer Packages (.msi files) obtained from Internet locations. Allows or blocks installation based on Internet zones location.

MORE INFO   To learn more about Software Restriction Policies, consult the following webpage: *http://technet.microsoft.com/en-us/library/dd349795(WS.10).aspx.*

EXAM TIP   Remember that hash rules must be updated if you patch an application.

Setting Application Control Policies

You need to know how to configure AppLocker to control the execution of programs on computers running Windows 7.

True or False? You can use AppLocker Policies to block the execution of applications on computers running Windows 7 Professional.

Answer: *False.* You can use AppLocker Policies only with computers running Windows Enterprise and Ultimate. You can apply AppLocker Policies to user or group accounts. AppLocker Policies can apply to the current and future versions of an application without needing maintenance.

True or False? Default rules are path rules.

Answer: *True.* You can create AppLocker default rules automatically. Default rules are necessary because when you enable AppLocker, the built-in rule of last resort blocks the execution of any application, installer, or script that is not the subject of an existing Allow rule. You create default rules by right-clicking the Executable Rules,

Windows Installer Rules, or Script Rules node and then clicking Create Default Rules. Default Rules are path rules. The default rules for each rule type are as follows:

- **Default Executable Rules** The default executable rules are path rules. All users can execute all applications located in the Program Files folder and the Windows folder. Members of the local Administrators group also can execute any applications in any path.

- **Default Windows Installer Rules** Everyone can use digitally signed Windows Installer files, all Windows Installer Files in the %systemdrive%\ Windows\Installer folder. Members of the local Administrators group can run .msi and .msp files in any path.

- **Default Script Rules** All scripts in the Program Files and Windows folders can be executed, and members of the local Administrators group can run scripts in any path.

True or False? A path rule that blocks overrides a file hash rule that allows.

Answer: *True*. Explicitly defined Block rules always override Allow rules. This applies to publisher rules, path rules, or file hash rules. A path rule that blocks will override a publisher rule that allows. The exception to this is the AppLocker default Block rule. The default Block rule does not override explicitly defined Allow rules. You can use Block rules to block the execution of applications allowed through the Default rules.

True or False? DLL rules cover files with the .msi and .msp extensions.

Answer: *False*. AppLocker rules work based on file extension. You can create AppLocker rules for the following types of files:

- **Executable Rules** Apply to applications that use the .exe and .com extensions. A user who is not a member of the local Administrators group still can't directly run an application that requires elevated privileges.

- **Windows Installer Rules** Applies to files with the .msi and .msp extensions. Allowing a user to run an installer file doesn't mean that the user has permission to install software.

- **Script Rules** Applies to files that use the .ps1, .bat, .cmd, and .js extensions. Use hash rules with scripts that are rarely modified. Use path rules with scripts that are frequently updated.

- **DLL Rules** Applies to libraries that use the .dll and .ocx extensions. Not enabled by default. Enabling DLL rules will likely cause an impact on performance.

True or False? Publisher rules can be created only for specific versions of executable files.

Answer: *False*. By default, AppLocker rules apply to Everyone, but you can configure them to apply to specific users or security groups. AppLocker rules can identify files using the following conditions:

- **Publisher** Uses the publisher's signing certificate extracted from the reference application file. It's possible to use the following rule scopes:

- **Any Publisher** Any digitally signed file.
- **Publisher** Any file digitally signed by a specific publisher.
- **Product Name** A specific product digitally signed by a specific publisher.
- **File Name** A specific file name of a specific product digitally signed by a specific publisher.
- **File Version** Specific version (or this version and higher) of a specific file name of a specific product signed by a specific publisher.

- **Path** You can specify file location, folder, or folder and subfolders. The least secure type of AppLocker rule because an attacker might be able to move unauthorized executable into folder covered by scope of path rule if NTFS permissions have been incorrectly applied.

- **File hash** Cryptographic hash of file. More manageable in AppLocker than they are in Software Restriction Policies because instead of having to manually generate a hash for each file, you can automatically generate hashes for all files. It is still necessary to update hash files for applications after applying software updates.

True or False? You can use a file hash to specify an exception to a path-based executable rule.

Answer: *True.* You use exceptions to allow specific applications to be exempt from more general rules. You can use a different way of identifying rules when creating an exception. For example, you could use a path-based exception to a publisher-based rule. You can create exceptions for Block and Allow rules.

True or False? You can configure AppLocker rules to use Audit mode.

Answer: *True.* AppLocker rules can be configured either for Enforcement or Auditing. Auditing means that users can still execute applications blocked by the rule, but an event will be written in the AppLocker Event Log, located in the Applications and Service Logs\Microsoft\Windows node of Event Viewer.

> **MORE INFO** To learn more about AppLocker, consult the following webpage: *http://technet.microsoft.com/en-us/library/ee791916(WS.10).aspx.*

> **EXAM TIP** Remember the differences in what you can accomplish with AppLocker Policies and Software Restriction Policies.

Setting through Group Policy or Local Security Policy

You need to know when it is appropriate to configure AppLocker and Software Restriction Policies using domain-based Group Policy and when it is appropriate to use Local Security Policy.

True or False? You can configure AppLocker and Software Restriction Policies through the Local Security Policy editor.

Answer: *True*. AppLocker Policies are located in the Computer Configuration\
Windows Settings\Security Settings\Application Control Policies node of a GPO.
Software Restriction Policies are located in the Computer Configuration\Windows
Settings\Security Settings\Software Restriction Policies node of a GPO. You can
configure both AppLocker and Software Restriction Policies through Group Policy
applied when a computer is a member of an Active Directory Directory Services
domain, through local Group Policy, or through Local Security Policy.

MORE INFO To learn more about AppLocker Policies, consult the following webpage: *http://technet.microsoft.com/en-us/library/ee449480(WS.10).aspx*.

Can you answer these questions?

You can find the answers to these questions at the end of the chapter.

1. You want to block all applications written by a specific publisher on a
   computer running Windows 7 Professional. What steps should you take to
   accomplish this goal?

2. Several custom applications written by a partner organization need to run
   on your organization's Windows 7 Enterprise computers. These applications
   are updated frequently. How can you ensure that these applications can be
   executed while also ensuring that other nonauthorized applications are still
   blocked? You must minimize the amount of time spent maintaining policies.

3. You want to block all applications written by a specific publisher except one
   on computers running Windows 7 Enterprise. What steps would you take to
   accomplish this goal?

4. Which tools can you use to configure AppLocker rules on stand-alone
   Windows 7 Enterprise computers functioning as kiosks?

Objective 3.4: Configure Internet Explorer

This objective requires you to demonstrate that you know how to configure and
manage Internet Explorer. Although Windows 7 included Internet Explorer 8 as
its default browser, in the intervening time, Internet Explorer 9 has been released.
Internet Explorer 10 is likely to be available at around the time the next version of
Windows client is released to manufacturing. At some point, the 70-680 exam is
likely to be updated to reflect the newest version of Internet Explorer that is compatible with Windows 7. Keep this in mind when studying for the exam.

Exam need to know

- Configuring Compatibility View

  For example: How to configure Internet Explorer so that Compatibility View is
  disabled for intranet sites.

- Configuring security settings

  For example: How to configure zone settings.

- Configuring providers

  For example: How to configure Windows 7 so that users can use a different search provider.

- Managing add-ons

  For example: How to configure Windows 7 to allow only specific add-ons to be used with Internet Explorer.

- Controlling InPrivate mode

  For example: How to block users from being able to access InPrivate browsing.

- Certificates for secure websites

  For example: How to configure Internet Explorer to require use of TLS 1.2.

Configuring Compatibility View

You need to know how to manage the Internet Explorer Compatibility View functionality, including how to enable and disable it for different classes of websites.

True or False? With Compatibility View, users can view pages designed for previous versions of Internet Explorer.

Answer: *True.* With Compatibility View, Internet Explorer can properly display sites designed for previous versions of Internet Explorer, such as Internet Explorer 6. Users can switch to Compatibility View by clicking the broken page item in the address bar. You can view a list of sites for which you have enabled Compatibility View in the Compatibility View Settings dialog box. You can manually add and remove sites from this list. You can use this dialog box to choose to enable some or all of the following:

- Include a list of updated websites from Microsoft.
- Display all intranet websites in Compatibility View. This is a default option.
- Display all websites in Compatibility View.

True or False? You can configure a list of websites that should use Compatibility View for all computers running Windows 7 through Group Policy.

Answer: *True.* You can configure the policies in the \Administrative Templates\ Windows Components\Internet Explorer\Compatibility View node.

- **Turn on Internet Explorer 7 Standards Mode**   Even though the policy mentions Internet Explorer 7, it also works with subsequent versions. It forces all sites to be displayed in Compatibility View.
- **Turn Off Compatibility View**   Disables Compatibility View.
- **Turn Off Compatibility View Button**   Disables the Compatibility View button.

- **Include Updated Web Sites Lists From Microsoft** Uses updated lists of sites from Microsoft.

- **Use Policy List Of Internet Explorer 7 Sites** A set of sites automatically added to the list of sites used with Compatibility View. Users can add extra sites, but not remove any of the sites specified by this policy. Works with later versions of Internet Explorer.

MORE INFO To learn more about Compatibility View, consult the following web-page: *http://windows.microsoft.com/en-US/windows7/How-to-use-Compatibility-View-in-Internet-Explorer-9.*

EXAM TIP Remember that users can't remove sites from the list of compatible sites configured through Group Policy.

Configuring security settings

You need to know how to use security zones to control website functionality based on website addresses.

True or False? Adding a site to the Restricted Sites zone means that users can't use Internet Explorer.

Answer: *False*. With zones, you can configure different security settings based on a website's address. These security settings determine how Internet Explorer responds to content, such as ActiveX controls and scripts. The zones available in Internet Explorer on computers running Windows 7 are as follows:

- **Internet** Applies to all websites by default. Default setting is Medium High. Not used for websites that are explicitly added to the Local Intranet, Trusted Sites, or Restricted Sites zones.

- **Local Intranet** Default setting attempts to detect intranet sites based on site address and name. You can configure this site to automatically include local sites not listed in other zones, all sites that bypass the proxy server, and sites accessed by UNC address. The default setting is Medium.

- **Trusted Sites** A special setting for sites that you explicitly trust not to dam-age your computer. The default setting is Medium.

- **Restricted Sites** Does not block users from using the site, but does block the site from running scripted or active content. The default setting is High and cannot be changed.

You can configure all sites that use a specific zone to use Protected Mode. Pro-tected Mode forces Internet Explorer to run as a low-integrity process that restricts the application from interacting with processes running at higher integrity levels. Protected Mode is enabled by default for the Internet and Restricted Sites zones.

MORE INFO To learn more about Internet Explorer security settings, consult the following webpage: *http://windows.microsoft.com/en-US/windows7/Change-Internet-Explorer-Security-settings.*

The available security levels are Low, Medium-Low, Medium, Medium-High, and High. You can use the Custom Level button to configure settings for a security zone, modifying the default settings. You can tighten or loosen some security settings without having to switch to another setting completely.

MORE INFO To learn more about advanced Internet Explorer security settings, consult the following webpage: *http://technet.microsoft.com/en-us/library/ dd883248(WS.10).aspx.*

EXAM TIP Remember that you can't modify the security level assigned to the Restricted Sites zone.

Configuring providers

You need to know how to manage which search providers are used on computers running Internet Explorer on Windows 7.

True or False? You can configure an authorized list of search providers using Group Policy.

Answer: *True*. You can specify how you search for information on the Internet using the Internet Explorer 9 address bar. In Internet Explorer 9, users type a query directly into the address bar instead of into a specific search box, as was the case in previous versions. You can configure a list of providers using the following policy, located in the \Windows Components\Internet Explorer Group Policy node:

- **Add A Specific List Of Search Providers To The User's Search Provider List** You can add specific providers to the list, and users can add and remove providers as long as the provider is on the list.

MORE INFO To learn more about search providers, consult the following webpage: *http://windows.microsoft.com/en-US/windows7/Search-with-the-Internet-Explorer-9-Address-bar.*

Managing add-ons

You need to know how to control which add-ons can and can't be installed for Internet Explorer on computers running Windows 7.

True or False? You can block users from installing all unauthorized add-ons.

Answer: *True*. Add-ons enhance Internet Explorer's functionality, often through providing extra toolbars. ActiveX controls are referred to as *plug-ins*. You can manage add-ons by using the Manage Add-Ons dialog box and selecting the Toolbars And Extensions Add-On Type. Search Providers, Accelerators, and Tracking Protection are also types of add-ons. You can configure add-ons through the following policies, located in the \Windows Components\Internet Explorer node:

- **Disable Add-On Performance Notifications** Stops Internet Explorer from warning the user about add-ons that take more than an average amount of time to load.

- **Automatically Enable Newly Installed Add-Ons** When enabled, new add-ons are active after installation. If the policy is disabled, users must provide consent to activate add-ons.

- **Do Not Allow User To Enable Or Disable Add-Ons** You can block users from managing add-ons.

There are additional policies located in the \Windows Components\Internet Explorer\Security Features\Add-on Management node. These policies include the following:

- **Add-On List** You can specify a list of add-ons that can be used with Internet Explorer.

- **Deny All Add-Ons Unless Specifically Allowed In The Add-On List** You can block the use of add-ons unless they are specifically allowed in Internet Explorer.

MORE INFO To learn more about managing add-ons, consult the following webpage: *http://windows.microsoft.com/en-US/windows7/Internet-Explorer-add-ons-frequently-asked-questions.*

True or False? Accelerators are used with the text on a webpage.

Answer: *True.* Accelerators are a special kind of add-on that enable you to select text on a webpage and then perform a function based on that text, such as performing a translation to another language or querying a mapping website for a street address. Accelerators categories include these:

- **Email** You can forward selected text into an email message.

- **Map** You can use a mapping service to display a location based on a highlighted address.

- **Translate** You can forward text to a translation service.

Accelerator Group Policy items are located in the \Windows Components\Internet Explorer\Accelerators node. You can configure the following accelerator-related policies:

- **Deploy Non-Default Accelerators** You can deploy accelerators. Users cannot remove accelerators deployed through this policy.

- **Deploy Default Accelerators** You can specify default accelerators. Although users can deploy additional accelerators, they can't modify the default accelerators.

- **Turn Off Accelerators** Disables all accelerators.

- **Use Policy Accelerators** Limits accelerator use to those specified by Group Policy.

MORE INFO To learn more about managing accelerators, consult the following webpage: *http://windows.microsoft.com/en-US/windows7/How-to-use-Accelerators-in-Internet-Explorer-9.*

Controlling InPrivate mode

You need to know how to manage InPrivate Filtering/Tracking Protection and InPrivate Browsing on computers running Windows 7.

True or False? InPrivate Browsing blocks users' activity being recorded by proxy servers.

Answer: *False.* InPrivate Browsing limits what data is stored by the browser. InPrivate Browsing does not stop proxy servers from recording a user's browsing activity. Users trigger InPrivate Browsing by clicking InPrivate on the Tools menu. When using InPrivate Browsing, the browser stores data, such as cookies provided when a user logs on to a site, during the session. When the session ends, Internet Explorer deletes that data.

True or False? InPrivate Filtering/Tracking Protection allows you to block third parties from tracking browsing activity across multiple sites.

Answer: *True.* InPrivate Filtering restricts how information can be tracked by external third parties. It does this by analyzing web content. If the same content is detected across a configurable number of websites, you will be given a prompt asking you whether you want to allow or to block that content. You can also configure InPrivate Filtering to automatically block any content provider or third-party website without requiring a prompt. InPrivate Filtering was replaced by Tracking Protection with the release of Internet Explorer 9.

> **MORE INFO** To learn more about **InPrivate browsing**, consult the following web-page: *http://windows.microsoft.com/en-US/windows7/InPrivate-frequently-asked-questions.*

Tracking Protection is a feature of Internet Explorer 9 that allows you to create a list that blocks content from specific websites that might affect your privacy because they track your web surfing activity across multiple websites. It builds on the functionality of InPrivate Filtering available in earlier versions of Internet Explorer.

> **MORE INFO** To learn more about **Tracking Protection**, consult the following web-page: *http://windows.microsoft.com/en-US/internet-explorer/products/ie-9/features/tracking-protection.*

You can manage InPrivate Filtering, Tracking Protection, and InPrivate Browsing using the following Group Policies located in the Administrative Templates\Windows Components\Internet Explorer\Privacy node:

- **Turn Off InPrivate Filtering** Disables InPrivate Filtering for computers running Internet Explorer 8.
- **Turn Off Tracking Protection** Disables Tracking Protection on computers running Internet Explorer 9 or later.
- **Turn Off InPrivate Browsing** Disables InPrivate browsing on computers running Internet Explorer.

- **Do Not Collect InPrivate Filtering Data**   Disables collection of private filtering data on computers running Internet Explorer 8.

- **Disable Toolbars And Extensions When InPrivate Browsing Starts**   Additional toolbars and extensions will be disabled in InPrivate Browsing sessions.

- **InPrivate Filtering Threshold**   The number of different sites containing the same third-party content that triggers InPrivate Filtering on computers running Internet Explorer 8.

- **Tracking Protection Threshold**   The number of different first-party sites that a third-party item can reference before Tracking Protection is triggered.

EXAM TIP   Remember that InPrivate Filtering and Tracking Protection are different versions of the same feature.

Certificates for secure websites

You need to know how to configure Internet Explorer to check the validity of certificates used to identify websites and protect secure sessions to websites.

True or False? You can configure Internet Explorer to check to see whether the signing certificate of the CA that issued the SSL certificate is valid.

Answer: *True.* You can view a list of Trusted Root Certification Authorities, Trusted Publishers, and Untrusted Publishers by clicking the Publishers button on the Content tab of Internet Options. You can configure Internet Explorer to trust a new Root CA by importing the CA certificate using this dialog box. You import code-signing certificates into the Trusted Publishers store when you want to trust digitally signed drivers or software from a specific vendor. Advanced Security Options related to certificates include the following:

- **Check For Publisher's Certificate Revocation**   Determines whether the publishing server's signing certificate is valid. Enabled by default.

- **Check For Server Certificate Revocation**   Determines whether the validity of SSL certificate on the web server is checked. Enabled by default.

- **Check For Signatures On Downloaded Programs**   Determines whether downloaded programs are digitally signed. Enabled by default.

- **Use SSL 2.0**   Not enabled by default. Enable only if infrastructure does not support SSL 3.0 because there are security risks in using SSL 2.0.

- **Use SSL 3.0**   Enabled by default. It is a more secure version of SSL than 2.0.

- **Use TLS 1.0**   Enabled by default.

- **Use TLS 1.1**   A more secure version of TLS 1.0; defined in 2006. Includes protection against cipher block chaining attacks. Not enabled by default.

- **Use TLS 1.2**   A more secure version of TLS 1.1; defined in 2008. Not enabled by default.

- **Warn About Certificate Address Mismatch**   Performs a check to see whether website certificate matches website address. Enabled by default.

MORE INFO To learn more about SSL certificates, consult the following webpage: *http://windows.microsoft.com/en-US/windows7/Get-information-about-Secure-Sockets-Layer-SSL-certificates.*

EXAM TIP Remember what steps you can take to configure Internet Explorer to trust a new Root Certificate Authority.

Can you answer these questions?

You can find the answers to these questions at the end of the chapter.

1. In which zone should you place sites if you want to minimize the chance of users being harmed by rogue scripts or ActiveX controls?

2. Which steps could you take to ensure that users can trust the SSL certificate used on a partner organization's intranet if that SSL certificate was issued by that organization's internal CA?

3. Which steps would you take to ensure that users can use only a specific set of authorized add-ons with Internet Explorer?

4. Which technology would you configure to block a specific third-party organization from tracking browsing activity across multiple sites for users of Internet Explorer 9?

Answers

This section contains the answers to the "Can you answer these questions?" sections in this chapter.

Objective 3.1: Configure devices

1. A user who is not a member of the local Administrators group can roll back a device driver as long as the device class related to the device the driver is for is listed in the Allow Limited Users To Install Drivers For These Device Classes policy.

2. You must uninstall version 2.2 of the driver and remove it from the driver store. You can then install version 2.1 of the device driver. You can't roll back to version 2.1 because it wasn't installed on the computer in the first place.

3. You can use msinfo32.exe and Device Manager to view device resource conflicts.

4. You can use Driver Verifier (verifier.exe) to stress-test a driver to determine whether it functions problematically in low-resource scenarios.

Objective 3.2: Configure application compatibility

1. You should use shims because using Windows XP mode would require an increase in the number of operating systems to which you need to apply software updates every month.

2. You could use Windows XP mode, or you could create and deploy a shim for the application. Either solution would resolve the problem.
3. Windows 7 Professional, Enterprise, and Ultimate support Windows XP mode.
4. The Internet Explorer Compatibility Test Tool.

Objective 3.3: Configure application restrictions

1. Configure a Software Restriction Policy Certificate rule.
2. Configure path rules either in Software Restriction Policies or AppLocker Policies.
3. Create an AppLocker Executable rule that uses a publisher certificate for file identification. Create an exception for the application you want to exempt.
4. You can use the either the Local Group Policy Editor or the Local Security Editor to configure AppLocker Rules on stand-alone Windows 7 Enterprise computers functioning as kiosks.

Objective 3.4: Configure Internet Explorer

1. You place sites in the Restricted Sites zone if you want to block ActiveX controls and scripts from running on untrusted websites.
2. Add the certificate for the partner organization's CA to the list of trusted Root CA in Internet Options.
3. Configure the Add-On List and Deny All Add-Ons unless specifically allowed in the Add-On List Policies. This will ensure that only authorized add-ons are run with Internet Explorer.
4. You configure Tracking Protection to block a specific third-party organization from tracking browsing activity across multiple sites for users of Internet Explorer 9.

CHAPTER 4

Configuring Network Connectivity

Approximately 14 percent of the 70-680 exam focuses on the topic of configuring network connectivity. That means that you need to have a good grasp of how to configure IPv4 and IPv6 addresses, network settings, Windows Firewall, Windows Firewall with Advanced Security, and remote management technologies.

This chapter covers the following objectives:

- Objective 4.1: Configure IPv4 network settings
- Objective 4.2: Configure IPv6 network settings
- Objective 4.3: Configure network settings
- Objective 4.4: Configure Windows Firewall
- Objective 4.5: Configure remote management

Objective 4.1: Configure IPv4 network settings

This objective requires you to demonstrate that you know how to configure IPv4 address settings so that computers running Windows 7 can interact with the LAN.

Exam need to know

- Connecting to a network

  For example: How to configure a wired network adapter to support 802.1X authentication.

- Configure name resolution

  For example: How to use command-line utilities to set a preferred DNS server.

- Setting up a connection for a network

  For example: How to configure Windows 7 to connect to a Bluetooth personal area network.

- Network locations

  For example: How to describe the different network locations used with Windows 7.

- Resolving connectivity issues

  For example: How to choose the appropriate tool to diagnose a connectivity problem.

- APIPA

  For example: How to determine when Windows 7 has been assigned an APIPA address.

Connecting to a network

You need to know how to configure a static IP address or how to configure Windows 7 to use a dynamic IP address.

True or False? A computer needs a dynamically assigned IP address to communicate on a LAN.

Answer: *False.* Computers running Windows 7 need an IP address to communicate on the local area network. This can be an IPv4 or an IPv6 address, and can be assigned dynamically or statically. You will learn more about IPv6 later in this chapter. Computers running Windows 7 use dynamic IP addresses by default. To configure an IPv4 address for a computer running Windows 7, perform the following steps:

1. Edit the network adapter's properties. Choose Internet Protocol Version 4 (TCP/IPv4) and then click the Properties button.
2. To have IP address configuration assigned automatically, choose Obtain An IP Address Automatically. To specify a static IP address, choose Use The Following IP Address and then specify an IP address, subnet mask, and default gateway.

To configure an adapter's IP address from an elevated command prompt, determine the adapter's name, usually Local Area Connection, and then use the netsh interface ipv4 set address command. For example, to set the address 192.168.15.101 with the subnet mask 255.255.255.0 and the default gateway as 192.168.15.1 on adapter Local Area Connection, use the following command:

```
Netsh interface ipv4 set address "Local Area Connection" static
192.168.15.101 255.255.255.0 192.168.15.1
```

To configure interface "Local Area Connection" to use Dynamic Host Configuration Protocol (DHCP), use the following command from an elevated command prompt:

```
Netsh interface ipv4 set address "Local Area Connection" dhcp
```

True or False? A computer will use an APIPA address if it is configured to use a dynamically assigned address but cannot communicate with a DHCP server.

Answer: *True*. You can determine whether the DHCP server has responded to the client's request for an IP address by checking the IP address configuration. If the computer has been assigned an APIPA address, the computer cannot contact the DHCP server. This may be because there is a problem with the physical network connection, such as a failed UTP drop cable between the computer and the wall point, a failure between the wall point and the switch, a switch failure, the failure of a router, or the failure of the DHCP server.

> **MORE INFO**   To learn more about IP address configuration, consult the following webpage: *http://windows.microsoft.com/en-US/windows7/Change-TCP-IP-settings*.

> **EXAM TIP**   The default gateway address must be on the same IPv4 subnet as the adapter's IPv4 address.

True or False? You can determine whether the Wired AutoConfig service is running by viewing a wired network adapter's properties.

Answer: *True*. 802.1X authentication requires that the computer authenticate to the wireless access point or the wired switch before it can establish a connection to the network. 802.1X authentication usually requires a certificate or smart card. To configure a computer running Windows 7 to support 802.1X authentication on a wired network, perform the following steps:

1. Open the Services console. Start the Wired AutoConfig service and set it to start automatically.
2. Edit the properties of the network connection that will be using 802.1X authentication. Starting the Wired AutoConfig service makes the Authentication tab available.
3. Choose the appropriate network authentication method for the 802.1X network to which you will be connecting.

To use 802.1X authentication with wireless networks, open the Manage Wireless Networks console and edit the properties of the wireless network for which you want to configure 802.1X authentication. On the Security tab of the wireless network's properties, choose the appropriate authentication method.

> **MORE INFO**   To learn more about configuring Windows 7 clients for 802.1X configuration, consult the following webpage: *http://windows.microsoft.com/en-US/windows7/Enable-802-1X-authentication*.

Configuring name resolution

You need to know how to configure name resolution for computers running Windows 7.

True or False? You can configure which DNS servers a client uses by using the Ipconfig.exe command-line utility.

Answer: *False*. DNS resolution enables the translation of IP addresses into fully qualified domain names (FQDNs) and FQDNs into IP addresses. You configure DNS resolution for computers running Windows 7 by setting preferred and alternate DNS servers. You can do this by editing the Internet Protocol Version 4 (TCP/IPv4) properties on the adapter properties in the GUI or by using the netsh interface ipv4 set dnsservers command. For example, to set the network adapter "Local Area Connection" to use the IP address 192.168.15.10 as the primary DNS server, run the following from an elevated command prompt:

```
Netsh interface ipv4 set dnsservers "Local Area Connection" static
192.168.15.10 primary
```

In most organizations, DHCP servers provide clients with DNS server addresses. You can choose this option by editing the Internet Protocol Version 4 (TCP/IPv4) properties or by executing the following command from an elevated command prompt:

```
Netsh interface ipv4 set dnsservers "Adapter Name" source=dhcp
```

True or False? Windows Internet Name Service (WINS) is used for NetBIOS name resolution.

Answer: *True*. WINS resolution enables the translation of IP addresses into NetBIOS names. You configure WINS resolution for computers running Windows 7 by editing the Internet Protocol Version 4 (TCP/IPv4) properties on the adapter properties in the GUI or by using the netsh interface ipv4 set winsserver command. For example, to set the network adapter "Local Area Connection" to use the IP address 192.168.15.100 as the WINS server, run the following from an elevated command prompt:

```
Netsh interface ipv4 set winsserver "Local Area Connection" static
192.168.15.100
```

In most organizations, DHCP servers provide clients with the address of the WINS server. You can choose this option by editing the Internet Protocol Version 4 (TCP/IPv4) properties or by executing the following command from an elevated command prompt:

```
Netsh interface ipv4 set winsserver "Adapter Name" source=dhcp
```

> **MORE INFO**   To learn more about configuring name resolution from the command line, consult the following webpage: *http://technet.microsoft.com/en-us/library/cc731521(WS.10).aspx*.

> **EXAM TIP**   Remember the difference between WINS and DNS.

Setting up a connection for a network

You need to know how to set up wired and wireless network connections using the Set Up A Connection Or Network Wizard.

True or False? Windows 7 supports setting up a PAN across Bluetooth connections.

Answer: *True.* You can use the Set Up A Connection Or Network Wizard to set up different types of network connections for computers running Windows 7. The Set Up A Connection Or Network Wizard, available through the Network and Sharing Center, gives you the following options:

- **Connect To The Internet**   You can configure a connection to the Internet using a wireless network, broadband, or dial-up connection. For example, if you directly connect a DSL modem to your computer, you will be able to provision that modem with a user name, password, and phone number.

- **Set Up A New Network**   You can configure a new router or wireless access point. For example, configure wireless access point settings such as network name, password, authentication scheme, and whether the wireless access point distributes IP addresses.

- **Manually Connect To A Wireless Network**   You can set up a connection to a hidden wireless network or to create a new wireless profile.

- **Connect To A Workplace**   You can create a dial-up or VPN connection. You'll learn more about creating VPN connections in Chapter 6, "Configuring Mobile Computing."

- **Set Up A Dial-Up Connection**   You can connect to the Internet by setting up a modem.

- **Set Up A Wireless Ad Hoc (Computer To Computer) Network**   You can set up a temporary network for sharing an Internet connection or files. It is available only if the computer has a wireless adapter.

- **Connect To A Bluetooth Personal Area Network (PAN)**   You can set up a connection to a Bluetooth device or network. It is available only if the computer running Windows 7 has Bluetooth capability.

MORE INFO   To learn more about connecting to a Bluetooth PAN, consult the following webpage: *http://windows.microsoft.com/en-US/windows7/Connect-to-a-Bluetooth-personal-area-network-PAN.*

Network locations

You need to know the available network locations that you can assign to Windows 7 network interfaces.

True or False? Administrators can manually configure the networks Windows 7 assigns to the domain network location.

Answer: *False.* You can differentiate networks based on their characteristics, so you can configure rules for Windows Firewall and Windows Firewall with Advanced Security (WFAS) that will apply to some network types and not others. Windows 7 remembers the properties of networks, so that once you assign a network type to a particular connection, the same network type will be assigned to the connection in the future. Windows 7 supports the following network locations:

- **Domain**   Profile is used when the computer is joined to an Active Directory domain. You cannot apply this profile manually. It is assigned to adapters, including VPN and DirectAccess connections, where Windows 7 detects a domain controller. Generally the most permissive profile.

- **Home/Work (Private)**   A manually selectable location type used for networks that are indirectly connected to the Internet. Network is assumed to be secure, but not as permissive as the domain profile. Can be set manually.

- **Public**   Used with insecure networks, including direct connections to the Internet and public access points. This profile is least permissive. Can be set manually.

Windows 7 supports more than one active network location type at a time. Computers running earlier versions of Windows support only one active network location type and apply the most restrictive profile when they detected multiple networks. Supporting more than one active location means that multiple profiles can be functioning at the same time. You will learn about Windows Firewall and WFAS later in this chapter.

> **MORE INFO**   To learn more about network location awareness, consult the following webpage: *http://technet.microsoft.com/en-us/library/cc753545(WS.10).aspx.*

Resolving connectivity issues

You need to know which diagnostic tools you can use to diagnose and resolve network connectivity issues.

True or False? You can use the ipconfig command to determine whether a DHCP server has provided the computer with an IP address.

Answer: *True.* Windows 7 includes a large number of command-line utilities that can be used to diagnose network connectivity problems.

- **Ipconfig**   Displays the IP address configuration. You can use the following options in diagnosing and resolving network connectivity issues:
  - **ipconfig /all**   To determine whether the computer has been correctly assigned an IP address from a DHCP server and to determine the default gateway, MAC address, and DNS server address.

- **ipconfig /release**   To release the currently leased address.
- **ipconfig /renew**   To renew the currently leased address.
- **ipconfig /flushdns**   To flush the DNS resolver cache.

- **Ping**   You can check point-to-point connectivity between computers running Windows 7. Use the -4 parameter to ensure that you are using IPv4 with Ping. If you can't ping a specific network host on a remote network, attempt to ping the default gateway address that you obtained running the ipconfig / all command.

- **Nslookup**   You can check the resolution of FQDN to IP address and IP address to FQDN. Use Nslookup when you suspect that connectivity problems might be caused by DNS problems. Use the command ipconfig /flushdns to flush the DNS resolver cache before attempting to use Nslookup.

- **Tracert**   You can see the path taken from the computer running Windows 7 to a destination host. You can determine if there is a problem between the computer running Windows 7 and the destination host, such as a failed router.

- **Pathping**   A tool that combines the functionality of Ping and Tracert. You can view the reliability of each hop on the path between two hosts. Useful if you want to determine whether a specific router is suffering reliability problems.

- **Route**   You can view and modify the computer's routing table.

- **Arp**   You can view the Address Resolution Protocol (ARP) cache. The ARP cache stores IP addresses and their resolved Ethernet addresses, also known as MAC address. Use it to determine whether Windows 7 can resolve the Ethernet addresses of other computers on the LAN.

- **Netstat**   Displays all active TCP connections. This tool can also display Ethernet statistics and the IP routing table.

MORE INFO   To learn more about troubleshooting and testing network connections, consult the following webpage: *http://technet.microsoft.com/en-us/library/dd163567.aspx*.

True or False? The Network Troubleshooter can automatically diagnose and repair common network problems.

Answer: *True*. The Network Troubleshooter provides a user-friendly interface for diagnosing network problems. The Network Troubleshooter performs common network troubleshooting tasks, such as attempting to renew a DHCP lease automatically. With Network Troubleshooter, non-IT professionals can resolve common network problems. Network Troubleshooter can diagnose problems with the following:

- Internet Connections
- Shared Folders
- HomeGroup

- Network Adapter
- Incoming Connections
- Connection To A Workplace Using DirectAccess

Network Troubleshooter is most useful for help desk support staff who can use it as first steps in a network troubleshooting routine during a support call. Users do not need to be members of the local Administrators group to use Network Trouble-shooter. Each time Network Troubleshooter runs, it generates a problem report. IT professionals can reference this report when performing a more thorough fault diagnosis.

MORE INFO To learn more about basic troubleshooting techniques, consult the following webpage: *http://windows.microsoft.com/en-US/windows7/Using-the-Network-troubleshooter-in-Windows-7.*

EXAM TIP The exam is more likely to ask you about diagnosing problems with specific utilities than to ask you about the Network Troubleshooter.

APIPA

You need to know how to determine whether the computer has been assigned an APIPA address and what modifications to make to Windows 7 to block APIPA address assignment.

True or False? A computer that has the IPv4 address 192.168.169.254 is using an APIPA address.

Answer: *False.* APIPA addresses fall in the range 169.254.0.1 to 169.254.255.254. Windows 7 computers that can't obtain a dynamically configured IPv4 address from a DHCP server use APIPA addresses. This can occur for a multitude of reasons, from the DHCP server not being functional to problems with the network adapter or intervening network infrastructure. You can use APIPA addresses to allow computers running Windows 7 on a LAN to communicate when no DHCP server is present. Computers with APIPA addresses can't use that address to send and receive traffic from hosts on the Internet.

You can disable APIPA on a computer running Windows 7 by editing the registry and adding the DWORD key IPAutoConfigurationEnabled, and setting the value to 0x0 under HKEY_LOCAL_MACHINE\SYSTEM\CurrentControlSet\Services\Tcpip\ Parameters\Interfaces\AdapterGUID, where AdapterGUID is the GUID of the specific network adapter.

MORE INFO To learn more about APIPA, consult the following webpage: *http:// msdn.microsoft.com/en-us/library/aa505918.aspx.*

EXAM TIP Remember that an APIPA address indicates that a computer that has a dynamically assigned IP address can't receive an address from DHCP. You can resolve the situation either by setting an address manually or resolving the issue that blocked the dynamic address from being allocated.

Can you answer these questions?

You can find the answers to these questions at the end of the chapter.

1. Which service must you configure to allow Windows 7 clients to use 802.1X authenticated wired connections?

2. What is the APIPA address range?

3. What command would you use to assign the IP address 10.10.0.101 that uses the subnet mask 255.255.255.0 and default gateway 10.10.0.1 to the "Local Area Connection" interface?

4. What command would you use to configure the interface "Local Area Connection" to use DHCP to obtain the address of DNS servers?

Objective 4.2: Configure IPv6 network settings

This objective requires you to demonstrate that you know how to configure IPv6 name resolution, network connections, and network locations; and how to resolve connectivity issues.

Exam need to know

- Configuring name resolution

  For example: How to configure Windows 7 with the IPv6 address of a DNS server.

- Connecting to a network

  For example: How to configure Windows 7 with an IPv6 address using the command line.

- Setting up a connection for a network

  For example: How to connect to networks that require certificate-based authentication.

- Network locations

  For example: How to know which network location is associated with a global unicast IPv6 address.

- Resolving connectivity issues

  For example: How to choose the appropriate tool to diagnose IPv6 connectivity problems.

- Link local multicast name resolution

  For example: How to determine when Windows 7 will use link-local multicast name resolution.

Configuring name resolution

You need to know how to configure IPv6 name resolution for computers running Windows 7.

True or False? You can use the Netstat command-line utility to configure IPv6 name resolution on a computer running Windows 7.

Answer: *False.* IPv6 name resolution works in a similar manner to IPv4 name resolution. You can configure a preferred and alternate DNS server that has an IPv6 address by editing the properties of a network adapter and then opening the Internet Protocol Version 6 (TCP/IPv6) Properties dialog box. You can also configure IPv6 DNS server configuration using the netsh interface IPv6 add dnsserver command from an elevated command prompt. For example, to add a DNS server with the IP address FEC0:0:0:FFFF::1 to the "Local Area Connection" interface, use this command:

```
Netsh interface ipv6 add dnsserver "Local Area Connection" FEC0:0:0:FFFF::1
```

You can use netsh to delete a DNS server for a configured interface. For example, to remove DNS server FEC0:0:0:FFFF::1 from the "Local Area Connection" interface, use the following command:

```
Netsh interface ipv5 delete dnsserver "Local Area Connection"
FEC0:0:0:FFFF::1
```

> **MORE INFO** To learn more about configuring IPv6 from the command line, consult the following webpage: *http://technet.microsoft.com/en-us/library/cc753156(WS.10).aspx.*

> **EXAM TIP** WINS only uses IPv4 and does not use IPv6. You can't configure WINS name resolution for IPv6.

Connecting to a network

You need to know how to configure an adapter to use an automatically assigned or static IPv6 address.

True or False? Unique local IPv6 addresses use the address prefix fc00::/7.

Answer: *True.* IPv6 generally uses auto-configured IP addresses. Configuring the provision of IPv6 addresses usually occurs through the configuration of routers or DHCP servers. There are three types of IPv6 addresses:

- **Unicast** Address used by a single network interface. Windows 7 supports the following types of unicast addresses:
  - **Global** Address prefix 2000::/3. Can also start with a 3000::/3. Used in the same way as a public IPv4 address for communication across the Internet.
  - **Link-local** Address prefix fe80::/64. Used in the same way as an IPv4 APIPA address for traffic on the same network that will not be routed. Used when IPv6 addresses are not automatically configured.
  - **Site-local** Address prefix fec0::/10. Can also start with Fed0::/10. Used in the same way as private IP address space, but deprecated by RFC 3879. Use unique local addresses instead of site-local.

- **Unique local**   Address prefix fc00::/7. Can also start with fd00::/7. Used in the same way as private IP address space. Routable within the organization.
- **Multicast**   Used by multiple nodes across the network and uses the FF prefix.
- **Anycast**   Used by multiple nodes, but traffic only received by nearest node to transmission according to routing metrics.

EXAM TIP   Remember IPv6 address prefixes for unicast addresses.

To configure a network interface to use a static or automatically assigned IPv6 address, perform the following steps:

1. Edit the properties of a network adapter. Select the Internet Protocol Version 6 (TCP/IPv6) Properties dialog box and then click Properties.

- To get IP address settings automatically, select Obtain An IPv6 Address Automatically.

- To use a static IPv6 address, choose Use The Following IPv6 Address and enter the IPv6 address, subnet prefix length, and default gateway.

To configure IPv6 addresses for interfaces from an elevated command prompt, use the netsh interface ipv6 add address command. For example, to add the address FC80::3 to the "Local Area Connection" interface, use this command:

```
Netsh interface ipv6 add address "Local Area Connection" FC80::3
```

MORE INFO   To learn more about configuring Windows 7 to use an IPv6 address, consult the following webpage: *http://windows.microsoft.com/en-US/windows7/ Change-TCP-IP-settings.*

True or False? IPv6 addresses can be automatically configured based on router advertisements.

Answer: *True.* Unlike IPv4, which uses DHCP servers to dynamically assign IP addresses, IPv6 uses auto-configuration to provision clients with addresses. IPv6 supports two different types of auto-configuration:

- **Stateful Auto-configuration**   Uses a DHCP server to provision clients with IPv6 addresses. Suitable for organizational networks.

- **Stateless Auto-configuration**   Uses router advertisements to inform hosts of appropriate IPv6 address prefix. Suitable for small organizations and individuals.

MORE INFO   To learn more about IPv6 auto-configuration, consult the following webpage: *http://msdn.microsoft.com/en-us/library/ms172318.aspx.*

EXAM TIP   Remember the difference between stateful and stateless auto-configuration.

Setting up a connection for a network

You need to know how to set up a connection for an IPv6 network.

True or False? You can specify an IPv6 address as the destination Internet address when configuring up a VPN connection.

Answer: *True*. Setting up a connection for a network uses the same process whether the network uses IPv4, IPv6, or both network-addressing schemes. For example, when setting up a VPN connection you can use an FQDN, IPv4, or IPv6 address as the destination Internet address. To set up a connection or network, use the Setup A Connection Or Network Wizard and choose one of the following options:

- Connect To The Internet
- Set Up A New Network
- Manually Connect To A Wireless Network
- Connect To A Workplace
- Set Up A Dial-Up Connection
- Set Up A Wireless Ad Hoc (Computer To Computer) Network
- Connect To A Bluetooth Personal Area Network (PAN)

Network locations

You need to know which network profiles are used by IPv6 networks.

True or False? IPv6-only networks use the same network profiles as IPv4-only networks.

Answer: *True*. A computer uses the same network locations independently of whether it is connecting to an IPv4 network, an IPv6 network, or a network that supports both IPv4 and IPv6. These network locations are as follows:

- **Domain** Profile is used with network adapters when Windows 7 determines that an Active Directory domain controller is directly contactable. This profile cannot be applied manually.
- **Home/Work (Private)** A manually selectable location type used for networks that are indirectly connected to the Internet, such as those that use link-local or unique unicast addresses.
- **Public** Used when the adapter is assigned a IPv6 global unicast address or when connecting to a potentially hostile network.

> **MORE INFO** To learn more about IPv6 and network profiles, consult the following webpage: *http://technet.microsoft.com/en-us/network/bb545475*.

Resolving connectivity issues

You need to know which tools you can use to resolve IPv6 connectivity issues.

True or False? The Nslookup utility cannot be used to resolve the IPv6 addresses of fully qualified domain names.

Answer: *False.* The tools that you use to diagnose IPv4 problems also work with IPv6. You can use the following tools to diagnose IPv6 connectivity issues:

- **Ipconfig** Displays the IP address configuration. Use Ipconfig to determine if the computer is using an appropriate IP address.

- **Ping** You can check point-to-point connectivity between computers running Windows 7 and another host. Use the -6 parameter to ensure that you are using IPv6 with Ping (for example, ping -6 www.contoso.com).

- **Nslookup** You can check the resolution of FQDN to IP address and IP address to FQDN. Use the –q=aaaa option to return only IPv6 addresses (for example, nslookup –q=aaaa www.contoso.com).

- **Tracert** You can see the path taken from the computer running Windows 7 to a destination host. Use the -6 option with IPv6 (for example, tracert -6 www.contoso.com).

- **Pathping** A combination of the Ping and Tracert tools. You can view the path between two hosts and the reliability of each hop in that path. Use the -6 option to force IPv6 (for example, pathping -6 www.contoso.com).

MORE INFO To learn more about network troubleshooting tools, consult the following webpage: *http://technet.microsoft.com/en-us/magazine/ee924647.aspx.*

EXAM TIP Remember that most of the tools that work for diagnosing problems on IPv4 networks will work on IPv6 networks.

Link local multicast name resolution

You need to know the situations in which link-local multicast name resolution (LLMNR) will be used by computers running Windows 7.

True or False? LLMNR is never used if a Windows 7 client is configured with the IPv6 address of a DNS server.

Answer: *False.* LLMNR is a protocol that allows IPv6 (and IPv4) hosts to perform name resolution on the local network segment without forwarding a query to a DNS server. LLMNR sends a link-local scope name request message to IPv6 multicast address FF02::1:3. All Windows 7 clients listen on this address and respond when their host name matches the name request. Computers running Windows 7 will fall back to using an LLMNR query if they can't resolve a name to an IP address through a DNS query.

MORE INFO To learn more about LLMNR, consult the following webpage: *http://technet.microsoft.com/en-au/library/bb878128.aspx.*

EXAM TIP Remember that LLMNR is used on the local network segment when DNS is not present or DNS cannot be used to successfully resolve a name.

Can you answer these?

You can find the answers to these questions at the end of the chapter.

1. What is the address prefix of a global unicast address?
2. What is the address prefix of a link-local address?
3. What is the address prefix of a unique local address?
4. Which protocol allows IPv6 name resolution on the local network segment without the presence of a DNS server?

Objective 4.3: Configure network settings

This objective requires you to demonstrate that you know how to add a wired or wireless device, connect automatically to a wireless network, configure network security settings, set preferred wireless networks, configure network adapters, and configure location-aware printing.

Exam need to know

- Adding a physically connected (wired) or wireless device

  For example: How to configure a Windows 7 client to discover a new storage device added to the network.

- Connecting to a wireless network

  For example: How to list available wireless networks from the command line.

- Configuring security settings on the client

  For example: How to configure 802.1x settings for network connections.

- Set preferred wireless networks

  For example: How to configure Windows 7 to use one network over another when multiple networks are available.

- Configuring network adapters

  For example: How to enable and disable clients, protocols, and services on a per-network adapter basis.

- Configuring Location Aware printing

  For example: How to configure Windows 7 to use a different default printer depending on which network the client connected to.

Adding a physically connected or wireless device

You need to know what steps to take to add a device, such as a storage device or printer, to an existing wired or wireless network.

True or False? You can see connected devices through View Network Computers And Devices on a Windows 7 client when Network Discovery is disabled.

Answer: *False*. Many devices, such as network storage devices, network-enabled printers, and network scanners, can be discovered by Windows 7 once they are connected to the same network segment. To add a physically connected device to the network, such as a storage device or network printer, perform the following steps:

1. Power on the device. Connect the device to a hub, switch, or router using a network cable.

2. On your Windows 7 client, in the Search Programs And Files text box on the Start menu, type **View Network Computers And Devices**. You should be able to connect to the device.

3. If the device is not visible, turn on Network Discovery through the Advanced Sharing Settings item in the Network And Sharing Center.

Wireless devices require more configuration to add to an existing network because you will need to provide them with the details and authentication credentials for the wireless network. To add a wireless device to the network, such as a wireless printer or storage device, perform the following steps:

1. Power on the device.

2. Configure the device to join a wireless network according to the instructions that shipped with the device.

3. Use the View Network Computers And Devices item in Windows 7 to verify the presence of the device on the network. If the device is not visible, verify that you have enabled Network Discovery.

MORE INFO To learn more about adding devices or computers to a network, consult the following webpage: *http://windows.microsoft.com/en-US/windows7/Add-a-device-or-computer-to-a-network*.

EXAM TIP Remember that you must enable Network Discovery on the Windows 7 client for devices on the network to be visible in View Network Computers And Devices.

Connecting to a wireless network

You need to know how to configure a Windows 7 client to connect to a wireless network.

True or False? You can view available wireless networks from the command prompt.

Answer: *True*. Windows 7 clients can connect to wireless networks using the following methods:

- **Network notification area icon** Click this icon to connect from the Windows 7 taskbar.

- **Set Up A Connection Or Network Wizard** You can choose to connect to a wireless network from Network and Sharing center. You can use this method to prepopulate wireless networks without having to initiate a connection.

- **Manage Wireless Networks dialog box**   You can add new wireless networks or delete existing remembered wireless network connections. You can use this method to prepopulate wireless networks without having to initiate a connection. You can use this method to create an ad hoc wireless network.

- **Group Policy**   Administrators can specify wireless network settings for domain-joined computers.

- **Netsh wlan command-line utility**   You can view and join wireless networks from the command line. For example, the command Netsh wlan show networks displays available wireless networks.

To connect to a network that is not broadcasting its SSID, you must specify the SSID name. You can do this by choosing the Other Network option when connecting from the taskbar or through the Manually Connect To A Wireless Network option in Set Up A Connection Or Network.

Windows 7 supports the following wireless access point security types:

- **802.1x**   IEEE 802.1X authentication with WEP. Also known as dynamic WEP. Uses WEP for traffic encryption.

- **No Authentication (Open)**   Open system authentication. No traffic encryption.

- **WEP**   Open system authentication with Wired Equivalent Privacy (WEP). Uses WEP for traffic encryption.

- **WPA-Enterprise**   Wi-Fi Protected Access (WPA) with IEEE 802.1X authentication. Can use AES or TKIP to encrypt traffic.

- **WPA2-Enterprise**   WPA2 with IEEE 802.1X authentication. Can use AES or TKIP to encrypt traffic.

- **WPA-Personal**   WPA with a preshared key. Can use AES or TKIP to encrypt traffic.

- **WPA2-Personal**   WPA2 with a preshared key. Can use AES or TKIP to encrypt traffic.

MORE INFO   To learn more about connecting to wireless networks, consult the following webpage: *http://technet.microsoft.com/en-us/library/ff802404.aspx.*

EXAM TIP   WPA2-Personal is the strongest wireless security method you can use with a preshared key.

Configuring security settings on the client

You need to know how to configure security settings such as 802.1X authentication on network connections.

True or False? Wired network connections on Windows 7 clients are enabled for 802.1X authentication by default.

Answer: *False*. With 802.1X authentication, you can limit network access to clients that have performed authentication. As you learned earlier, you can configure 802.1X authentication for wired network connections by configuring the Wired AutoConfig service. When this service is active, the Authentication tab becomes available on a network adapter's properties. On the Authentication tab, you can configure the following settings:

- Enable IEEE 802.1X authentication
- Choose A Network Authentication Method
  - Microsoft: Smart Card Or Other Certificate
  - Microsoft: Protected EAP (PEAP)
- Remember My Credentials For This Connection Each Time I'm Logged On
- Fallback To Unauthorized Network Access

True or False? You can configure 802.1X authentication to use either user or computer authentication.

Answer: *True*. By configuring Advanced Settings on the Authentication tab of a network adapter's properties, you can configure the following advanced settings:

- **Specify Authentication Mode** Used when you want to configure specific types of 802.1X authentication. You can choose between the following:
  - **User Or Computer Authentication** User or computer can perform 802.1X authentication.
  - **Computer Authentication** Computer credentials are used for 802.1X authentication.
  - **User Authentication** User credentials are used for 802.1X authentication.
  - **Guest Authentication** Allows limited guest access to the network.
- **Enable Single Sign On For This Network** Determines how single sign in functions with 802.1X authentication. You can configure the following single sign in options:
  - Perform Immediately Before User Logon
  - Perform Immediately After User Logon
  - Maximum Delay
  - Allow Additional Dialogs To Be Displayed During Single Sign On
  - This Network Uses Separate Virtual LANs for Machine And User Authentication

MORE INFO To learn more about 802.1X authentication, consult the following web-page: *http://technet.microsoft.com/en-us/library/cc730878(WS.10).aspx.*

EXAM TIP Remember that you need to enable 802.1X authentication when connecting to authenticating switches in secure environments.

Set preferred wireless networks

You need to know how you can configure a Windows 7 client to connect to one wireless network in preference over another when both are in range.

True or False? You can configure a Windows 7 client to connect to a particular wireless network when more than one wireless network that you regularly connect to is available.

Answer: *True.* You can configure Windows 7 to remember the credentials that you use to connect to different wireless networks. You can use the Manage Wireless Networks dialog box to set preferred wireless networks, with wireless networks toward the top of the list preferred over wireless networks lower on the list. When the Windows 7 client is in range of one or more existing networks for which credentials are stored, it connects to the preferred wireless network.

> *MORE INFO* To learn more about preferred wireless networks, consult the following webpage: *http://windows.microsoft.com/en-US/windows7/View-your-preferred-wireless-networks.*

> *EXAM TIP* Remember that wireless networks closer to the top of the list have higher priority than wireless networks farther down the list.

Configuring network adapters

You need to know how to enable and disable Clients, Services, and Protocols on a per-network adapter basis.

True or False? IPv6 is disabled by default on all network adapters.

Answer: *False.* By editing the network adapter properties, you can configure existing Clients, Services, and Protocols or install a new Client, Service, or Protocol. Network adapters in Windows 7 come with the following clients and protocols enabled:

- **Client For Microsoft Networks** A client can access resources on Microsoft networks.
- **QoS Packet Scheduler** Enables network traffic control, including rate-of-flow and traffic prioritization.
- **File And Printer Sharing For Microsoft Networks** Enables the Windows 7 client to share files and printers.
- **Internet Protocol Version 6 (TCP/IPv6)** Enables the computer to use IPv6. Click Properties to configure IPv6 address configuration.
- **Internet Protocol Version 4 (TCP/IPv4)** Enables the computer to use IPv4. Click Properties to configure IPv4 address configuration.
- **Link-Layer Topology Discovery Mapper I/O Driver** Enables the Windows 7 client to discover network infrastructure components such as other clients and devices.
- **Link-Layer Topology Discovery Responder** Enables the Windows 7 client to be discovered on the network.

Although all these items are enabled by default, it is possible to disable them when necessary. You can add additional clients for third-party network operating systems using this dialog box. You can configure the authentication options of a network adapter only if the Wired AutoConfig service is started.

> **EXAM TIP** Remember that both the Link-Layer Topology Discovery Mapper I/O Driver and the Link-Layer Topology Discovery Responder must be enabled for the computer to be able to discover and be discovered on the LAN.

Configuring Location Aware Printing

You need to know what steps to take to configure a computer running Windows 7 to use a different default printer when connected to different networks.

True or False? Windows 7 Professional edition supports Location Aware Printing.

Answer: *True*. With Location Aware Printing, Windows 7 clients can use a different default printer depending on the network to which they connect. Default printers are associated with network names. You configure default printers for each network name using the Manage Default Printers dialog box, which is accessible through the Devices And Printers Control Panel item. The Professional, Enterprise, and Ultimate editions of Windows 7 support Location Aware Printing.

> **MORE INFO** To learn more about Location Aware Printing, consult the following webpage: *http://technet.microsoft.com/en-us/library/ee424302(WS.10).aspx*.

> **EXAM TIP** Location Aware Printing is useful for computers that are regularly moved to different locations, such as an employee who works at different branch office locations during the week.

Can you answer these questions?

You can find the answers to these questions at the end of the chapter.

1. You have a laptop computer running Windows 7. What technology should you configure to ensure that your default printer used in your home office is different than the default printer used at your place of work?

2. A Windows 7 client has a single network adapter. Which service needs to be enabled on the network adapter's properties to ensure that other clients on the network can access the client's shared folders and printer?

3. Your office has three wireless networks: Alpha, Beta, and Gamma. How can you ensure that your computer connects to wireless network Gamma when all three networks are in range?

4. You have added a new network storage device to your wired home network. The device is visible in View Network Computers And Devices on one Windows 7 client, but not on another. Both clients are running Windows 7 Ultimate. What change should you make to ensure that the device is visible on the second Windows 7 client?

Objective 4.4: Configure Windows Firewall

This objective requires you to demonstrate that you know how to configure Windows Firewall and WFAS to support inbound and outbound connections to specific programs, services, and with specific ports. You should also be able to manage and configure connection security rules.

Exam need to know

- Allowing or denying an application

  For example: How to configure WFAS to block remote access to a specific service.

- Configuring rules for multiple profiles

  For example: How to configure Windows 7 to apply a firewall rule across multiple network profiles.

- Network profile specific rules

  For example: How to configure a firewall rule to apply only when the computer is using the Public network profile.

- Configuring notifications

  For example: How to configure Windows 7 to notify you when traffic to a program is blocked by Windows Firewall.

- Configuring authenticated exceptions

  For example: How to configure Windows 7 to allow remote access to a program or service when a connection is authenticated.

Allowing or denying an application

You need to know how to configure Windows Firewall and WFAS to allow or block an application based on the application's path.

True or False? You can allow programs through Windows Firewall by using the ipconfig command.

Answer: *False.* You can allow or block inbound network traffic to programs or features on a computer running Windows 7. To allow a program through Windows Firewall, open the Windows Firewall Control Panel item and then click Allow A Program Or Feature Through Windows Firewall. Either select the program or feature from the list, or click Allow Another Program and then navigate to the executable file for that program. To allow or block a program through the command line, use the netsh firewall add allowedprogram command. For example, to allow the program c:\app\program.exe, run the following command from an elevated command prompt:

```
Netsh firewall add allowedprogram "c:\app\program.exe" "My Program" enable
```

You can disable a program through the GUI by either removing the rule that allows the program or deselecting the profiles in which it is enabled. You can also disable rules using the netsh firewall set allowedprogram disabled command.

MORE INFO To learn more about configuring Windows Firewall from the command line, consult the following webpage: *http://technet.microsoft.com/en-us/library/cc771046(WS.10).aspx.*

EXAM TIP Remember that Windows Firewall has limited functionality, and you can block only inbound traffic to programs and features.

True or False? You can create rules in WFAS to block outbound traffic for specific applications.

Answer: *True*. You can use WFAS to block or allow programs, services, or traffic on specific ports. Unlike Windows Firewall, you can configure WFAS to allow or block both inbound and outbound traffic. WFAS does not block outbound connections by default, though this can be changed on a per-network profile basis by setting the Outbound connections drop-down from Allow (default) to Block.

To allow an application, perform the following steps.

1. In WFAS, choose Inbound Rule and then click New Rule. This will launch the New Inbound Rule Wizard.

2. Choose Program, specify the program path, and choose one of the following options:

   - **Allow The Connection** The connection is allowed if other conditions are met.
   - **Allow The Connection If It Is Secure** The connection is allowed only if it is secured using the settings in IPsec properties and a Connection Security Rule. You'll learn more about Connection Security Rules later in this chapter.
   - **Block The Connection** The connection is blocked.

3. Select the profiles in which the rule applies and give the rule a name.

To create a rule based on a Service, choose the Custom rule type in the New Inbound Rule Wizard. Creating outbound rules involves running the New Outbound Rule Wizard. The process for creating an outbound rule is the same as when you create a new inbound rule: You choose the rule type, whether to allow, allow if secure, or block the connection; and specify the network profiles in which the rule applies.

You can create WFAS rules from an elevated command prompt using the netsh in the advfirewall firewall context. The following command will create a WFAS rule named ProgramRule that will allow all inbound traffic to a program named app.exe located in the directory c:\app:

```
Netsh advfirewall firewall add rule name="ProgramRule" dir=in program="c:\app\app.exe" action=allow
```

To block traffic to the same program, issue the command:

```
Netsh advfirewall firewall add rule name="ProgramRule" dir=in program="c:\app\app.exe" action=block
```

MORE INFO To learn more about adding Windows Firewall with Advanced Security rules using netsh, consult the following webpage: *http://technet.microsoft.com/en-us/library/dd734783(WS.10).aspx.*

EXAM TIP Remember that with WFAS, you can block outbound traffic.

Configuring rules for multiple profiles

You need to know how to configure a firewall rule to apply across multiple network profiles in both Windows Firewall and Windows Firewall with Advanced Security.

True or False? A firewall rule can only apply in a single network profile.

Answer: *False.* Windows Firewall rules can apply across one or more network profiles. You can choose the network profiles in which a firewall rule applies for Windows Firewall by choosing Allow Program Or Feature Through Windows Firewall on the Windows Firewall Control Panel item, then clicking Change Settings, and then checking the profiles in which you want a specific allowed program or feature to be enabled. Firewall rules are represented by program and feature name. You can choose to enable firewall rules in the home/work (private) or public profiles. You can also choose to allow a program or feature for the domain network profile if your computer is a member of an Active Directory domain. You can configure the profiles in which a Windows Firewall rule applies using the netsh firewall set allowedprogram command with the profile option.

```
Netsh firewall set allowedprogram "C:\apps\program.exe" "Program"
profile=standard
```

True or False? You can configure WFAS rules to only apply to wireless network interfaces.

Answer: *True.* With WFAS, you can control the network profiles in which a rule applies. You can configure this by editing the properties of the WFAS rule or by specifying the network profiles during rule creation. You also can configure the following additional limits on rules:

- **Interface Types** You can specify that the rule applies to one or all of the following interface types: Local Area Network, Remote Access, Wireless.
- **Edge Traversal** You can block or allow traffic that has passed across a Network Address Translation router or firewall.
- **Scope** You can specify local and remote IP addresses and IP address ranges. WFAS will block traffic that does not meet the specified local and remote IP address scope condition.
- **Users** You can specify user accounts or group accounts when you configure a firewall rule that allows only secure connections. WFAS will block network traffic from users not on this list.
- **Computers** You can specify a list of computers or security groups when you configure a firewall rule that allows only secure connections. WFAS will block network traffic computers not on this list.

MORE INFO To learn more about WFAS advanced properties, consult the following webpage: *http://technet.microsoft.com/en-us/library/cc731927.aspx.*

EXAM TIP Remember that you can configure a firewall rule to apply to a specific interface type.

You can configure rules to function in specific profiles from the command line by using the netsh advfirewall firewall set rule command with the profile option. For example, to set the rule named Alpha to apply in the domain profile, use this command:

```
Netsh advfirewall firewall set rule name="Alpha" new profile=Domain
```

Network profile specific rules

You need to know how to configure a Windows Firewall or WFAS rule to apply only in specific profiles.

True or False? Windows Firewall rules must always apply to the public profile.

Answer: *False.* You can configure a firewall rule to apply in a single network profile. You can do this by choosing Allow Program Or Feature Through Windows Firewall on the Windows Firewall Control Panel item, then clicking Change Settings, and then checking the profile in which you want a specific allowed program or feature to be enabled. You can configure the profiles in which a Windows Firewall rule applies using the netsh firewall set allowedprogram command with the profile option. The allowed profile settings are as follows:

- **Current** Applies to all currently active network profiles
- **Domain** Applies only to the domain profile
- **Standard** Applies only to the private profile
- **All** Applies to all profiles except the private profile

True or False? The private profile applies to both the home and work locations.

Answer: *True.* You can configure the network profiles in which a WFAS rule applies on the Advanced tab of the rule's properties. You can choose for the rule to apply in the domain, private (home or work), or public profiles. You can modify an existing WFAS rule using the netsh advfirewall firewall set rule command with the profile option and choose among the following options:

- **Public** Applies to the public network profile
- **Private** Applies to the work and home network profiles
- **Domain** Applies to the domain network profile
- **Any** Applies to all network profiles

MORE INFO To learn more about applying WFAS rules in specific profiles, consult the following webpage: *http://technet.microsoft.com/en-us/library/cc731927.aspx.*

EXAM TIP Remember that you can use the domain profile only for computers that are members of Active Directory domains.

Configuring notifications

You need to know how to enable and disable notifications in Windows Firewall and WFAS.

True or False? You can enable notifications in Windows Firewall on a per-network location basis.

Answer: *True.* Notifications inform the user that Windows Firewall has blocked a new program. You configure notifications for Windows Firewall by performing the following steps:

1. Open the Windows Firewall console and then click Change Notification Settings.
2. In the Customize Settings dialog box, choose whether to enable the Notify Me When Windows Firewall Blocks A New Program option for each network location.

MORE INFO To learn more about notification settings for Windows Firewall, consult the following webpage: *http://windows.microsoft.com/en-US/windows7/Understanding-Windows-Firewall-settings.*

True or False? You can configure WFAS notifications only for the domain profile.

Answer: *False.* You configure notifications for WFAS by editing WFAS properties and clicking the Customize button in the Settings area for each profile. You can then choose whether a notification is displayed when a program is blocked from receiving inbound connections.

MORE INFO To learn more about notification settings for WFAS, consult the following webpage: *http://technet.microsoft.com/en-us/library/cc753002.aspx.*

EXAM TIP Remember that notifications can be configured on a per-profile basis.

Configuring authenticated exceptions

You need to know how to configure a connection security rule so that connections from specific computers do not require authentication.

True or False? Authentication exemptions enable you to bypass WFAS rules that require authentication.

Answer: *True.* Authentication exemptions allow you to exempt computers or IP address ranges from needing to authenticate even when other connection security rules are being applied. You need to use authentication exemptions only when you are using connection security rules and you have configured WFAS rules with the Allow The Connection If It Is Secure action. An authentication exemption makes all such rules function as if the Allow The Connection action were chosen, but only for the computers specified in the authentication exemption rule. To create an authentication exemption, open the WFAS console and perform the following steps:

1. Select the Connection Security Rules node and click New Rule on the Actions pane.
2. On the Rule Type page, select Authentication Exemption.
3. On the Exempt Computers page, click Add and then enter an IP address, an IP subnet, or one of the following from the predefined list:
   - Default gateway
   - WINS servers
   - DHCP servers
   - DNS servers
   - Local subnet
4. Specify the profiles in which the exemption applies and give the exemption a name.

MORE INFO To learn more about authentication exemptions, consult the following webpage: *http://technet.microsoft.com/en-us/library/cc811521(WS.10).aspx.*

True or False? You can create authentication exemptions using the netsh command-line utility.

Answer: *True.* You can create authentication exemptions using the netsh command-line utility. You must run this command from an elevated command prompt and use the netsh advfirewall consec option. When using this command you must specify endpoint1 as "any" and endpoint2 as the addresses of the computers for which you want to configure the authentication exemption. For example, to create authentication exemptions from all computers on the subnet 192.168.16.0/24, use the following command:

```
Netsh advfirewall consec add rule name=Exemptions endpoint1=any
endpoint2=192.168.16.0/24 action=noauthentication
```

MORE INFO To learn more about configuring authentication exemptions, consult the following webpage: *http://technet.microsoft.com/en-us/library/dd736198(WS.10). aspx.*

EXAM TIP Authentication exemptions are most useful when you want to configure a management computer that can make remote connections when the authentication infrastructure has failed.

Can you answer these questions?

You can find the answers to these questions at the end of the chapter.

1. What steps would you take to block outgoing traffic from a specific application when the computer is connected to a public Wi-Fi access point?

2. You have a network application in the c:\networkapp1 directory that uses the executable name networkapp1.exe. You want to create a WFAS rule named NetworkApplication that allows inbound traffic to this application. What command should you use to accomplish this goal?

3. What command-line command would you run to configure the WFAS rule named Epsilon to apply in the domain profile?

4. What command-line command would you run to create an authentication exemption for all computers on the subnet 10.10.100.0/24?

Objective 4.5: Configure remote management

This objective requires you to demonstrate that you know how to use and configure Windows 7 remote management technologies including PowerShell remoting, WinRS, Remote Desktop, and Remote Assistance.

Exam need to know

- Remote management methods

  For example: How to select an appropriate remote management method.

- Configuring remote management tools

  For example: How to configure Windows 7 to accept Remote Desktop connections.

- Executing PowerShell commands

  For example: How to use PowerShell remoting to run a single command on multiple computers.

Remote management methods

You need to know the appropriate remote management method for a specific task.

True or False? You can perform remote management of computers running Windows 7 only if they are members of the same domain.

Answer: *False.* You can perform remote management of computers running Windows 7 using several different technologies, each of which is appropriate for specific scenarios. Each remote management technology can be used when the remote and the local computers are members of the same Active Directory domain or when they are stand-alone systems. The remote management technologies that you can use with Windows 7 include these:

- **Remote Assistance** Used in screen-sharing support scenarios. The remote user is given permission to connect by the currently logged-in user.

- **Remote Desktop** Allows remote full-screen login to a computer running Windows 7. The remote user requires local credentials that have Remote Desktop privileges.

- **WinRS** Allows remote execution of scripts and command-line utilities. Remote user requires local credentials with permission to execute command-line utilities and scripts.

- **PowerShell Remoting** Allows remote execution of PowerShell commands and scripts. Requires local credentials with permission to execute PowerShell commands and scripts.

MORE INFO To learn more about remote management methods for computers running Windows 7, consult the following webpage: *http://technet.microsoft.com/en-us/library/dd443489(WS.10).aspx.*

Configuring remote management tools

You need to know how to configure Windows 7 to support Remote Assistance, Remote Desktop, and remote PowerShell sessions.

True or False? It is possible to remotely log in through Remote Assistance without the logged-in user's permission.

Answer: *False.* Remote Assistance is a support tool that enables support staff, usually referred to as *helpers*, to view the screen of a user logged in to a computer running Windows 7. Remote Assistance requires the helper to have an invitation issued by the computer user. The computer user can terminate the Remote Assistance session at any time.

True or False? Helpers remotely connected using Remote Assistance can respond to User Account Control (UAC) prompts.

Answer: *True.* With Easy Connect, you can connect without using Remote Assistance invitations. You can use Easy Connect only when both computers are running Windows 7, both computers have Internet access, and routers support the Peer Name Resolution Protocol (PNRP). If Easy Connect is unavailable, you can forward an invitation file through an email message or by transferring the invitation file through another method such as a file share or USB storage device. When connecting, a helper must enter a password that displays on the user's screen. You can transmit this password with the invitation, but Microsoft recommends using a separate method such as an SMS message or reading the password over a telephone call. You can specify the period of invitation validity through the Remote Assistance Settings dialog box. In domain-based environments, the user can choose to allow a helper to respond to UAC prompts when accepting the connection.

MORE INFO To learn more about Remote Assistance, consult the following webpage: *http://windows.microsoft.com/en-US/windows7/Windows-Remote-Assistance-frequently-asked-questions.*

EXAM TIP Remote Assistance requires an invitation, and you can view the logged-in user's desktop. Remote Desktop does not require an invitation, and you can't view the logged-in user's desktop.

True or False? Computers running Windows 7 Home Premium support incoming Remote Desktop connections.

Answer: *False.* With Remote Desktop, clients that use the Remote Desktop Connection software or a compatible third-party alternative to make remote connections to computers running Windows 7 can view and interact with the desktop of the host computer. Remote Desktop has the following properties:

- All editions of Windows 7 include Remote Desktop Connection client software.
- Remote Desktop Connection is disabled by default.
- You can remotely connect only to computers running Windows 7 Professional, Enterprise, or Ultimate.
- You can remotely log in to a Windows 7 computer if no user is locally logged in.
- If a user locks the screen of a Windows 7 computer, that user can remotely connect and resume the locked session using Remote Desktop.
- A currently logged-in user can deny access to someone attempting console login or remote login.
- Remote users on the Internet can make connections to Windows 7 computers with Remote Desktop enabled on internal networks through Windows Server 2008 R2 computers that host the Remote Desktop Gateway role.
- Enabling Remote Desktop automatically configures the firewall rules that allow inbound connections.

MORE INFO To learn more about Remote Desktop, consult the following webpage: *http://windows.microsoft.com/en-US/windows7/Remote-Desktop-Connection-frequently-asked-questions.*

True or False? You can configure Remote Desktop so that only Remote Desktop clients that support Network Level Authentication can connect.

Answer: *True.* When you enable Remote Desktop, you choose between allowing connections from any version of Remote Desktop or restricting connections to Remote Desktop clients that support Network Level Authentication. The Remote Desktop clients available in Windows Vista, Windows 7, and Windows Server 2008 support Network Level Authentication.

True or False? By default, only members of the local Administrators group can make a Remote Desktop connection to a computer running Windows 7.

Answer: *False.* Members of the administrators and Remote Desktop Users local groups can connect through Remote Desktop to computers running Windows 7. When you add specific users or groups through the Remote Desktop Users dialog box, you can alter which groups and users can log in by editing the Computer Configuration\Windows Settings\Security Settings\Local Policies\User Rights Assignment\Allow Log On Through Remote Desktop Services policy.

MORE INFO To learn more about Remote Desktop, consult the following TechNet document: *http://technet.microsoft.com/en-us/magazine/ff404238.aspx.*

EXAM TIP Remember the difference between allowing connections from computers running any version of Remote Desktop and computers running Remote Desktop with Network Level Authentication.

True or False? You enable Windows Remote Shell (WinRS) by running the Windows Remote Management (WinRM) Quickconfig command.

Answer: *True.* With WinRS, you can execute command-line utilities on a remote computer. To configure a computer to accept remote commands, run the following command from an elevated command prompt:

```
Winrm quickconfig
```

To manage computers that are not part of the same Active Directory domain, you need to configure a bi-directional trust by executing the following command:

```
Winrm set winrm/config/client @{TrustedHosts="trusted FQDN or IP address"}
```

You can configure WinRM settings through the \Computer Configuration\ Administrative Templates\Windows Components\Windows Remote Management and \Computer Configuration\Administrative Templates\Windows Components\ Windows Remote Shell group policy nodes.

True or False? You use the WinRS command to execute command-line utilities on remote computers.

Answer: *True.* You use the WinRS command to execute command-line utilities or scripts on the remote computer. You also specify the name of the remote computer using the –r parameter. For example, to run the command hostname on the computer Win7-B, using the Kim_Akers account, use this command:

```
WinRS -r:Win7-B -u:Win7-B\Kim_Akers hostname
```

MORE INFO To watch a Remote Shell video tutorial, consult the following webpage: *http://technet.microsoft.com/en-us/library/dd163506.aspx.*

When the computer is on the local network, specify the NetBIOS name. If the computer is on a remote network, use the fully qualified domain name and address the http or https listener. You can configure the http and https listener using the WinRM command. For example, to run the hostname command on the computer win7-b.contoso.com across the Internet using the Kim-Akers local account, use this command:

```
WinRS -r:http://win7-b.contoso.com -u:win7-b\kim_akers hostname
```

MORE INFO To learn more about Remote Shell, consult the following webpage: *http://technet.microsoft.com/en-us/library/dd163506.aspx.*

Executing PowerShell commands

You need to know what steps to take to enable PowerShell remoting and to execute PowerShell commands on remote computers running Windows 7.

True or False? You can enable PowerShell remoting by running the Enable-PSRemoting cmdlet when the Windows Remote Management service is configured.

Answer: *True*. To set up PowerShell for remoting when the WinRM service is running, open an elevated PowerShell session and run the following command:

```
Enable-PSRemoting -force
```

True or False? You need to configure remotely managed computers to be trusted when attempting to use PowerShell remoting for computers that are in different Active Directory environments.

Answer: *True*. When managing computers not in the same Active Directory domain, you will need to configure remotely managed computers to be trusted. Do this from an elevated command prompt by issuing the following command:

```
Winrm set winrm/config/client @{TrustedHosts="Remote Computer or IP
Address"}
```

To open an interactive session, run the Enter-PSSession cmdlet with the Computer-Name parameter. For example, to open an interactive session to computer Win7-680, use this command:

```
EnterPSSession -ComputerName:Win7-680
```

To end the session, run the Exit-PSSession cmdlet.

True or False? You can run one PowerShell command or script against multiple computers.

Answer: *True*. With PowerShell remoting, you can execute commands in parallel to more than one destination computer. You do this by using the Invoke-Command cmdlet with the Computername parameter. For example, to run the cmdlet Get-Hotfix on computers ALPHA, BETA, and GAMMA using the Kim_Akers local account credential, run this command:

```
Invoke-Command -scriptblock { Get-Hotfix } -computername ALPHA,BETA,GAMMA
```

> **MORE INFO**   To learn more about PowerShell remoting, consult the following web-page: *http://technet.microsoft.com/en-us/magazine/ff700227.aspx*.

Can you answer these questions?

You can find the answers to these questions at the end of the chapter.

1. Which remote management technology would you use if you needed to remotely train a user on a new application?

2. Which editions of Windows 7 support incoming Remote Desktop connections?

3. Rooslan wants to make a Remote Desktop connection to a computer running Windows 7 Enterprise, but he is not a member of the local Administrators group on this computer. What group should you add Rooslan's user account to in order to allow him to accomplish this goal?

4. PowerShell remoting is configured on computer Win7A and Win7B. What command would you use on Win7A to open an interactive PowerShell session on Win7B?

Answers

This section contains the answers to the "Can you answer these questions?" sections in this chapter.

Objective 4.1: Configure IPv4 network settings

1. You must configure the Wired AutoConfig service.

2. The APIPA range is 169.254.0.0 through 169.254.255.254.

3. Use this command: netsh interface ipv4 set address "Local Area Connection" static 10.10.0.101 255.255.255.0 10.10.0.1.

4. Use this command: netsh interface ipv4 set dnsservers "Local Area Connection" source=dhcp.

Objective 4.2: Configure IPv6 network settings

1. Global unicast addresses use the 2000::/3 prefix.

2. Link-local addresses use the FE80::/64 prefix.

3. Unique local addresses use the fc00::/7 prefix.

4. Link-local multicast name resolution (LLMNR).

Objective 4.3: Configure network settings

1. You should configure location-aware printing.

2. The File and Printer Sharing For Microsoft Networks service must be enabled on the network adapter for other clients on the network to be able to access the client's shared folders and printer.

3. Configure Gamma above Beta and Alpha in the Manage Wireless Networks list. This will configure Gamma as a preferred wireless network.

4. Turn on Network Discovery through the Advanced Sharing Settings item in Network and Sharing Center.

Objective 4.4: Configure Windows Firewall

1. Create a WFAS outbound rule that blocks traffic from the application on the public profile.

2. Use this command: netsh advfirewall firewall add rule name="NetworkApplication" dir=in program="c:\networkapp1\network-app1.exe" action=allow.

3. Use this command: netsh advfirewall firewall set rule name="Epsilon" new profile=Domain.

4. Use this command: netsh advfirewall consec add rule name=Exemptions endpoint1=any endpoint2=10.10.100.0/24 action=noauthentication.

Objective 4.5: Configure remote management

1. Remote Assistance enables screen sharing.

2. Windows 7 Professional, Enterprise, and Ultimate support incoming Remote Desktop connections.

3. Add Rooslan's account to the Remote Desktop Users group.

4. EnterPSSession -ComputerName:Win7B.

CHAPTER 5

Configuring Access to Resources

Approximately 13 percent of the 70-680 exam focuses on the topic of configuring access to resources. You need to have a good grasp of how to configure Microsoft Windows 7 to share resources to other users on the network, configure permissions on files and folders, and ensure that users can properly authenticate. You also need to understand how Windows 7 clients in branch offices can leverage BranchCache to speed up remote file and folder access.

This chapter covers the following objectives:

- Objective 5.1: Configure shared resources
- Objective 5.2: Configure file and folder access
- Objective 5.3: Configure User Account Control (UAC)
- Objective 5.4: Configure authentication and authorization
- Objective 5.5: Configure BranchCache

Objective 5.1: Configure shared resources

This objective requires you to demonstrate that you know how to configure folder redirections, set up shared folder permissions so that users have an appropriate level of access, configure shared printers, and manage HomeGroup settings.

Exam need to know

- Folder virtualization
  For example: How to configure Windows 7 to redirect commonly used folders to a network share.
- Shared folder permissions
  For example: How to configure shared folder permissions to enable one group of users to read documents without being able to modify them.

- Printers and queues

  For example: How to configure shared printer permissions so that one group of users can manage all documents in the printer queue.

- Configuring HomeGroup settings

  For example: How to configure a portable computer running Windows 7 Ultimate that is domain joined.

Folder virtualization

You need to know how to configure folder redirection for users who log on to computers running Windows 7.

True or False? Folder redirection can redirect the Documents folder to a file server.

Answer: *True.* With folder virtualization, part of user state virtualization and also known as folder redirection, a user's folders can be redirected to a specially configured file share. With folder redirection, common folders are available to the user independently of which computer is used. Folder redirection maps folders (for example, Favorites, Downloads, Documents, and AppData) to shared folders. Windows 7 improves the performance of folder redirection by leveraging offline files functionality, which means that content in redirected folders will be available if the connection between the computer running Windows 7 and the host server is disrupted.

True or False? You can use Group Policy to redirect the Favorites folder.

Answer: *True.* You can configure folder redirection through Group Policy by editing the items under the \User Configuration\Policies\Windows Settings\Folder Redirection node. You can configure redirection for the following folders:

- AppData (Roaming)
- Desktop
- Start Menu
- Documents
- Pictures
- Music
- Videos
- Favorites
- Contacts
- Downloads
- Links
- Searches
- Saved Games

When configuring these policies, you can choose between the following options:

- **Basic**   Each person's folder is redirected to the same location. When you choose this option, you can choose to do the following:
  - Redirect to the user's home directory
  - Create a folder for each user under the root path
  - Redirect to a specific location
  - Redirect to the local user profile location
- **Advanced**   Folders are redirected based on the user group. Although this option provides the same options as the Basic choice, you can differentiate these settings based on security group membership.

MORE INFO   To learn more about folder redirection, consult the following webpage: *http://technet.microsoft.com/en-us/library/cc771969.aspx.*

Shared folder permissions

You need to know which shared folder permissions can be configured by using both the Share and the Advanced Sharing options.

True or False? The owner permission is automatically assigned to the person who shares the folder.

Answer: *True.* When you choose to share a folder using simple sharing, you can choose the following permission levels:

- **Owner**   This permission is assigned to the person who shares the folder. This person can then change permissions.
- **Read**   The person accessing the shared folder can read the contents of the file, but cannot delete or modify the file.
- **Read/Write**   The person accessing the shared folder can read, modify, add, or delete the files.

Whenever possible, best practice is to assign share permissions to groups instead of individual users. This is straightforward when the computer is joined to a domain because you just use a domain-based group. If the computer is a member of a HomeGroup, you can configure permissions for the HomeGroup. You can also configure permissions for the Everyone group or for individual local user accounts on the computer running Windows 7.

True or False? The Change advanced share permission is functionally the same as the Read/Write simple share permission.

Answer: *True.* Advanced Sharing is available on the folder's properties page. You can share items, such as the entire volume, that you cannot share using simple sharing options. Using the Advanced Sharing dialog box, you can limit the number of users who can access the share. You can also configure additional permissions using the Advanced Sharing dialog box. Rather than configuring the Read, Read/Write, and

Owner share permissions, you instead configure Full Control, Change, and Read. The big difference is that you can assign an Allow or Deny permission, with Deny settings overriding Allow settings. The advanced Read share permission is the same as in simple sharing. The Change permission is the same as the Read/Write simple sharing permission because you can read, modify, delete, and add files to the shared folder. The Full Control permission confers the same rights as the Change permission, except that users also can modify existing permissions.

True or False? You can configure shared folders on computers running Windows 7 to support the offline files functionality.

Answer: *True.* You can configure caching from the Advanced Sharing dialog box so files shared by the computer running Windows 7 can have offline file access. You can configure the following options:

- **Only The Files And Programs That Users Specify Are Available Offline**   Users can access only those files that are specifically set by the user to be available offline.

- **No Files Or Programs From The Shared Folder Are Available Offline**   This setting blocks offline file access for files hosted on the computer running Windows 7.

- **All Files And Programs That Users Open From The Shared Folder Are Automatically Available Offline**   This setting ensures that users will have offline access to files hosted on the computer running Windows 7.

You can centrally manage all folders shared on a computer running Windows 7 by using the Shared Folders node of the Computer Management console. This console will provide you with the following information:

- **Shares node**   This node shows a list of all shares on the computer running Windows 7.

- **Sessions node**   This node shows which users are connected, how long they have been connected, and the location from which they are connecting.

- **Open Files node**   This node shows folders and files currently being accessed remotely.

You can use the Net Share command to manage shared folders from a command prompt. To create a shared folder, use the following command syntax:

```
Net share sharename=drive:path
```

You can assign permissions using the Net Share command by using the following syntax:

```
Net share sharename=[path] /grant:user,[Read/Change/Full]
```

You can also use this command to configure caching options.

> **MORE INFO**   To learn more about shared folders, consult the following webpage: *http://windows.microsoft.com/en-US/windows7/Share-files-with-someone.*

Printers and queues

You need to know how to share printers and how to assign permissions to manage printers.

True or False? You can distribute printer drivers for Windows XP when sharing a printer on a computer running Windows 7.

Answer: *True*. With shared printers, other users on the network can send documents to a printer managed by a computer running Windows 7. You can enable printer sharing in HomeGroup or in Advanced Sharing Settings after the printer is installed. If the printer needs to be accessible to computers running Windows XP or Windows Vista, you can add drivers for these operating systems by clicking the Additional Drivers button. After pressing this button, clients running those operating systems are automatically provisioned with the appropriate drivers when they remotely connect to the printer.

> **MORE INFO** To learn more about sharing printers with other operating systems, consult the following webpage: *http://windows.microsoft.com/en-US/windows7/help/sharing-files-and-printers-with-different-versions-of-windows.*

True or False? Users can restart the printer with the Manage Documents permission.

Answer: *False*. When a printer is shared, the Everyone group is granted the Print permission. All members of the HomeGroup (or any members of the domain if the computer is domain joined) can submit jobs to the printer. It is possible to assign specific permissions to printers beyond these default permissions. These permissions include the following:

- **Print** A user or group has permission to print. Users can rearrange the documents they submit to the printer.
- **Manage This Printer** A user or group can pause and restart the printer. Users can modify spooler settings, permissions, properties, and printer sharing.
- **Manage Documents** A user or group can pause, restart, resume, cancel, and reorder any documents in the current print queue.

> **MORE INFO** To learn more about printer permissions, consult this webpage: *http://windows.microsoft.com/en-US/windows7/Why-cant-I-change-the-printer-properties.*

Configuring HomeGroup settings

You need to know what can be shared with a homegroup and the conditions under which a homegroup can be created.

True or False? Domain-joined computers can't join homegroups.

Answer: *False.* Homegroups simplify file sharing by sharing libraries and folders, and printers on non domain networks. Using computers running Windows 7 Starter and Windows 7 Home Basic, you can join a homegroup, but you can't create one. Computers running Home Premium, Professional, Enterprise, and Ultimate editions can create homegroups as long as there is no existing homegroup or they are not members of a domain. If they are members of a domain, they can join an existing homegroup only. A user must have administrative privileges to enable, join, and leave a homegroup. Users without administrative privileges can select which libraries to share with the homegroup. You can block computers joining homegroups by configuring the \Computer Configuration\Policies\Administrative Templates\Windows Components\HomeGroup\Prevent The Computer From Joining A Homegroup Group Policy item.

> **MORE INFO** To learn more about homegroups, consult the following webpage: *http://windows.microsoft.com/en-US/windows7/What-is-a-homegroup.*

Can you answer these questions?

You can find the answers to these questions at the end of the chapter.

1. Which policy do you configure to prevent a domain-joined portable computer running Windows 7 from being able to join a homegroup?

2. You want to have the AdminAssistants group be able to pause and restart shared printers. Which permission should you assign to this group?

3. Which node of the Computer Management console provides you with information on which files hosted on shared folders are currently open?

4. A user has 10 important files hosted in the Documents folder. What steps can you take to ensure access to these files from any computer?

Objective 5.2: Configure file and folder access

This objective requires you to demonstrate that you know how to manage the Encrypting File System (EFS), manage NTFS File System (NTFS) permissions, and disentangle permissions when a user is a member of multiple groups that are assigned different permissions to the same resource. You also need to understand how the process of copying files differs from moving files.

Exam need to know

- Encrypting files and folders by using EFS

  For example: How to configure a folder so that all new files created in the folder will be encrypted using EFS.

- Configuring NTFS permissions

  For example: How to configure a folder so that it does not inherit the permissions of its parent folder.

- Resolving effective permissions issues

  For example: How to use the Effective Permissions tool to calculate a user's permission.

- Copying files versus moving files

  For example: How to understand what happens to permissions, encryption, and compression when a file is moved or copied between separate locations on the same volume.

Encrypting files and folders by using EFS

You need to know how to encrypt files and folders using EFS and how to configure recovery of those files and folders if the original owner can't do so.

True or False? You can use EFS to encrypt files stored on the FAT32 file system.

Answer: *False.* EFS provides per-user encryption of files and folders. EFS is available for the Professional, Enterprise, and Ultimate editions of Windows 7. EFS is different from BitLocker and BitLocker To Go, which offer full volume encryption. EFS can be used only on volumes formatted with NTFS. If you encrypt a file using EFS and then copy it to a USB stick formatted with the FAT32 file system, the file is automatically decrypted. Similarly, if you encrypt a file with EFS and then attach it to an email message, the file is decrypted during the attachment process. Encrypted files display in Windows Explorer with green text. If you encrypt a folder, all new files created in that folder are encrypted. Similarly, files copied and moved to that folder are also encrypted. If you copy an encrypted file to a compressed folder, the file remains encrypted and doesn't compress. You can use the cipher.exe command-line utility to manage EFS from the command line.

True or False? An EFS-encrypted file can be configured to be readable by multiple users.

Answer: *True.* Although it is possible to add the EFS certificates of multiple users to encrypt individual files, you can't do it at the folder level. To give additional users access to an EFS-encrypted file, you need to have access to their public EFS certificates. Doing so is possible on stand-alone computers running Windows 7 only if the user has previously encrypted a file. In domain environments, you can configure autoenrollment of EFS certificates so that public EFS certificates for all users are accessible through Active Directory.

True or False? You can configure a recovery agent certificate using the Cipher.exe command-line utility.

Answer: *True*. Recovery agents are special certificates that allow EFS-encrypted files to be decrypted. In domain environments, the first administrator account in the domain is configured by the Default Domain Policy as a recovery agent. You can create a separate recovery agent by using the following command:

`Cipher.exe /r:recoveryagent`

Running this command will create two files: recoveryagent.cer and recoveryagent.pfx. You can edit the \Computer Configuration\Windows Settings\Security Settings\Public Key Policies\Encrypting File System node and specify the location of the recoveryagent.cer file. By importing recoveryagent.pfx, a user can perform recovery of EFS recovery operations. If your organization has deployed a Microsoft Windows Server 2008 or Microsoft Windows Server 2008 R2 Active Directory Certificate Services CA, you can issue a special data recovery agent certificate and use it in place of the certificate generated with cipher.exe.

> **MORE INFO** To learn more about EFS, consult the following webpage: *http://technet. microsoft.com/en-us/library/cc700811.aspx.*

Configuring NTFS permissions

You need to know which NTFS permissions are available and how they can be used to control access to files and folders.

True or False? Users granted the Modify permission to a folder can execute program files in that folder.

Answer: *True*. NTFS permissions can be applied to folders and individual files. NTFS permissions can be applied only to files and folders hosted on the NTFS file system. You can't configure file and folder permissions for files and folders hosted on FAT or FAT32 volumes. Permissions are assigned to security principals. A security principal can be a user or a security group. You can assign the following NTFS permissions:

- **Full Control (FC)**   The security principal can view the contents of a file or folder, modify existing files and folders, create new files and folders, and run programs in a folder. Granting this permission also grants the Modify, Read & Execute, List Folder Contents, Read, and Write permissions.
- **Modify (M)**   The security principal can change existing files and folders, but can't create new files and folders. Granting this permission also grants the Read & Execute, List Folder Contents, Read, and Write permissions.
- **Read & Execute (RX)**   The security principal can view the contents of existing files and folders. The security principal can also run programs in the folder.
- **Read (R)**   The security principal can view the contents of folders and open files.

- **Write (W)** The security principal can create new files and folders as well as make modifications to existing files and folders.
- **List Folder Contents (LFC)** The security principal can view the contents of folders. This permission can be applied only to folders.

MORE INFO To learn more about permissions, consult the following webpage: *http://windows.microsoft.com/en-US/windows7/What-are-permissions.*

True or False? The Delete Subfolders and Files special permission is associated only with the Full Control permission.

Answer: *True.* The 6 common NTFS permissions are actually combinations of 14 special permissions, with FC including all 14 special permissions. These special permissions and the NTFS permissions that they are related to are as follows:

- **Traverse Folder/Execute File** FC, M, R&E, LFC
- **List Folder/Read Data** FC, M, R&E, LFC, R
- **Read Attributes** FC, M, R&E, LFC, R
- **Read Extended Attributes** FC, M, R&E, LFC, R
- **Create Files/Write Data** FC, M, W
- **Create Folders/Append Data** FC, M, W
- **Write Attributes** FC, M, W
- **Write Extended Attributes** FC, M, W
- **Delete Subfolders and Files** FC
- **Delete** FC, M
- **Read Permissions** FC, M, R&E, LFC, R, W
- **Change Permissions** FC
- **Take Ownership** FC
- **Synchronize** FC, M, R&E, LFC, R, W

MORE INFO To learn more about special permissions consult the following webpage: *http://technet.microsoft.com/en-us/library/cc732880.aspx.*

True or False? You can't back up NTFS permissions from the command line.

Answer: *False.* You can use the Icacls.exe command-line utility to view and modify NTFS permissions. Use the syntax Icacls.exe file /grant user_or_group:permission and use /deny to apply a Deny permission instead of an Allow permission. For example, to assign Kim Akers the Read and Execute permission on the d:\binaries folder, issue this command:

```
Icacls.exe d:\binaries /grant Kim_Akers:(OI)RX
```

You can also use Icacls.exe to back up permissions and restore them. For example, to back up all the permissions on the e:\shared_folder folder to a file named permissions, use this command:

```
Icacls.exe e:\shared_folder\* /save permissions /t
```

> **MORE INFO** To learn more about the Icacls.exe utility, consult the following webpage: *http://technet.microsoft.com/en-us/library/cc753525(WS.10).aspx*.

Resolving effective permissions issues

You need to know how to calculate security principals' actual permissions when they are assigned different permissions to the same file or folder, usually through being members of multiple security groups.

True or False? Effective permissions must always be calculated manually.

Answer: *False*. If users are members of multiple groups, they might have been assigned separate permissions to the same shared folder, NTFS folder, or file stored on an NTFS file system. The basic rules are these:

- Permissions work cumulatively.
- Deny permissions override Allow permissions.

The Effective Permissions tool allows you to determine a user or group's actual permissions for a specific file or folder. You can access the Effective Permissions tool through the Advanced button on the Security tab of the target item's properties.

> **MORE INFO** To learn more about effective permissions, consult the following webpage: *http://technet.microsoft.com/en-us/library/cc772184.aspx*.

> **EXAM TIP** Remember that a Deny permission overrides an Allow permission.

Copying files vs. moving files

You need to know what happens to permissions when a file is copied (as opposed to when it is moved).

True or False? A file inherits the permissions of the target folder when moved to a new folder on the same volume.

Answer: *False*. NTFS permissions work differently depending on whether a file is copied or moved on the same volume or to a different volume. For example:

- When you copy a file or folder from one folder to another, the file or folder will inherit the permissions of the target folder. This applies if the file is being copied within the same volume or to a different volume.
- A file or folder will retain its original permissions when you move that file or folder between folders on the same volume.
- A file or folder moved from one volume to a separate volume inherits the permissions of the destination volume.

You can use the robocopy.exe command-line utility to move files and folders from one volume to another while retaining existing permissions. Depending on the options used, robocopy.exe is an exception to the normal rules of moving and copying files. When you move files or folders to FAT or FAT32 volumes, the files lose all existing permissions.

MORE INFO To learn more about permissions when files and folders are copied, consult the following webpage: *http://support.microsoft.com/kb/266627.*

Can you answer these questions?

You can find the answers to these questions at the end of the chapter.

1. When moving a file from one folder to another folder on the same volume, what happens to that file's permissions?

2. Describe what happens when you move an EFS-encrypted file to a compressed folder on the same volume.

3. Rooslan is a member of three separate security groups assigned different NTFS permissions to the same folder. What tool can you use to calculate Rooslan's actual permissions to that folder?

4. Which permissions should you assign to a folder if you want to allow a user to edit existing files stored in that folder, but not to alter the permissions of those files?

Objective 5.3: Configure User Account Control (UAC)

This objective requires you to demonstrate that you know how to configure security policies related to UAC, including how to configure different behaviors for users with administrative privileged and nonprivileged accounts. You also need to know how to configure secure desktop functionality.

Exam need to know

- Configuring Local Security Policy

  For example: How to configure Windows 7 to require complex passwords

- Configuring admin versus standard UAC prompt behaviors

  For example: How to configure Windows 7 to require users with local administrator privileges to provide credentials.

- Configuring Secure Desktop

  For example: How to configure Windows 7 to ensure that all UAC prompts are displayed on the secure desktop.

Configuring Local Security Policy

You need to know how to use the Local Security Policy console to configure security policies on a computer running Windows 7 and what configuration options are available.

True or False? Secpol.msc can be used to configure password and account lockout policies.

Answer: True. By using the Local Security Policy console (accessible by typing **secpol.msc** in the Search Programs And Files dialog box), you can manage policy items that are usually located in the Computer Configuration\Windows Settings\ Security Settings node of a typical Group Policy object (GPO). Using the Local Security Policy console, you can configure the following settings:

- **Account Policies**   Includes password policies and account lockout policies. These determine the length and complexity of passwords as well as what happens when a user enters an incorrect password a specific number of times.

- **Local Policies**   Includes Audit Policy, User Rights Assignment, and Security Options. User Rights Assignment allows you to configure which users can perform tasks such as logging on locally and backing up files. You'll learn more about configuring rights later in this chapter. You can use security options to configure such things as whether users have to press Ctrl+Alt+Del to log on and what happens if a user that authenticated with a smart card ejects the card during a session.

- **Windows Firewall With Advanced Security**   You can configure firewall settings through policy. You learned about configuring Windows Firewall in Chapter 4, "Configuring Network Connectivity."

- **Network List Manager Policies**   You can specify the properties of networks, such as whether the network is Public or Private, and whether the logged-on user can modify this designation.

- **Public Key Policies**   You can configure EFS, BitLocker, and certificate enrollment policies.

- **Software Restriction Policies**   Administrators can control which software can be run on computers running Windows 7. You learned about Software Restriction Policies in Chapter 3, "Configuring Hardware and Applications."

- **Application Control Policies**   Application Control Policies (AppLocker) are the technological successors to Software Restriction Policies. You learned about Application Control Policies in Chapter 3.

- **IP Security Policies on Local Computer**   This is a policy option used to support older implementations of IPsec. As you learned in Chapter 4, IPsec is configured for computers running Windows 7 through connection security rules.

- **Advanced Audit Policy Configuration**   You can configure which advanced audit policies are active when advanced audit policy configuration is enabled. You'll learn more about advanced audit policies in Chapter 6, "Configuring Mobile Computing."

MORE INFO   **To learn more about using the Local Security Policy editor consult the following webpage:** *http://technet.microsoft.com/en-us/magazine/ee851677.aspx.*

Configuring admin vs. standard UAC prompt behaviors

You need to know which Group Policy items you need to configure to manage UAC behavior for standard and privileged users.

True or False? You can configure different UAC behavior depending on whether a user is a member of the local Administrators group on the computer running Windows 7.

Answer: *True.* UAC has two basic prompt behaviors: prompt for consent and prompt for credentials. When prompted for consent, users are asked a Yes or No question, to which they can respond by clicking one of the available options. When prompted for credentials, users must reauthenticate, usually by providing their password, to provide an affirmative response to the UAC dialog box. You control the behavior of the UAC prompt through two policies: one policy for users with local administrator privileges, and the other for users who don't have those privileges. These policies are as follows:

- User Account Control: Behavior of the elevation prompt for standard users
- User Account Control: Behavior of the elevation prompt for administrators in Admin Approval mode

True or False? You can configure UAC so that a standard user can respond to a UAC prompt by entering the credentials of a user who is a member of the local Administrators group.

Answer: *True.* You have the following options for controlling elevation prompt behavior for standard users:

- **Automatically Deny Elevation Requests**   Any attempt at privilege elevation is automatically blocked.
- **Prompt For Credentials On The Secure Desktop**   A nonprivileged user can provide the credentials of a privileged user when providing a response to a UAC prompt. This request occurs on the secure desktop.
- **Prompt For Credentials**   A nonprivileged user can provide the credentials of a privileged user on the standard interactive desktop. This can be overridden by User Account Control: Switch To The Secure Desktop When Prompting For Elevation policy and the secure desktop would be used.

True or False? You can force administrators to re-enter their credentials when responding to UAC prompts.

Answer: *True.* You have the following options when configuring the User Account Control: Behavior Of The Elevation Prompt For Administrators In Admin Approval Mode policy:

- **Elevate Without Prompting**   When this option is configured, the privileged user is automatically allowed to perform the task without having to provide consent or credentials.

- **Prompt For Credentials On The Secure Desktop** The privileged user must enter credentials to allow the elevation of privileges. This occurs on the secure desktop.

- **Prompt For Consent On The Secure Desktop** The privileged user must choose Yes or No on the secure desktop.

- **Prompt For Credentials** The privileged user provides credentials on the interactive desktop. This can be overridden by User Account Control: Switch To The Secure Desktop When Prompting For Elevation policy, and the secure desktop would be used.

- **Prompt For Consent** The privileged user is prompted for consent on the interactive desktop. This can be overridden by User Account Control: Switch To The Secure Desktop When Prompting For Elevation policy and the secure desktop would be used.

- **Prompt For Consent For Non-Windows Binaries** This option requires consent only when running programs that aren't part of Windows. Consent occurs on the interactive desktop, but it can be overridden by User Account Control: Switch To The Secure Desktop When Prompting For Elevation policy, and the secure desktop would be used.

MORE INFO To learn more about controlling UAC through Group Policy, consult the following webpage: *http://windows.microsoft.com/en-US/windows7/How-do-I-change-the-behavior-of-User-Account-Control-by-using-Group-Policy.*

Configuring Secure Desktop

You need to know how to configure UAC to use the secure desktop instead of the interactive desktop when dealing with UAC prompts.

True or False? Secure Desktop can protect against malware that can mask the UAC prompt.

Answer: *True.* Secure Desktop is a special mode that Windows 7 enters when providing a UAC consent or credentials prompt. When in Secure Desktop mode, the UAC dialog box appears on a dimmed screenshot of the desktop when the operating system invokes UAC. Secure Desktop ensures that users are responding directly to the UAC prompt and are not responding to malware that can mask the UAC prompt, inadvertently tricking the logged-on user to provide consent to elevate the malware's privileges. Secure Desktop can cause problems with some screen-sharing software, and it might be necessary to disable Secure Desktop in certain circumstances to be able to remotely perform administrative tasks. Remote Desktop and Remote Assistance fully support Secure Desktop, and remotely connected users can respond to prompts on the secure desktop as if they were logged on locally.

True or False? You can configure all prompts for consent or prompts for credentials to appear on the secure desktop.

Answer: *True.* You can configure the User Account Control: Switch To The Secure Desktop When Prompting For Elevation policy to ensure that all prompts for credentials and prompts for consent appear on the secure desktop. It occurs no matter which settings you configure in the following policies:

- User Account Control: Behavior Of The Elevation Prompt For Administrators In Admin Approval Mode
- User Account Control: Behavior of the Elevation Prompt For Standard Users

MORE INFO To learn more about UAC and Secure Desktop, consult the following webpage: *http://windows.microsoft.com/en-US/windows7/User-Account-Control-Switch-to-the-secure-desktop-when-prompting-for-elevation.*

Can you answer these questions?

You can find the answers to these questions at the end of the chapter.

1. Which Group Policy item would you configure to ensure that users logged on with accounts that do not have administrative privileges can provide the credentials of an account that has local administrative privileges?

2. Which Group Policy item would you configure to ensure that all UAC prompts occur on the secure desktop?

3. Currently administrators are prompted for consent by UAC when they need elevated permissions. What modification would you make to Group Policy to ensure that administrators must enter their password when they want to elevate permissions?

4. Which command would you type in the Search Programs And Files dialog box to open the Local Security Policy console?

Objective 5.4: Configure authentication and authorization

This objective requires you to demonstrate that you know how to resolve issues related to authentication, configure Group Policy so that specific users and groups are given appropriate rights, back up and modify saved credentials, manage certificates and smart cards, be able to elevate privileges as necessary, and configure Group Policies to support multifactor authentication.

Exam need to know

- Resolving authentication issues
  For example: How to configure a password reset disk.

- Configuring rights

  For example: How to configure Windows 7 so that only members of the local Administrators group can shut down a computer.

- Managing credentials

  For example: How to back up passwords used to access websites and local network resources.

- Managing certificates

  For example: How to know which tool to use to request a new certificate.

- Smart cards with PIV

  For example: How to configure Windows 7 to lock the screen if a user removes the smart card.

- Elevating user privileges

  For example: How to configure Windows 7 to run a program using administrator privileges.

- Multifactor authentication

  For example: How to configure Windows 7 to require that a user log on with a smart card.

Resolving authentication issues

You need to know how to manage forgotten passwords for users of computers running Windows 7.

True or False? A password reset disk can be configured to recover a user password after the user has forgotten that password.

Answer: *False.* The most common authentication problem faced by users of computers running Windows 7 is forgotten passwords. There are two ways to resolve this issue:

- **Password reset disk**   A password reset disk can be used to reset a local account hosted on a computer running Windows 7. You cannot use a password reset disk to reset a domain-based account. A password reset disk must be created prior to the password being forgotten. A password reset disk can be stored on a USB storage device; it doesn't have to be stored on a floppy disk (as the name implies).

- **Reset user account password**   It is possible to reset a user account password for a local user account only if there is a way for a user with local administrator privileges to log on to the computer. When a local user's password is changed, that user loses access to all EFS-encrypted files, personal certificates, and stored passwords hosted in the Windows Vault through Credential Manager. If Windows Vault has been backed up using Credential Manager, it is possible to recover these items.

If a user's account has been locked out because too many incorrect passwords were entered in succession, the account can be unlocked by a user with local administrative privileges. Unlocking an account does not reset the account password and doesn't affect stored credentials or EFS certificates.

MORE INFO To learn more about password reset disks, consult the following webpage: *http://windows.microsoft.com/en-US/windows7/Create-a-password-reset-disk.*

EXAM TIP Remember that you can't use password reset disks to reset domain-based user accounts.

Configuring rights

You need to know how to configure user rights through the User Rights Assignment node of a Group Policy object.

True or False? You can block nonadministrative users from shutting down the system by configuring Group Policy.

Answer: *True*. User rights are configured though the Computer Configuration\ Windows Settings\Security Settings\Local Policies\User Rights Assignment node of Group Policy. When configuring policies to assign rights, best practice is to specify a group instead of a user account. This way you can assign the right to a specific user by adding the user to a security group instead of modifying the Group Policy item. There are 44 policies available in this node. Although you should review all these policies as part of your exam preparation, important policies include the following:

- Allow Log On Through Remote Desktop Services
- Back Up Files And Directories
- Change The System Time
- Deny Log On Locally
- Deny Log On Through Remote Desktop Services
- Local And Unload Device Drivers
- Manage Auditing And Security Log
- Shut Down The System

True or False? The Power Users group does not provide any special administrative rights.

Answer: *True*. You can assign rights by adding users to the built-in local groups. The built-in local groups on a computer running Windows 7 are as follows:

- **Administrators** Provides unrestricted access to the settings of the computer.
- **Backup Operators** Users can override file and folder permissions to back up files.
- **Cryptographic Operators** Users can perform cryptographic operations. Used only when Windows 7 is deployed in Common Criteria mode.

- **Distributed COM Users** Users can manipulate distributed COM objects.
- **Event Log Readers** Users can read data stored in the event logs, except for the Security log, which requires membership in the Administrators group.
- **Network Configuration Operators** Users can alter TCP/IP address settings.
- **Performance Log Users** Users can schedule data collector sets.
- **Performance Monitor Users** Users can access performance data.
- **Power Users** Provided for backward compatibility. Does not confer rights.
- **Remote Desktop Users** Users can make remote connections to the computer through Remote Desktop Client.
- **Replicator** Users can use file replication in a domain environment.

MORE INFO To learn more about the default local groups, consult the following webpage: *http://technet.microsoft.com/en-us/library/cc771990.aspx.*

Managing credentials

You need to know how to use Credential Manager to store logon names and passwords for network resources.

True or False? You can store passwords for Remote Desktop Services servers in Windows Vault.

Answer: *True*. Credential Manager can store user names and passwords for file servers, websites, Remote Desktop Services, and other network resources. Credential Manager hosts this data in the Windows Vault. Windows Vault can be backed up so that saved credentials can be transferred from one computer running Windows 7 to another. You can add credentials to Windows Vault by choosing Remember My Credentials when presented with the Windows Security dialog box. This dialog box is available in Windows Internet Explorer, Windows Explorer, and Remote Desktop Connection.

MORE INFO To learn more about Credential Manager, consult the following webpage: *http://windows.microsoft.com/en-US/windows7/What-is-Credential-Manager.*

Managing certificates

You need to know how to manage user and computer certificates used for authentication.

True or False? You cannot use the Certificates console to import a previously exported certificate.

Answer: *False*. You can open the Certificates console by typing **certmgr.msc** in the Search Programs And Files text box. You can use the Certificate Services console to import or export certificates. The most efficient way of deploying certificates to users is to use autoenrollment. This is not appropriate in all cases, such as the issuance of sensitive certificates. In this case, the Certificates console can be used to request certificates that the user has permission to enroll in. The request is forwarded to the CA, where it is either automatically approved or will be approved or rejected depending on the decision of the certificate services administrator.

> **MORE INFO** To learn more about importing and exporting certificates, consult the following webpage: *http://windows.microsoft.com/en-US/windows7/Import-or-export-certificates-and-private-keys.*

Smart cards with PIV

You need to know how to use smart cards with personal identity verification (PIV) with computers running Windows 7.

True or False? You can have Windows 7 lock the screen if a user removes the smart card while logged on.

Answer: *True.* Smart cards host digital certificates that you can use authenticate with computers running Windows 7. Windows 7 supports the PIV standard. This means that you can use smart cards directly with Windows 7 without having to install third-party software. Group policies related to smart cards are located in the Computer Configuration\Windows Settings\Security Settings\Local Policies\Security Options node. These policies have the following functionality:

- **Interactive Logon: Require Smart Card** Enable this policy to force a user to log on with a smart card. Used when implementing multifactor authentication.
- **Interactive Logon: Smart Card Removal Behavior** Configure this policy to specify how the operating system will react if a smart card is removed while the user is logged on. You can choose between locking the computer, forcing logoff, and disconnecting an active Remote Desktop session.

> **MORE INFO** To learn more about using smart cards with Windows 7, consult the following webpage: *http://technet.microsoft.com/en-us/library/dd367851(WS.10).aspx.*

Elevating user privileges

You need to know how to configure UAC to display an elevation prompt for credentials when a normal user performs an action that requires elevated privileges.

True or False? A user who is logged on with a user account that does not have administrative privileges can't elevate privileges.

Answer: *False.* There are several ways to elevate user privileges. Some applications, which require elevated privileges, will automatically prompt the user with a UAC prompt. If users are logged on with local administrative credentials, they can respond to this prompt either by providing consent or credentials. If users aren't logged on with an account that has local administrative credentials, their request for elevation is either automatically denied or they can provide alternative credentials, depending on how Group Policy is configured. You learned about these Group Policy configuration options earlier in this chapter.

A user can also elevate a process by right-clicking the process and choosing the Run As Administrator option. This option triggers a UAC prompt to which the user must respond. You use the Run As Administrator option to elevate a command prompt or PowerShell session when you start it.

A user can also use the runas.exe command from the command line to run programs with another user's credentials. For example, to run the application program. exe as user Kim_Akers on computer Adelaide, issue this command:

```
Runas.exe /user:Adelaide\Kim_Akers "program.exe"
```

> **MORE INFO** To learn more about elevating permissions, consult the following webpage: *http://technet.microsoft.com/en-us/magazine/ff431742.aspx.*

Multifactor authentication

You need to know how to support multiple authentication methods, such as smart card and password, on computers running Windows 7.

True or False? You can't force users to log on to computers running Windows 7 with a smart card.

Answer: *False.* The most common form of multifactor authentication used with Windows 7 is logging on with user name, password, and smart card. It is possible, if you install third-party tools, to use biometric authentication, such as a fingerprint reader, as part of a multifactor authentication scheme. Windows 7 does not provide native support for this form of authentication. If you want to ensure that multifactor authentication is used, enable the Interactive Logon: Require Smart Card policy.

> **MORE INFO** To learn more about planning the deployment of smart cards with Windows 7, consult the following webpage: *http://technet.microsoft.com/en-us/library/ee706526(WS.10).aspx.*

Can you answer these questions?

You can find the answers to these questions at the end of the chapter.

1. What steps can you take to ensure that you can run command-line utilities that require elevation?

2. What step would you take to ensure that users could log on to a computer running Windows 7 only if they had a smart card?

3. How can you ensure that users are logged off if they remove their smart card when logged on to a computer running Windows 7?

4. Which tool would you use to request a new certificate from a CA for which you had permission to enroll?

Objective 5.5: Configure BranchCache

This objective requires you to demonstrate that you know how to configure Branch-Cache through Group Policy and the command line, know which BranchCache mode is appropriate for a given environment, understand the network infrastructure requirements for BranchCache, and what the certificate requirements are for Hosted Cache mode.

Exam need to know

- Distributed Cache mode vs. Hosted mode

  For example: How to determine when Distributed Cache mode is more appropriate than Hosted mode.

- Network infrastructure requirements

  For example: How to determine what steps need to be taken to support Hosted Cache mode at a branch office.

- Configuring settings

  For example: How to configure Windows 7 to use Distributed Cache mode from the command line.

- Certificate management

  For example: How to configure certificates to support Hosted Cache mode.

Distributed Cache mode vs. Hosted mode

You need to know when you should choose to use Distributed Cache mode instead of Hosted Cache mode.

BranchCache is a technology available to computers running Windows 7 Enterprise and Ultimate that allows them to store content accessed across a wide area network (WAN) link and share it with other Windows 7 clients on the branch office network. BranchCache can be used with data stored on Windows Server 2008 R2 web and file servers, and can't be used with data stored on file or web servers running earlier versions of Windows Server.

True or False? All computers in Distributed Cache mode at a branch office host copies of the entire cache.

Answer: *False.* Distributed Cache mode involves a group of computers running Windows 7 at a branch office sharing the cache. Each member of the Distributed Cache holds part of the cache, but no single client computer at the branch office holds all the cache. When a Windows 7 client accesses content across the WAN, it stores that content in its local cache. The next Windows 7 client at the branch office accessing the same content across the WAN will instead access that content from the local cache on the peer computer. Distributed Cache mode has the advantage of not requiring a computer running Windows Server 2008 R2 to be deployed at the branch office.

True or False? You can use a server running Windows Server 2008 as a Hosted Cache mode server.

Answer: *False.* Hosted Cache mode uses a central branch office cache hosted on a server running Windows Server 2008 R2. An advantage of Hosted Cache mode over Distributed Cache mode is that the cache is centralized and available as long as the server is online. Clients must be configured with the address of the local Hosted Cache server by using netsh.exe or through Group Policy. You must also ensure that each computer running Windows 7 trusts the SSL certificate issued to the Hosted Cache mode server.

> **MORE INFO** To learn more about BranchCache modes, consult the following webpage: *http://technet.microsoft.com/en-us/library/dd637832(WS.10).aspx.*

> **EXAM TIP** Remember which editions of Windows 7 support BranchCache.

Network infrastructure requirements

You need to know what server and client operating systems need to be present to support a BranchCache deployment.

True or False? BranchCache can be used by computers running Windows 7 Professional.

Answer: *False.* BranchCache can be used only with computers running Windows 7 Enterprise and Ultimate. If you are using Hosted Cache mode, you must deploy a server running Windows Server 2008 R2 with the BranchCache feature installed on the branch office network. This server must have an SSL certificate installed that is trusted by all BranchCache clients. When the certificate is installed, you need to link the certificate to BranchCache. You will learn how to do this later in this chapter. By default, BranchCache will use up to 5 percent of the active partition on the Hosted Cache Size. You can modify this amount by using the following command, where *X* is the percentage value of the active partition that you want to devote to the Hosted Cache:

```
Netsh branchcache set cachesize size=80 percent=true
```

> **MORE INFO** To learn more about configuring Windows Server 2008 R2 to support BranchCache, consult the following webpage: *http://technet.microsoft.com/en-us/library/dd637785(WS.10).aspx.*

Servers hosting BranchCache content must be running Windows Server 2008 R2 and must have the BranchCache feature installed. BranchCache can be used with file shares and Internet Information Server (IIS) content, including Windows Server Update Services content. When configuring a file server to support BranchCache, you must also install the BranchCache For Network Files role service and configure the \Computer Configuration\Administrative Templates\Network\Lanman Server\ Hash Publication For BranchCache policy.

Configuring settings

You need to know the Group Policy items and command-line tools that you can use to support BranchCache.

True or False? The default round trip delay that triggers BranchCache is 150 milliseconds.

Answer: *False.* To configure a Windows 7 computer as a BranchCache client, you need to enable BranchCache, choose between Hosted Cache mode and Distributed Cache mode, and then configure the appropriate Windows Firewall with Advanced Security rules. The BranchCache policies are located in the \Computer Configuration\Administrative Templates\Network\BranchCache node of a GPO. You can use the following Group Policy items to configure BranchCache:

- **Turn On BranchCache**   Enables BranchCache.
- **Set BranchCache Distributed Cache Mode**   Configures Windows 7 to use Distributed Cache mode. Requires that the Turn On BranchCache policy be enabled.
- **Set BranchCache Hosted Cache Mode**   Configures Windows 7 to use Hosted Cache mode. Requires that the Turn On BranchCache policy be enabled.
- **Configure BranchCache For Network Files**   Configures the round-trip latency that triggers the use of BranchCache. The default value is 80 milliseconds.
- **Set Percentage Of Disk Space Used For Client Computer Cache**   Specifies amount of client disk space used to store BranchCache files. The default is 5 percent.

True or False? You must run netsh.exe from an elevated command prompt when configuring BranchCache to use Distributed Cache mode.

Answer: *True.* You can manually configure BranchCache using the netsh.exe utility. When you configure BranchCache using netsh.exe, you must run all commands except for netsh.exe show status, from an elevated command prompt. You can use the following commands to manage BranchCache:

- **Netsh.exe BranchCache reset**   Resets and disables the current configuration.
- **Netsh.exe BranchCache show status**   Displays the Current Service mode and configuration details.
- **Netsh.exe BranchCache set service mode=distributed**   Configures the client to use Distributed Cache mode. Configures appropriate firewall rules.
- **Netsh.exe BranchCache set service mode=local**   Local mode is a special mode in which remote content is cached, but not shared with other Windows 7 clients on the branch office network.

- **Netsh.exe BranchCache set service mode=hostedclient location=hostedserver** Configures Hosted Cache mode; you can specify the location of the Hosted Cache mode server.
- **Netsh.exe BranchCache set cachesize** You can configure the size of the local cache.

True or False? A BranchCache client must always allow inbound and outbound traffic on TCP port 80, irrespective of whether it is using Hosted Cache or Distributed Cache mode.

Answer: *True*. The firewall rules that you configure for BranchCache on the client depend on whether you are using Distributed Cache mode or Hosted Cache mode. The firewall rules related to BranchCache are as follows:

- **BranchCache – Content Retrieval (Uses HTTP)** Allows inbound and outbound traffic on TCP port 80. Used with both Hosted Cache and Distributed Cache modes.
- **BranchCache – Peer Discovery (Uses WSD)** Allows inbound and outbound traffic on UDP port 3702. Used only with Distributed Cache mode.
- **BranchCache – Hosted Cache Client (HTTPS-Out)** Allows outbound traffic on TCP port 443. This rule is required only when using Hosted Cache mode.

You need to configure appropriate firewall rules when you configure Branch-Cache using Group Policy. If you configure BranchCache manually using the netsh. exe command-line utility, the appropriate firewall rules are generated automatically.

> **MORE INFO** To learn more about client settings for BranchCache, consult the following webpage: *http://technet.microsoft.com/en-us/library/dd637820(WS.10).aspx*.

Certificate management

You need to know how to manage the certificates that you need to deploy to support BranchCache.

True or False? You need to install an EFS certificate on a computer that functions as a Hosted Cache server.

Answer: *False*. The Hosted Cache mode server needs to have an SSL certificate installed where the subject name of the certificate is set to the fully qualified domain name of the server. The certificate needs to be trusted by all the BranchCache clients that will use the Hosted Cache mode server. The simplest way to accomplish this goal is to use an enterprise CA in the local domain to issue the SSL certificate because trust is automatically established. Once the certificate has been imported into the Hosted Cache mode server's local certificate store, determine the certificate thumbprint. Once you have the thumbprint, bind the certificate to BranchCache using the following command:

```
NETSH HTTP ADD SSLCERT IPPORT=0.0.0.0:443 CERTHASH=<thumbprint>
APPID={d673f5ee-a714-454d-8de2-492e4c1bd8f8}
```

MORE INFO To learn more about configuring certificates for a Hosted Cache server, consult the following webpage: *http://technet.microsoft.com/en-us/library/ dd637793(WS.10).aspx.*

Can you answer these questions?

You can find the answers to these questions at the end of the chapter.

1. When using Hosted Cache mode, where should you install SSL certificates?

2. What is the syntax of the netsh.exe command that you would use to config- ure a client to use Hosted Cache mode with the server sydney.contoso.com functioning as the branch office Hosted Cache server?

3. Which firewall rules should you enable for a client configured to use Branch- Cache in Hosted Cache mode?

4. Which firewall rules should you enable for a client that is using BranchCache in Distributed Cache mode?

Answers

This section contains the answers to the "Can you answer these questions?" sections in this chapter.

Objective 5.1: Configure shared resources

1. Configure the Prevent The Computer From Joining A Homegroup policy.

2. Assign the Manage This Printer permission because the AdminAssistants group can pause and restart the shared printer.

3. The Shared Folders\Open Files node provides information on which files, hosted on shared folders, are currently being accessed.

4. Configure folder redirection for the Documents folder. Ensure that the 10 important files are copied to this documents folder.

Objective 5.2: Configure file and folder access

1. Files retain permissions when moved from one folder to another on the same volume.

2. The file remains encrypted and retains its permissions.

3. You can use the Effective Permissions tool to calculate a user's actual permis- sions to a resource when they are a member of multiple groups.

4. You should assign the Read & Write permission if you want to allow a user to edit an existing file, but not to alter the permissions of that file.

Objective 5.3: Configure User Account Control (UAC)

1. Configure the User Account Control: Behavior of the Elevation Prompt For Standard Users so that it will prompt for credentials.

2. You would configure the User Account Control: Switch To The Secure Desktop When Prompting For Elevation policy to ensure that all prompts for credentials and prompts for consent use Secure Desktop.

3. Configure the User Account Control: Behavior Of The Elevation Prompt For Administrators In Admin Approval Mode policy and set it to prompt for credentials or prompt for credentials on the secure desktop.

4. You would use secpol.msc to open the Local Security Policy console.

Objective 5.4: Configure authentication and authorization

1. You can open a command prompt using the Run As Administrator option to trigger an elevated command prompt.

2. You would configure the Interactive Logon: Require Smart Card policy to ensure that users logged on to a computer running Windows 7 with a smart card.

3. You can ensure that users log off when they remove their smart card from a computer running Windows 7 by configuring the Interactive Logon: Smart Card Removal Behavior policy and setting the Force Logoff option.

4. You can use the Certificates console to request a new certificate from a CA for which you had permission to enroll.

Objective 5.5: Configure BranchCache

1. You should install SSL certificates on the Hosted Cache mode server.

2. You would use the following command:

```
Netsh.exe BranchCache set service mode=hostedclient location=Sydney.
contoso.com
```

3. You should enable the BranchCache – Peer Discovery (Uses WSD) rule and the BranchCache – Hosted Cache Client (HTTPS-Out) rule to support clients when in Hosted Cache mode.

4. You should enable the BranchCache – Peer Discovery (Uses WSD) rule and the BranchCache – Content Retrieval (Uses HTTP) rule.

CHAPTER 6

Configuring Mobile Computing

Approximately 10 percent of the 70-680 exam focuses on the topic of configuring mobile computing. So you need to have a good grasp of how to configure mobile computers running Microsoft Windows 7, such as laptops and tables, with features such as BitLocker, DirectAccess, offline files, and VPN connections.

This chapter covers the following objectives:

- Objective 6.1: Configure BitLocker and BitLocker To Go
- Objective 6.2: Configure DirectAccess
- Objective 6.3: Configure mobility options
- Objective 6.4: Configure remote connections

Objective 6.1: Configure BitLocker and BitLocker To Go

Both portable computers and USB flash drives are likely to contain important confidential organizational data. If these devices aren't protected through a technology such as BitLocker or BitLocker To Go, it is incredibly easy for unauthorized third parties to recover the data stored on these devices.

Exam need to know

- Configuring BitLocker and BitLocker To Go policies

  For example: How to know which BitLocker policy you would configure to ensure that users can't write data to BitLocker To Go protected USB flash drives from other organizations.

- Managing Trusted Platform Module (TPM) PINs

  For example: How to configure Windows 7 to require that a user enter a TPM PIN to successfully start the computer.

- Configuring startup key storage

  For example: How to configure BitLocker to require a startup key.

- Data recovery agent support

  For example: How to configure BitLocker and BitLocker To Go to use a specific data recovery agent certificate to simplify the process of recovering data from protected drives.

Configure BitLocker and BitLocker To Go policies

You need to be familiar with what you can and can't accomplish using the BitLocker related group policies.

True or False? You can configure BitLocker so that the computer can boot successfully only if a specially prepared USB storage device is connected.

Answer: *True.* BitLocker protects unauthorized parties from recovering data from computers using an offline attack. It accomplishes this by providing full volume encryption that is transparent to an authorized user of the computer. Data cannot be recovered from a volume encrypted using BitLocker unless the person attempting the recovery has the BitLocker recovery key or access to a specially configured data recovery agent (DRA). BitLocker also offers boot integrity protection, requiring a user to enter the BitLocker recovery key if the boot environment has been altered.

BitLocker can be made more secure through the use of a Trusted Platform Module (TPM) chip, personal identification number (PIN), and a BitLocker startup key. A TPM chip is a special chip that can store the BitLocker encryption key and also can store boot integrity information. A startup key is a special cryptographically generated file that can be stored on a removable USB device. You can use these in the following combinations to secure a computer:

- **TPM only mode** Does not require a PIN or startup key. User is unaware that BitLocker is functioning unless the boot environment is modified.
- **TPM with startup key** Successful boot requires that the user must connect a USB device that hosts a preconfigured startup key to the computer powering on.
- **TPM with PIN** Successful boot requires that users enter a PIN to successfully boot the computer. Group Policy can be configured to determine whether this is simply a four-digit number or if a password containing alphanumeric characters and symbols is required.
- **TPM with PIN and startup key** Successful boot requires that the user connect a USB device that hosts a preconfigured startup key prior to boot and enters a PIN during boot.
- **Startup key without a TPM** This combination provides hard disk encryption, but doesn't provide boot integrity protection. Successful boot requires that the user must connect a USB device that hosts a preconfigured startup key prior to the computer powering on.

BitLocker policies are located in the Computer Configuration\Administrative Templates\Windows Components\BitLocker Drive Encryption node. You should review these policies on a computer running Windows 7 prior to taking the exam. You should especially review the following policy:

- **Provide The Unique Identifiers For Your Organization** You can specify an organizational ID. Use this ID with other policies to limit the use of BitLocker to drives encrypted within your organization.

Under this node, there are nodes for policies related to Fixed Data Drives, Operating System Drives, and Removable Data Drives. The policies available under each of these nodes are generally the same. You should review these policies prior to taking the exam. The most important of these policies are as follows:

- **Require Additional Authentication At Startup** You can specify startup authentication options including whether BitLocker must be used with a TPM, with a startup key, and with a TPM startup PIN.

- **Allow Enhanced PINs for Startup** You can use alphanumeric passwords with symbols as TPM startup PINs.

- **Configure Minimum PIN Length For Startup** You can specify the minimum length for the TPM startup PIN.

- **Choose How BitLocker-Protected Operating System Drives Can Be Recovered** You can set a DRA, a 48-digit recovery password and a 256-bit recovery key as well as backup of password and keys to Active Directory.

- **Deny Write Access To Fixed Drives Not Protected By BitLocker** Blocks users from writing data to drives (other than the operating system drive) not protected by BitLocker).

- **Configure Use Of Password For Fixed Data Drives** Determines whether a password is required to unlock BitLocker-protected fixed data drives (as opposed to operating system drives). You can configure password complexity.

True or False? Windows XP clients can be configured to write to BitLocker To Go protected removable drives.

Answer: *False*. BitLocker To Go provides full volume encryption for removable volumes including flash drives and removable hard disk drives. BitLocker To Go is available to clients running the Enterprise and Ultimate editions of Windows 7. Computers running the other editions of Windows 7 can read and write data on BitLocker To Go protected drives, but cannot be used to configure a drive to use BitLocker To Go.

BitLocker To Go doesn't require a TPM chip or require that Group Policy be configured to require an authentication method such as a startup key. BitLocker To Go can be configured so that clients running the Windows Vista and Windows XP operating systems can read data from protected disks. Clients running Windows Vista and Windows XP can't be configured to write data to BitLocker To Go protected disks.

BitLocker To Go can be used with the following Group Policy items:

- **Allow Access To BitLocker-Protected Removable Data Drives From Earlier Versions of Windows** Blocks or allows Windows Vista and Windows XP clients to read data from FAT-formatted, BitLocker-protected, removable drives.

- **Choose How BitLocker-Protected Removable Drives Can Be Recovered** Configures a DRA or recovery password for BitLocker To Go protected removable drives.

- **Configure Use Of Passwords For Removable Data Drives** Determines whether a password is required to unlock BitLocker To Go protected drives. Can be used to force password complexity policies to be applied.

- **Configure Use Of Smart Cards On Removable Data Drives** You can enable or require the use of a smart card to authenticate access to a removable storage device.

- **Control Use Of BitLocker On Removable Drives** You can control whether users can apply BitLocker protection to removable drives and whether users can remove BitLocker protection from removable drives.

- **Deny Write Access To Removable Drives Not Protected By BitLocker** You can block users from writing data to any drive not protected by BitLocker. You can also limit the writing of data to drives to those protected by BitLocker that were configured within your organization.

MORE INFO To learn more about BitLocker and BitLocker To Go group policies, consult the following webpage: *http://technet.microsoft.com/en-us/library/ee706521(WS.10).aspx.*

EXAM TIP Remember that computers running Microsoft Windows XP can read data only from drives configured with BitLocker To Go and then only under certain conditions.

Managing Trusted Platform Module (TPM) PINs

You need to know how to configure a TPM to require a PIN for successful boot and how to set, back up, and recover those PINs.

True or False? You can require that TPM PINs be backed up to Active Directory.

Answer: *True.* TPM Pin must be entered for the computer to successfully boot. TPM PINs can be a standard numerical password or can be alphanumeric with symbols. If a user forgets the TPM PIN, the computer won't boot into Microsoft Windows 7. It is important to ensure that the TPM PINs or passwords are backed up and are recoverable, and Active Directory, properly configured, provides a method through which this goal can be accomplished. You can ensure that TPM recovery information is backed up to Active Directory by enabling the Turn On TPM Backup To Active Directory Domain Services policy and selecting the Require TPM Backup to AD DS check box. This policy can be found in the Computer Configuration\Administrative Templates\System\Trusted Platform Module Services node.

True or False? You can turn the TPM off using the TPM Management console.

Answer: *True.* With the TPM Management console, you can back up TPM recovery information in Active Directory Domain Services (AD DS), clear the TPM, reset TPM lockout, and enable or disable the TPM. You can also use the console to change the TPM owner password and reset the TPM to factory default settings. The TPM Management console is accessible through the BitLocker Drive Encryption Control Panel.

> **MORE INFO** To learn more about TPM management, consult the following web-page: *http://technet.microsoft.com/en-us/library/cc755108(WS.10).aspx.*

True or False? You must update the Active Directory schema to support TPM backup if your domain is running at the Microsoft Windows Server 2008 functional level.

Answer: *False.* If your organization's domain controllers are running Microsoft Windows Server 2003 Service Pack 1 or Service Pack 2, you must update the Active Directory schema to support backing up of TPM module recovery information. If your organization's domain controllers are running Windows Server 2008 or Windows Server 2008 R2, it is not necessary to update the schema to support this functionality.

> **MORE INFO** To learn more about backing up TPM recovery information to Active Directory, consult the following webpage: *http://technet.microsoft.com/en-us/library/dd875529(WS.10).aspx.*

> **EXAM TIP** Remember that it is possible to force the backup of TPM recovery information to Active Directory.

Configuring startup key storage

You need to know how to manage and recover BitLocker startup keys.

True or False? Startup key files can be backed up to Active Directory.

Answer: *False.* BitLocker startup keys are special cryptographically generated files that are stored on USB flash drives. A computer running Windows 7 can be configured to require that a startup key be present when the computer boots or resumes from hibernation. When you use a startup key in combination with a TPM, part of the encryption key that unlocks BitLocker-protected volumes is stored by the TPM, and part is stored on a USB flash drive. BitLocker can also be configured on computers that do not have TPMs if a startup key is used. The startup key can be stored on a USB flash drive formatted using the FAT, FAT32, or NTFS file system. If the startup key is lost, you can recover by entering the recovery password or recovery key. Individual startup keys are not backed up to Active Directory.

MORE INFO To learn more about startup keys, consult the following webpage: *http://windows.microsoft.com/en-US/windows7/Can-I-use-a-BitLocker-startup-key-with-a-TPM.*

Data recovery agent support

You need to know how to configure BitLocker and BitLocker To Go so that a DRA can be used to recover BitLocker encrypted volumes.

True or False? A data recovery agent (DRA) is a special digital certificate that you can use to recover specially prepared BitLocker encrypted drives.

Answer: *True.* Typically you use either a 48-digit recovery password or a 256-bit recovery key that is unique to the BitLocker-protected volume to recover data from a BitLocker-protected drive. You can use a DRA to recover information even if the recovery password is lost. The advantage of a DRA is that you need to use only one certificate to perform recovery rather than having to extract a specific recovery key.

To configure BitLocker to support a DRA, perform the following steps:

1. Specify the user account enrolled with a DRA certificate to the Computer Configuration\Windows Settings\Security Settings\Public Key Policies\Bit-Locker Drive Encryption node.

2. Configure the Computer Configuration\Administrative Templates\Windows Components\BitLocker Drive Encryption\Provide The Unique Identifiers For Your Organization policy. BitLocker can manage and update DRAs only when the identification field on the drive matches the value configured in this policy.

3. Configure the following policies to allow particular volume types to be recoverable with a DRA:

   - Choose How BitLocker-Protected Operating System Drives Can Be Recovered
   - Choose How BitLocker-Protected Fixed Drives Can Be Recovered
   - Choose How BitLocker-Protected Removable Drives Can Be Recovered

4. To verify that a BitLocker-protected volume is configured for recovery using a DRA, run the manage-bde –protectors –get command. The output of this command will display the certificate thumbprint associated with the DRA.

True or False? You can use the manage-bde command to unlock a BitLocker-protected volume.

Answer: *True.* If you have enabled BitLocker on a volume prior to configuring a DRA, you can use the manage-bde –SetIdentifier command to make it recoverable via DRA. To recover a BitLocker-encrypted volume, ensure that the DRA certificate is present in the certificate store and then run the manage-bde.exe –unlock <drive> -Certificate –ct <certificate thumbprint> command from an elevated command prompt.

MORE INFO To learn more about using a DRA with BitLocker, consult the following webpage: *http://technet.microsoft.com/en-us/library/dd875560(WS.10).aspx.*

EXAM TIP Remember that it is possible to recover BitLocker-protected volumes using a 48-digit recovery password, a 256-bit recovery key, or a specially configured DRA.

Can you answer these questions?

You can find the answers to these questions at the end of the chapter.

1. Which method would you use to ensure that BitLocker-protected drives can be recovered without having to recover the keys associated with an individual computer?

2. Which method can you use to enable BitLocker on a computer that does not have a TPM?

3. Which polices would you configure to ensure that both a recovery password and a recovery key are required for operating system drives and that those items are backed up to Active Directory?

4. Which policy would you configure to enable users to use alphanumeric and symbol characters for their TPM Startup PIN?

Objective 6.2: Configure DirectAccess

The primary difference between DirectAccess and a typical VPN is that DirectAccess performs authentication at the computer level and doesn't require any form of user authentication. With DirectAccess, a user simply powers on his or her computer, connects to an Internet access point, and then automatically gains access to the organization's internal network.

Exam need to know

- Configuring client side

  For example: How to know which editions of Windows 7 support DirectAccess.

- Configuring authentication

  For example: How to know what type of certification authority (CA) you should use to automatically issue computer certificates to support DirectAccess authentication.

- Network infrastructure requirements

  For example: How to describe the versions of Microsoft Windows Server that must be deployed on the organizational network to support DirectAccess.

Configuring client side

You need to know what steps to take to prepare a computer running Windows 7 to function as a DirectAccess client.

True or False? DirectAccess requires user authentication.

Answer: *False.* DirectAccess is a special type of IPv6, encrypted VPN connection that makes an automatic connection when an Internet connection is detected. DirectAccess does not require the user to authenticate when establishing a connection as authentication occurs using a computer certificate. DirectAccess is bidirectional, so Group Policies and other management technologies can manage the computer as though it were connected to a LAN. DirectAccess can be integrated with NAP to ensure that mobile clients are kept up to date with software updates and antimalware software and definitions.

True or False? Windows 7 Professional supports DirectAccess.

Answer: *False.* Windows 7 Enterprise and Windows 7 Ultimate support DirectAccess. These computers must be members of an Active Directory domain and must have a computer certificate for IPsec authentication installed. When configuring a computer for DirectAccess, the computer account must be a member of a specially configured security group. This group is specified when running the DirectAccess Wizard during initial configuration on the DirectAccess server. DirectAccess configuration is pushed to the client through Group Policy.

True or False? You need to manually configure Group Policy to support DirectAccess.

Answer: *False.* Group Policies for DirectAccess are configured when you run the DirectAccess Client Setup Wizard on the DirectAccess server during initial configuration. Two GPOs are created: One applies to the DirectAccess clients and the other to the DirectAccess server. You don't have to edit the policies manually; they are configured based on your responses to the DirectAccess Setup Wizard.

True or False? DirectAccess clients on the Internet need a globally routable IPv6 address to make a successful connection.

Answer: *False.* The method that the client uses to connect to the DirectAccess server depends on its local connectivity (for example, if the client's Internet connection point provides the following):

- A globally routable IPv6 address: DirectAccess will use this address.
- A public IPv4 address: DirectAccess will use 6to4.
- A private IPv4 address: DirectAccess will use Teredo unless the NAT device also provides 6to4 gateway functionality. In that case, DirectAccess will use 6to4.
- If these methods fail, the client will fall back to using IP-HTTPS.

MORE INFO To learn more about DirectAccess requirements, consult the following webpage: *http://technet.microsoft.com/en-us/library/ee382305(WS.10).aspx.*

Configuring authentication

You need to know what steps you need to take to ensure that DirectAccess clients can authenticate.

True or False? You have to modify the properties of the default computer certificate template to enable automatic enrollment.

Answer: *True.* DirectAccess uses computer certificates for authentication. Although it is possible to use certificates from a trusted third-party CA because all computers using DirectAccess must be members of an Active Directory domain, you should use computer certificates issued from an internal CA to support this authentication. If you want to use certificate autoenrollment to simplify the certificate deployment process, you'll have to use an enterprise root or enterprise subordinate CA. You'll have to make a duplicate of the existing computer certificate template and con- figure the duplicate to support autoenrollment. The certificates used by the clients should be trusted by the DirectAccess server. The certificate used on the DirectAccess server must be trusted by the DirectAccess clients.

True or False? DirectAccess requires that users authenticate using a smart card.

Answer: *False.* You can configure DirectAccess to use smart cards to authenticate re- mote users. This isn't necessary because DirectAccess usually authenticates the com- puter before the user logs on, although this grants access only to domain controllers and DNS servers. Once the user logs on, DirectAccess authenticates the user, and the user can access network resources in a normal manner. By default, this is done through user account and password credentials, but it is also possible to configure user authentication to require smart cards. Configuring this method of authentica- tion requires the same steps as configuring smart cards for access to the LAN.

MORE INFO To learn more about using DirectAccess and smart card authentica- tion, consult the following webpage: *http://technet.microsoft.com/en-us/library/ dd637823(WS.10).aspx.*

True or False? If you are using a single CA to issue certificates for all DirectAccess components, the CRL distribution point (CDP) needs to be accessible only on the internal network.

Answer: *False.* You need to ensure that the certificate revocation list (CRL) distribu- tion points (CDPs) are accessible to DirectAccess clients. You can configure multiple CDPs for a single CA. You configure CDPs on the Extensions tab of the CA properties dialog box. If you are using Windows Server 2008 R2 CAs, you can also use one or more Online Certificate Status Protocol (OCSP) arrays as CDPs. CDPs are used in the following parts of the DirectAccess process:

- DirectAccess clients check CRLs to validate the DirectAccess server certificate when using IP-HTTPS connections. Without access to the CDP, IP-HTTPS communication will fail. This CDP needs to be accessible to clients on the Internet.
- DirectAccess clients must perform a certificate revocation check to validate the SSL certificate on the network location server. This CDP needs to be accessible to clients on the internal network.

MORE INFO To learn more about configuring CDPs, consult the following webpage: *http://technet.microsoft.com/en-us/library/ee382302(WS.10).aspx.*

EXAM TIP Remember that if you want to use autoenrollment for computer certificates, you'll need to modify the properties of the existing certificate template.

Network infrastructure requirements

You need to know what components must be present on the organizational network to support a DirectAccess deployment.

True or False? The Internet interface of the DirectAccess server must be assigned two consecutive public IPv4 addresses.

Answer: *True.* The DirectAccess server is a server running Windows Server 2008 R2 with the DirectAccess Management Console feature installed. To function as a Direct-Access server, the host must meet the following requirements:

- The DirectAccess server must be a member of an Active Directory domain.
- The DirectAccess server must have a minimum of two network adapters.
- At least one of the network adapters on a DirectAccess server must be connected to the public Internet and must be assigned two consecutive public IPv4 addresses.
- At least one of the network adapters on the DirectAccess server must be connected to the internal network.
- The DirectAccess server must have a digital certificate that supports server authentication installed. This certificate must match the fully qualified domain name that is assigned to the public IP addresses used by the server's external network interface.

True or False? At least one domain controller running Windows Server 2008 R2 must be a member of the same domain as the DirectAccess clients.

Answer: *True.* You must configure an internal website that is protected by an SSL certificate trusted by both the DirectAccess server and the DirectAccess clients. This website must be configured so that it can be accessed only by clients on the organization's internal network. Clients attempt to connect to this website to determine whether they are on the organizational network or on the Internet. On top of the requirements for the DirectAccess server, the internal network must have the following:

- At least one domain controller must be running Windows Server 2008 R2 or Windows Server 2008.

- A DNS server running Windows Server 2008 R2 or Windows Server 2008 with hotfix Q958194 or Service Pack 2 installed.

- A server running Windows Server 2008 or Windows Server 2008 R2 with the Active Directory Certificate Services role installed that is configured as either an enterprise root or an enterprise subordinate CA.

To ensure that DirectAccess clients can communicate with internal network resources, you need to do one of the following:

- Configure all internal resources with IPv6 addresses.

- Configure ISATAP on the intranet so DirectAccess clients can tunnel IPv6 traffic over an internal IPv4 intranet.

- Configure a NAT-PT device, so those devices that only support IPv4 can be accessible to DirectAccess clients.

You must also ensure that all application servers that you want DirectAccess clients to interact with allow ICMPv6 traffic inbound and outbound.

> **MORE INFO** To learn more about DirectAccess requirements consult the following webpage: *http://technet.microsoft.com/en-us/library/ee382305(WS.10).aspx.*

> **EXAM TIP** Remember which editions of Windows 7 support DirectAccess.

Can you answer these questions?

You can find the answers to these questions at the end of the chapter.

1. You are planning the deployment of CDPs to support certificate revocation checks for clients. From which location does the CDP need to be accessible for clients that are using IP-HTTPS with DirectAccess?

2. What kind of certificate needs to be installed on a DirectAccess client?

3. What methods can a DirectAccess client that is issued the IP address 192.168.15.101 to connect to the Internet from a hotel DHCP server where NAT does not support 6to4 gateway functionality use to make a DirectAccess connection?

4. What requirements must a Windows 7 computer meet to use DirectAccess?

Objective 6.3: Configure mobility options

The configuring mobility options objective deals with configuring mobile computers to support the use of offline files, transparent caching, and migrating power policies.

Exam need to know

- Configuring offline file policies
  For example: How to configure Windows 7 to support offline files.

- Transparent caching

  For example: How to configure Windows 7 to use transparent caching.

- Creating and migrating power policies

  For example: How to import and export a power policy.

Configuring offline file policies

You need to know what offline file policies are available and how you can use them to accomplish specific objectives.

True or False? Users can make files available for offline access.

Answer: *True.* With Offline Files, a Windows 7 client can locally cache files that are hosted in shared folders so that the user can access those files when the computer can't initiate a direct connection to the hosting server. Unless an administrator has configured a shared folder to block the use of offline files, users can make files available offline by right-clicking the file and then clicking the Always Available Offline option. The Offline Files feature in Windows 7 can be used in the following operating modes:

- **Online**   Changes made to files are written first to the host file share and then to the local cache. Read requests are handled by the local cache. Synchronization occurs automatically and can be triggered manually. This is the default mode.

- **Auto-offline**   When a network disconnection or error is detected, Windows 7 will go to auto-offline mode. File read and write operations occur against the offline files cache. Windows 7 will attempt reconnection every 2 minutes. If a connection is established, client returns to online mode.

- **Manual offline**   User forces the transition to offline mode by selecting Work Offline in Windows Explorer. When the computer is put in offline mode manually, it must be returned to online mode manually.

- **Slow-link**   This mode is enabled automatically when the link speed falls below a default value of 64,000 bits per second. When this happens, the client treats the network as if a disconnection has occurred. When the link speed improves, the client returns to online mode.

True or False? Administrators can configure a list of files and folders that are always available for offline use through Group Policy.

Answer: *True.* Offline files policies are located in the Computer Configuration\Administrative Templates\Network\Offline Files node of a GPO. Offline files policies are also available under the User Configuration\Administrative Templates\Network\Offline Files node of a GPO. The offline files policies that are available for computers running Windows 7 are as follows:

- **Administratively Assigned Offline Files**   An administrator can specify network files and folders that are always available for offline use.

- **Configure Background Sync**   You can configure a sync schedule for folders in "slow-link" mode.

- **Limit Disk Space Used By Offline Files**   You can configure how much disk space, in megabytes, is reserved to store offline files.
- **Allow Or Disallow Use Of The Offline Files Feature**   You can block or allow the use of offline files.
- **Encrypt The Offline Files Cache**   Ensures that files stored in the offline files cache are encrypted.
- **Event Logging Level**   You can specify the amount of detail related to Offline Files recorded in the event log.
- **Exclude Files From Being Cached**   You can specify file types, based on file extension, that you want to block from being made available through Offline Files.
- **Remove 'Make Available Offline'**   You can block users from making network files and folders available offline.
- **Enable Transparent Caching**   Used to enable transparent caching. You'll learn more about this topic later in the chapter.
- **Turn On Economical Application Of Administratively Assigned Offline Files**   When enabled, only new files and folders in administratively assigned folders will sync at logon. Older files will be synchronized later.
- **Configure Slow-Link Mode**   When Offline Files operates in slow-link mode, all network file requests will be satisfied from the Offline Files cache even though the computer is still technically online.

MORE INFO   To learn more about offline files, consult the following webpage: *http:// technet.microsoft.com/en-us/library/gg277982(WS.10).aspx.*

Transparent caching

You need to know how to enable transparent caching and the difference between it and Offline Files and BranchCache.

True or False? Transparent caching stores files in the Offline Files cache.

Answer: *True.* Transparent caching optimizes bandwidth consumption on WAN links for mobile users and users at branch office sites that are accessing network files and folders that have not been explicitly made available offline. This makes it different from BranchCache and Offline Files. After a user has opened a file off a remote server where the network latency exceeds the configured value, the file is stored in the Offline Files cache on the local hard disk drive. Subsequent file access is from the cached file, although checks are performed to verify that the cached file is up to date. Modifications to the file are written back to the server, not to the cache.

True or False? Transparent caching is enabled by default on computers running Windows 7 Enterprise and Ultimate.

Answer: *False.* Files subject to transparent caching are not available to the user when the user is offline. You enable transparent caching by configuring the Enable Transparent Caching policy that is available in the Computer Configuration\Administrative Templates\Network\Offline Files node of a Group Policy. The default value is to cache files if there is a 32,000-millisecond network latency, though this can be adjusted. Transparent caching is not enabled by default. Transparent caching is also automatically enabled when you enable BranchCache. You learned about Branch-Cache in Chapter 5, "Configuring Access to Resources."

MORE INFO   To learn more about transparent caching, consult the following webpage: *http://technet.microsoft.com/en-us/library/ff633429(WS.10).aspx.*

EXAM TIP   Remember the difference between transparent caching and Branch-Cache.

Creating and migrating power policies

You need to know how to create a new power scheme, as well as how to import and export an existing power scheme.

True or False? You can create a new power scheme using the powercfg.exe utility.

Answer: *True.* Power policies are also known as power schemes. You create new power policies by duplicating existing policies and then modifying them. To do this from the GUI, open the Power Options Control Panel item, click Create A Power Plan, and then select the plan you want to use as the basis for the new plan. Enter a name for the plan and click Create.

You can create a new power scheme using powercfg.exe by using the –duplicate-scheme parameter. You must supply the GUID of the scheme that you want to duplicate. To get a power scheme's GUID, use the powercfg.exe –list command from an elevated command prompt. This command will output all current power schemes and their GUIDs. You'll learn more about configuring power in Chapter 7, "Monitoring and Maintaining Systems that Run Windows 7."

MORE INFO   To learn more about creating power plans, consult the following webpage: *http://windows.microsoft.com/en-US/windows7/Change-create-or-delete-a-power-plan-scheme.*

True or False? You import and export power schemes using powercfg.exe.

Answer: *True.* You export and import power schemes from the command line using the powercfg.exe utility. You cannot export or import a power scheme using the Power Options Control Panel item. To export a power scheme, you must know the scheme's GUID. To export a power scheme, use this command: powercfg –export name.pow <GUID>, where name.pow is the name of the power scheme that you want to export. To import a power scheme, issue the command powercfg –import name.pow. You can either supply a GUID, or allow Windows 7 to generate and use a new GUID.

EXAM TIP   Remember that you use powercfg.exe to import and export power schemes.

Can you answer these questions?

You can find the answers to these questions at the end of the chapter.

1. What command can you run to display the GUIDs of all power schemes on a computer running Windows 7?
2. What method would you use to export a power scheme?
3. What steps do you need to take to enable transparent caching on a computer running Windows 7?
4. What policy should you configure to ensure that .mp3 files are not available as offline files?

Objective 6.4: Configure remote connections

Unless an organization has already deployed DirectAccess, it is likely that mobile computers will use a VPN to remotely access the organizational network. Setting up remote access involves understanding VPN protocols and authentication, dial-up, Network Access Protection quarantine, and Remote Desktop (RD) Gateway functionality.

Exam need to know

- Establishing VPN connections and authentication
  For example: How to configure Windows 7 to use SSTP as a VPN protocol.
- Enabling a VPN Reconnect
  For example: How to understand the requirements for deploying VPN Reconnect.
- Advanced security auditing
  For example: How to configure Windows 7 to use advanced auditing policies.
- NAP quarantine remediation
  For example: How to understand the NAP remediation process.
- Dial-up connections
  For example: How to configure a dial-up connection.
- Remote Desktop
  For example: How to configure Windows 7 to use a RD Gateway server.
- Published apps
  For example: How to configure RemoteApp applications to work from the Internet through the RD Gateway.

Establishing VPN connections and authentication

You need to know what the VPN options are for computers running Windows 7 and what authentication options are appropriate for a given set of circumstances.

True or False? The IKEv2 VPN protocol supports VPN Reconnect.

Answer: *True.* Every edition of Windows 7 supports VPNs that use the following protocols:

- **PPTP** The least secure form of VPN. Does not require access to digital certificates. Can use MS-CHAP, MS-CHAPv2, EAP, and PEAP authentication protocols. Windows 7 uses PPTP to support incoming VPN connections.

- **L2TP/IPsec** Requires a certificate services infrastructure or can be used with preshared keys. Traditionally, certificate services is deployed to provision both VPN clients and servers with certificates for authentication. Most third-party VPN solutions support L2TP/IPsec.

- **SSTP** SSTP tunnels over port 443, meaning that it can pass across almost all firewalls that allow Internet access, something that is not true of other VPN protocols. SSTP requires a VPN server running Windows Server 2008 or Windows Server 2008 R2.

- **IKEv2** Can be used only with computers running Windows 7 and Windows Server 2008 R2. Allows VPN Reconnect. (You'll learn more about VPN reconnect later in this chapter.) IKEv2 does not support PAP, CHAP, or MS-CHAPv2 (without EAP) authentication protocols.

MORE INFO To learn more about VPN protocols, consult the following webpage: *http://technet.microsoft.com/en-us/library/ff687723(WS.10).aspx.*

True or False? By default, a VPN connection will use only the L2TP/IPsec VPN protocol.

Answer: *False.* Creating a VPN involves specifying the address of the remote VPN server and providing authentication credentials. Users without local administrative privileges can create new VPN connections by clicking Set Up A New Connection Or Network and then Connect To A Workplace in the Network And Sharing Center. By default, newly created VPN connections use the automatic VPN type, which means that the client will attempt to use the most secure protocol. If that is not available or is unsupported, they switch to a less secure protocol. After you have created the connection, you can edit the VPN connection's properties and specify that a specific protocol is used, but the connection can use only that protocol and no others. Administrators can also simplify the deployment of VPNs by creating Connection Manager Administration Kit (CMAK) profiles that automate the setup of remote access connections.

MORE INFO To learn more about the CMAK, consult the following webpage: *http://technet.microsoft.com/en-us/library/cc753977(WS.10).aspx.*

True or False? PEAP-MS-CHAPv2 is a password-based authentication protocol.

Answer: *True*. Windows 7 supports the following authentication protocols for both VPN and dial-up connections:

- **Password Authentication Protocol (PAP)**   Uses unencrypted passwords. Not enabled by default. Not supported by remote access servers running Windows Server 2008 or Windows Server 2008 R2. Used when connecting to older third-party VPN servers. Least secure option.

- **Challenge Authentication Protocol (CHAP)**   Password-based authentication protocol. Not supported by remote access servers running Windows Server 2008 or Windows Server 2008 R2. Enabled by default for Windows 7 VPN connections.

- **Microsoft Challenge Handshake Authentication Protocol (MS-CHAPv2)**   Password-based authentication protocol. VPN connection can use credentials of currently logged-on user for authentication.

- **Protected Extensible Authentication Protocol with Transport Layer Security (PEAP-EAP-TLS)**   Certificate-based authentication protocol. Requires deployment of computer certificate on VPN server.

- **PEAP-EAP-MS-CHAPv2**   Most secure password-based authentication protocol for Windows 7 VPN clients. Requires deployment of computer certificate on VPN server.

- **Smart Card or Other Certificate**   Use when supporting authentication of VPN connections is a smart card or other certificate.

Enabling a VPN Reconnect

You need to know how to configure Windows 7 to use the IKEv2 VPN protocol to automatically connect when the VPN connection is disrupted.

True or False? IKEv2 requires the user to manually reconnect when switching Internet connections.

Answer: *False*. VPN Reconnect uses the IKEv2 VPN protocol. With VPN Reconnect, the underlying network connection can be disrupted for up to 8 hours without the user losing the existing VPN tunnel. This automatic restoration can occur, even when the computer switches Internet connections. If the computer is placed into hibernation, the VPN connection must be manually reestablished.

> **MORE INFO**   To learn more about remote access with VPN Reconnect, consult the following webpage: *http://technet.microsoft.com/en-us/library/dd637803(WS.10).aspx*.

True or False? IKEv2 requires a Routing and Remote Access server running Windows Server 2008 R2.

Answer: *True*. Only Routing and Remote Access servers running Windows Server 2008 R2 support IKEv2. You can configure IKEv2 with mobility to support a network outage time of up to 8 hours. If the disruption lasts longer than 8 hours, the user will have to reconnect manually. You need to configure a special certificate template with Enhanced Key Usage (EKU) options to support IKEv2.

MORE INFO To learn more about configuring IKEv2-based remote access, consult the following webpage: *http://technet.microsoft.com/en-us/library/ff687731(WS.10).aspx.*

EXAM TIP Remember that the only VPN protocol you can use to switch Internet connections while maintaining the VPN link is IKEv2.

Advanced security auditing

You need to know how to enable advanced auditing.

True or False? You must enable a special policy to use advanced auditing options.

Answer: *True.* With the Computer Configuration\Windows Settings\Security Settings\ Local Policies\Security Options\Audit: Force Audit Policy Subcategory Settings policy, you can perform advanced auditing on computers running Windows 7. Advanced auditing is much more specific than the general audit categories. You configure auditing by configuring the policies that are located in the Computer Configuration\Windows Settings\Security Settings\Advanced Audit Policy Configuration\System Audit Policies node. Advanced audit policies are available in the following categories:

- **Account Logon** Includes the following audit policies: Audit Credential Validation, Audit Kerberos Authentication Service, Audit Kerberos Service Ticket Operations, and Audit Other Account Logon Events.
- **Account Management** Includes the following audit policies: Audit Application Group Management, Audit Computer Account Management, Audit Distribution Group Management, Audit Other Account Management Events, Audit Security Group Management, and Audit User Account Management.
- **Detailed Tracking** Includes the following audit policies: Audit DPAPI Activity, Audit Process Creation, Audit Process Termination, and Audit RPC Events.
- **DS Access** Includes the following audit policies: Audit Detailed Directory Service Replication, Audit Directory Service Access, Audit Directory Service Changes, and Audit Directory Service Replication.
- **Logon/Logoff** Includes the following audit policies: Audit Account Lockout, Audit IPsec Extended Mode, Audit IPsec Main Mode, Audit IPsec Quick Mode, Audit Logoff, Audit Logon, Audit Network Policy Server, Audit Other Logon/Logoff Events, and Audit Special Logon.
- **Object Access** Includes the following audit policies: Audit Application Generated, Audit Certification Services, Audit Detailed File Share, Audit File Share, Audit File System, Audit Filtering Platform Connection, Audit Filtering Platform Packet Drop, Audit Handle Manipulation, Audit Kernel Object, Audit Other Object Access Events, Audit Registry, and Audit SAM.

- **Policy Change** Includes the following audit policies: Audit Audit Policy Change, Audit Authentication Policy Change, Audit Authorization Policy Change, Audit Filtering Platform Policy Change, Audit MPSSVC Rule-Level Policy Change, and Audit Other Policy Change Events.

- **Privilege Use** Includes the following audit policies: Audit Non Sensitive Privilege Use, Audit Other Privilege Use Events, and Audit Sensitive Privilege Use.

- **System** Includes the following audit policies: Audit IPsec Driver, Audit Other System Events, Audit Security State Change, Audit Security System Extension, and Audit System Integrity.

- **Global Object Access Auditing** Includes the following audit policies: File System and Registry.

MORE INFO To learn more about advanced audit policy configuration, consult the following webpage: *http://technet.microsoft.com/en-us/library/dd408940(WS.10).aspx.*

NAP quarantine remediation

You need to know what methods you can use to remediate Windows 7 clients that don't meet Network Access Protection (NAP) health benchmarks.

True or False? Administrators can require that a firewall be present on all network connections as a criterion for allowing network access to VPN clients.

Answer: *True.* With NAP, administrators can limit network access, in this case VPN access, to client computers that meet a minimum health benchmark. Remediation is the process through which those clients are updated so that they meet the NAP requirements and are granted access to the network. NAP requirements can include the following:

- Does the client have active antispyware software, and is that software up-to-date?

- Does the client have active antivirus software, and is that software up-to-date?

- Are automatic updates enabled, and has the computer recently checked for updates?

- Is a firewall enabled for all network connections?

Administrators specify which of these criteria must be met by configuring security health validators (SHVs). Administrators can also configure NAP to perform remediation so that clients that don't meet these benchmarks can perform the necessary checks and software updates required to bring them to an acceptable standard. Windows 7 clients can take steps toward remediation as long as the Security Center service is enabled. This service interacts with the Windows 7 Action Center, which can trigger the necessary software updates and activate disabled applications and firewalls. There is a limit to what can be accomplished through remediation. For example, although Windows 7 Action Center can enable a disabled antivirus program during remediation, it can't locate and install an antivirus application.

MORE INFO To learn more about VPN remote access connections and NAP quarantine, consult the following webpage: *http://technet.microsoft.com/en-us/library/cc984479.aspx.*

Dial-up connections

You need to know how to configure Windows 7 to support incoming and outgoing dial-up connections.

True or False? You can create a dial-up connection for a Windows 7 computer if it has a built-in cellular modem.

Answer: *True.* Windows 7 supports dial-up connections using a modem to an ISP or other host. Windows 7 also supports incoming dial-up connections. Windows 7 can be used with both traditional landline modems and cellular modems. To configure an outbound dial-up connection, in Network And Sharing Center, click Set Up A New Connection Or Network and then select Set Up A Dial-Up Connection. You'll need to enter the phone number of the ISP as well as a user name and password. You can click Dialing Rules to specify options such as country code, carrier code, and whether a specific number needs to be provided to access an external line.

True or False? Windows 7 supports incoming PPTP VPN connections.

Answer: *True.* If you have a modem attached to your computer, you can configure your computer to accept incoming modem calls by clicking New Incoming Connection from the Change Adapter Settings dialog box available from the Network And Sharing Center Control Panel item. You can also use this method to configure a computer running Windows 7 to support incoming PPTP VPN connections through a NIC.

MORE INFO To learn more about incoming VPN or dial-up connections, consult the following webpage: *http://windows.microsoft.com/en-US/windows7/Set-up-an-incoming-VPN-or-dial-up-connection.*

Remote Desktop

You need to know how to configure Windows 7 clients to use RD Gateway to access internal Remote Desktop services.

True or False? A client must establish a VPN connection prior to connecting to an RD Gateway Server.

Answer: *False.* With RD Gateway, clients on the Internet can make Remote Desktop connections to servers on protected internal networks through an RD Gateway server on a perimeter network. Clients can establish these connections without having to initiate a VPN connection. The client opens the specially configured Remote Desktop Connection application and can initiate the connection as if opening a

Remote Desktop Connection to a Remote Desktop host on the internal network. To configure Remote Desktop Client to use an RD Gateway, navigate to the Advanced tab of the Remote Desktop Connection Properties dialog box and click Settings under Connect From Anywhere. Specify the RD Gateway server name and whether you want the client to bypass the RD Gateway server for local addresses. You can also configure RD Gateway settings through the User Configuration\Administrative Templates\Windows Components\Remote Desktop Services\RD Gateway node of a GPO. The policies in this node include the following:

- **Enable Connection Through RD Gateway** When enabled, the client attempts a connection through the specified RD Gateway server if it cannot directly connect to the target Remote Desktop Services server.
- **Set RD Gateway Server Address** You can specify the address of the RD Gateway Server.

MORE INFO To learn more about RD Gateway, consult the following webpage: *http://technet.microsoft.com/en-us/library/dd560672(WS.10).aspx.*

Published apps

You need to know how to ensure that remote Windows 7 clients can connect to RemoteApp applications over the Internet.

True or False? You configure the RD Gateway Server address prior to deploying RemoteApp applications to Windows 7 clients.

Answer: *True.* With the RemoteApp technology, individual Remote Desktop Services applications can be published to client computers. RemoteApp applications can be used by clients on the Internet if the application is published with the address of an RD Gateway Server. Administrators can configure this address on the RD Gateway tab of the RemoteApp Deployment Settings dialog box.

MORE INFO To learn more about RemoteApp, consult the following webpage: *http://technet.microsoft.com/en-us/library/cc772415.aspx.*

Can you answer these questions?

You can find the answers to these questions at the end of the chapter.

1. What is the most secure password-based authentication protocol?
2. What conditions can NAP check for?
3. Which VPN protocol supports VPN Reconnect?
4. Which VPN protocol does Windows 7 support for incoming connections?

Answers

This section contains the answers to the "Can you answer these questions?" sections in this chapter.

Objective 6.1: Configure BitLocker and BitLocker To Go

1. You would configure a DRA to ensure that BitLocker-protected drives can be recovered without having to provide individual recovery keys.

2. You can use BitLocker without a TPM if a startup key is configured.

3. You would configure the Store BitLocker Recovery Information In Active Directory Domain Services and Choose How BitLocker-Protected Operating System Drives Can Be Recovered policy to accomplish this goal.

4. Allow Enhanced PINs for Startup.

Objective 6.2: Configure DirectAccess

1. The CDP for clients using IP-HTTPS with DirectAccess needs to be accessible from the Internet.

2. A computer certificate that will be used for authentication needs to be installed on the DirectAccess client.

3. Clients on NAT networks where the NAT device does not support 6to4 functionality need to use Teredo or IP-HTTPS to make a DirectAccess connection.

4. Needs a computer certificate installed, must be a member of the domain, must be a member of the designated DirectAccess security group, and must be running either the Enterprise or Ultimate version of the operating system.

Objective 6.3: Configure mobility options

1. You run the powercfg.exe –List command to view the GUIDs of all power schemes on a computer.

2. You need to use the powercfg.exe command-line utility to export a power scheme. It is necessary to know the GUID of the power scheme that you are going to export. You can't perform this task from the Power Options Control Panel item.

3. Transparent caching is enabled by configuring the Enable Transparent Caching Group Policy.

4. You can use the Exclude Files From Being Cached to block specific file types, based on file extension, from being made available offline.

Objective 6.4: Configure remote connections

1. PEAP-EAP-MS-CHAPv2.

2. NAP can check for the following conditions: Does the client have active anti-spyware software and is that software up to date? Does the client have active antivirus software and is that software up to date? Are automatic updates enabled, and has the computer recently checked for updates? Is a firewall enabled for all network connections?

3. The IKEv2 VPN protocol supports VPN Reconnect.

4. Windows 7 supports the PPTP protocol for incoming connections.

CHAPTER 7

Monitoring and Maintaining Systems that Run Windows 7

Approximately 11 percent of the 70-680 exam focuses on the topic of monitoring and maintaining Windows 7, so you need to have a good grasp of how to configure Windows Update settings, how to use the options for Windows 7 volumes, what you can do with Windows 7 event logs and data collector sets, and how to monitor and improve Windows 7 performance.

This chapter covers the following objectives:

- Objective 7.1: Configure updates to Windows 7
- Objective 7.2: Manage disks
- Objective 7.3: Monitor systems
- Objective 7.4: Configure performance settings

Objective 7.1: Configure updates to Windows 7

Although it is important to retain control over what updates are deployed to Windows 7, the more automated you can make the update deployment process, the less direct work you'll have to perform on individual computers. If you get the deployment of updates right, you'll save yourself hundreds of hours of work over the Windows 7 operating system's deployment lifetime.

Exam need to know

- Configure update settings

  For example: How to configure Windows 7 to use a WSUS server at the address *http://wsus.contoso.internal.*

- Determine source of updates

  For example: How to configure Windows 7 to use WSUS.

- Configuring Windows Update policies

  For example: How to configure WSUS groups.

- Review update history

  For example: How to determine which updates aren't installed on a computer running Windows 7.

- Check for new updates

  For example: How to force Windows 7 to check for new updates.

- Rolling back updates

  For example: How to hide an update.

Configure update settings

You need to know how and where to configure settings related to Windows Update. This means not only being familiar with the Windows Update item in Control Panel but also with the relevant Group Policies used to control Windows Update behavior.

True or False? A user who is not a member of the local Administrators group on a Windows 7 computer can check for updates.

Answer: *True.* The Windows Update Control Panel is the primary tool you use to manage software updates on clients running Windows 7. Through this Control Panel, a user with Administrator privileges can check for updates, change update settings, review installed updates, and review hidden updates. A user who can't elevate privileges can use this Control Panel to check for and install updates. Windows Update relies on the Windows Update service, which is enabled by default on all clients running Microsoft Windows.

True or False? Only a user who is a member of the local Administrators group can change Windows Update settings.

Answer: *True.* You can manually configure how Windows Update deals with updates by clicking the Change Settings item. With this item, you can configure how Windows 7 deals with important updates, the frequency at which updates are checked, whether recommended updates are treated in the same fashion as important updates, and whether users without administrative privileges can install updates on the computer. Only users with administrative privileges can change Windows Update settings. The options that you can configure with this dialog box are as follows:

- **Install Updates Automatically (Recommended)**   Windows Update installs updates automatically at the time specified. This is the default setting for Windows Update.

- **Download Updates But Let Me Choose Whether To Install Them**   Updates are downloaded to the computer, and the user is notified that the updates are available for installation.

- **Check For Updates But Let Me Choose Whether To Download And Install Them**   The user is notified that updates are available for download and install.

- **Never Check For Updates (Not Recommended)**   Windows Update does not check for updates, but updates can still be checked for and installed manually.

- **Give Me Recommended Updates The Same Way I Receive Important Updates** This means that recommended updates are treated in the same manner as important updates. Optional updates still need to be installed manually.
- **Allow All Users To Install Updates On This Computer** This option is enabled by default. If you disable this option, only user accounts that are members of the local Administrators group can install updates.

MORE INFO To learn more about configuring update settings, consult the following webpage: *http://technet.microsoft.com/en-us/library/ee126108(WS.10).aspx.*

EXAM TIP Remember that permissions are required to update Windows 7 with a critical update.

Determine source of updates

You need to know how to set Windows Update to retrieve updates either from Microsoft Update or an alternate source such as a Windows Server Update Services (WSUS) server.

True or False? By default, Windows Update on Windows 7 uses the proxy server settings configured through Internet Options in the Control Panel.

Answer: *False.* Occasionally, on networks that have specific firewall and proxy configurations, Windows Update clients can't contact the Microsoft Update servers on the Internet. There are several ways to deal with this problem. The first is to deploy a WSUS server on the local area network (LAN) and have the clients download updates from the WSUS server. When setting up the WSUS server, you can configure it to use the proxy. Alternatively, it is possible to configure a client running Windows 7 manually so that Windows Update can communicate with the Microsoft Update servers through the proxy. Although you can configure Internet Explorer to use a proxy through Internet Options, Windows Update can't use these settings directly. You can configure clients running Windows 7 to determine proxy settings in two ways:

- **Web Proxy Auto Detect (WPAD)** This feature allows computer services to locate an available proxy by querying a Dynamic Host Configuration Protocol (DHCP) option or checking a Domain Name System (DNS) record.
- **Netsh.exe command-line tool** Although Windows Update does not use the Internet Options settings directly, you can use the netsh.exe command-line tool to import the proxy settings configured for Internet Explorer. To accomplish this goal, use the following command from an elevated command prompt:

```
netsh winhttp import proxy source=ie
```

MORE INFO For more information on configuring Web Proxy Auto Detect on DNS and DHCP servers, consult the following document on Microsoft TechNet: *http://technet. microsoft.com/en-us/library/cc713344.aspx.*

True or False? You can use the Windows Update Stand-alone Installer (Wusa.exe) utility to manually install updates downloaded from the Microsoft website.

Answer: *True.* In some cases, such as when you are dealing with stand-alone computers that are not connected to a network, it is necessary to install update files directly. You can download Windows 7 update files directly from the Microsoft website. You can find these updates related to each update's security bulletin. Update files have the .msu extension. If you want to script the installation of a number of .msu files, you can use the Wusa.exe utility. When chaining the update installation, you should use the */norestart* parameter after each update except the last one that you want to install. For example, you might have a script that installs three updates with these commands:

```
Wusa.exe d:\windows6.1-kb123456-x64.msu /quiet /norestart
Wusa.exe d:\windows6.1-kb123457-x64.msu /quiet /norestart
Wusa.exe d:\windows6.1-kb123458-x64.msu /quiet
```

MORE INFO For more information about Wusa.exe, consult the following article: *http://support.microsoft.com/kb/934307.*

True or False? WSUS groups are security groups you create using Active Directory Users And Computers.

Answer: *False.* WSUS allows administrators to organize client computers into groups, which allows staggered update deployment. You can deploy updates on some computers, but not on others. You create groups on the WSUS server. After the groups are created on the WSUS server, you can configure a client to join a group by configuring the Enable Client Side Targeting policy, which you will learn about later in this lesson, or by manually assigning computers to groups using the WSUS console.

True or False? You can roll back the deployment of an update using WSUS.

Answer: *True.* WSUS also allows administrators centrally to roll back the installation of an update across all computers in the organization. For example, if an update causes a problem in an organization that relies only on Microsoft Update, administrators have to uninstall and then hide the update on each computer in the organization manually. If an update causes a problem in an organization that uses WSUS, the update administrator can roll back the update from WSUS, which removes that update from all client computers in the organization. It is not necessary to hide a rolled-back update because the WSUS server makes approved updates available only to Windows Update clients.

MORE INFO To learn more about WSUS, consult the Windows Server Update Services TechCenter at the following address: *http://technet.microsoft.com/en-us/wsus/default. aspx.*

Configuring Windows Update policies

You need to be familiar with the Group Policy items related to Windows Update and what you can accomplish with those policies.

True or False? You can join a computer to an existing WSUS group using the Enable Client Side Targeting policy.

Answer: *True*. You configure most Windows Update settings by configuring Group Policy. The Computer Configuration\Administrative Templates\Windows Components\Windows Update Group Policy node contains 16 policies. You can configure Windows Update using these policies as follows:

- **Do Not Display "Install Updates And Shut Down" Option In Shut Down Windows Dialog Box**   You can configure whether the Shut Down menu displays the Install Updates And Shut Down option. The default setting has this option available.

- **Do Not Adjust Default Option To "Install Updates And Shut Down" In Shut Down Windows Dialog Box**   When this policy setting is enabled, the user's last shutdown choice is the default shutdown option. When this policy setting is disabled or is not configured, Install Updates And Shut Down is the default option if updates are available for installation. This policy is deprecated when the Do Not Display "Install Updates And Shut Down" Option In Shut Down Windows Dialog Box policy is enabled.

- **Enabling Windows Update Power Management To Automatically Wake The System To Install Scheduled Updates**   This policy allows Windows Update to wake a hibernating computer to install updates. Updates do not install if the computer is hibernating on battery power.

- **Configure Automatic Updates**   You can configure update detection, download, and installation settings. Several of these settings are similar to the ones that you can configure through the Windows Update Control Panel. You can configure the following settings using this policy:

  - **Notify For Download And Notify For Install**   Windows Update does not download updates; it notifies the user that updates are available for download and installation.

  - **Auto Download And Notify For Install**   Windows Update downloads updates and notifies the user that updates are available for installation.

  - **Auto Download And Schedule The Install**   Windows Update downloads and installs updates without user intervention.

  - **Allow Local Admin To Choose Setting**   Configuring this setting allows a local administrator to override Windows Update settings..

  - **Install Day and Install Time**   Use these settings to configure the day and time that Windows Update will install updates.

- **Specify Intranet Microsoft Update Service Location**   You can specify the location of an internal update server, such as one running WSUS. This policy is the only way that you can configure Windows Update to use an alternate update server. Using this policy, you can specify the update server and the statistics server. In most cases, these are the same servers. The *updates server* is where the updates are downloaded from, and the *statistics server* is the server in which clients report update installation information.

EXAM TIP   Remember the function of the Specify Intranet Microsoft Update Service Location policy.

- **Automatic Updates Detection Frequency**   Configure this policy to specify how often Windows Update checks the local intranet update server for updates. This policy doesn't work if you configure a client to retrieve updates from the Windows Update servers.
- **Allow Non-Administrators To Receive Update Notifications**   This policy specifies whether users who are not members of the local Administrators group can install updates.
- **Turn On Software Notification**   When you enable this policy, Windows Update presents users with information about optional updates.
- **Allow Automatic Updates Immediate Installation**   When you enable this policy, updates that do not require a restart install automatically. Updates that do require a restart are not installed until the conditions set in the Configure Automatic Updates policy are met.
- **Turn On Recommended Updates Via Automatic Updates**   Use this policy to configure Windows Update to install recommended updates as well as important updates.
- **No Auto-Restart With Logged On Users For Scheduled Automatic Updates Installation**   When you enable this policy, Windows Update waits until the currently logged-on user logs off if Windows Update installs updates that require a restart. If you disable or don't configure this policy, and the Configure Automatic Updates policy is set to install updates at a specific time, Windows Update gives the logged-on user a 5-minute warning prior to restarting to complete the installation.
- **Re-Prompt For Restart With Scheduled Installations**   Use this policy to set the amount of time in which a user can postpone a scheduled restart when the Configure Automatic Updates policy is set to install updates at a specific time.
- **Delay Restart For Scheduled Installations**   Through this policy, you can specify the amount of time that Windows waits before automatically restarting after a scheduled installation. This policy applies only if the Configure Automatic Updates policy is set to install updates at a specific time.

- **Reschedule Automatic Updates Scheduled Installations**   You can use this policy to configure a computer that has missed a scheduled update to perform the update a specific number of minutes after startup. For example, use this policy to ensure that a computer that was switched off at the scheduled update time installs updates 1 minute after starting up. Disabling this policy means that updates install at the next scheduled time.

- **Enable Client-Side Targeting**   You can place computers into different software update groups. Different software update groups allow the software update administrator to target the deployment of updates, allowing updates to be deployed to specific groups of computers in the organization rather than all computers in the organization.

- **Allow Signed Updates From An Intranet Microsoft Update Service Location**   This policy allows updates from third-party vendors to be distributed from the Automatic Updates location as long as those updates are digitally signed by a trusted publisher.

EXAM TIP   Remember how to assign computers to different WSUS groups.

Review update history

You need to be able to determine which updates are installed on a particular computer and when those updates were installed.

True or False? Recommended updates address critical security issues.

Answer: *False.* Updates can have one of the three following classifications:

- **Important Updates**   These updates often address critical security issues. In some cases, updates with the important classification address security issues in which an exploit is already available to attackers on the Internet.

- **Recommended Updates**   These updates often address functionality issues.

- **Optional Updates**   These updates provide items such as driver updates and language packs.

Use the View Update History Control Panel to view a list of all updates that have been successfully or unsuccessfully installed on a computer, as well as the date they were installed and their importance classification. By clicking an update within the View Update History Control Panel, you can find out more information about the update. This information provides a summary of the update and also provides a link to a Knowledge Base article that also provides detailed information about the update. Knowledge Base articles also provide information about any potential problems that an update might cause. If you install an update on a client running Windows 7 and start experiencing problems, you should consult the Knowledge Base article related to the update to determine whether these problems have been documented and whether there are any workarounds to deal with the issues related to the update. Knowing the Knowledge Base ID of an update is also important if you want to delete the update. The Knowledge Base ID is a six-digit number, often preceded by the letters *KB*, such as KB123456.

True or False? When you hide an update, it will be presented for installation the next time a check occurs.

Answer: *False.* When reviewing updates that are available for installation, you can also right-click an update and select Hide Update. Choosing to hide an update effectively declines the update, so the update does not install, and Windows Update does not present that particular update for installation through Windows Update in the future. Only users with administrative privileges can hide updates. Declining an update does not mean that the update can't be installed at a later stage. By using the Restore Hidden Updates item in the Windows Update Control Panel, you can restore updates that were hidden in the past. Restoring a hidden update means that the update will be available the next time an update check occurs.

True or False? You can't manually uninstall an update using the Windows Update Control Panel item.

Answer: *True.* It is possible to uninstall an update that has already been installed. A user who is a member of the local Administrators group can uninstall an update through the Programs And Features Control Panel item. You can also access this panel by clicking the Installed Updates item in the Windows Update Control Panel. Unlike the View Update History dialog box, you are presented only with the Knowledge Base identifier of the update. So you must know the Knowledge Base identifier of an update to uninstall it. You can determine the Knowledge Base identifier of a particular update by using the View Update History Control Panel and double-clicking the update. It displays an update information dialog box from which you can determine the Knowledge Base ID. When you uninstall an update, it will be available the next time an update check occurs.

Check for new updates

You need to know how to force the Windows Update client to check for new updates, but also know how to set update checks to occur at specific times.

True or False? You can initiate a Windows Update check from the command line.

Answer: *True.* Administrators and standard users can manually check for updates by clicking the Check For Updates item in the Control Panel. The computer needs to be able to contact the update source to be able to check for updates. The update source can be the Microsoft Update servers on the Internet or a local update server. After you check for updates, the Windows Update Control Panel lists all available updates that can be installed. When you manually check for updates, as opposed to waiting until the scheduled update time, Windows Update checks only for updates. Manually checking for updates does not automatically download and install updates. You can also manually check for updates from the command line by issuing the following command:

```
Wuauclt.exe /detectnow
```

True or False? An account needs to be a member of the Enterprise Admins group if it is to be used to scan computers for missing updates using the Microsoft Baseline Security Analyzer (MBSA).

Answer: *False.* The MBSA tool can check a computer to see whether it is missing updates based on updates published by Microsoft Update or can scan a computer based on a list of updates that are approved on a WSUS server. You can also use the MBSA tool to determine whether there are problems with a computer's security configuration, such as whether common administrative vulnerabilities are present and weak passwords are set. You can use the MBSA tool to scan servers as well as clients, so it is possible to check for other vulnerabilities, such as those that are present in Internet Information Server (IIS) and Microsoft SQL Server. To scan a computer, you need to have Administrator access on the local computer and on any remote computer that you are scanning. This requirement ensures that you cannot use the MBSA tool as an attack tool to scan other people's computers to determine which vulnerabilities they may possess. You must use version 2.2 or later of the MBSA to scan computers running Windows 7.

> **MORE INFO**   To get more information about the MBSA, consult the following Microsoft TechNet webpage: *http://technet.microsoft.com/en-au/security/cc184923.aspx.*

> **EXAM TIP**   Remember what tools you can use to check for missing updates.

Rolling back updates

You need to know how to uninstall deployed updates from one or more computers.

True or False? If you roll back an update, it will be presented for installation next time an update check occurs.

Answer: *True.* When you uninstall an update, it does not appear in the list of hidden updates, but it does become available again if you check for new updates. It is important to remember to hide any update after you uninstall it. For example, you might install an update only to find that it causes a conflict with some custom software deployed in your organization. You choose to uninstall the update to restore the functionality of the custom software. You can then use the Hide Update function to hide the update until the software vendor can develop a fix that makes the custom software compatible with the update, ensuring that other users who can install updates do not inadvertently install the update until the custom software fix is available.

> **EXAM TIP**   Remember what tools you can use to roll back a deployed update.

Can you answer these questions?

You can find the answers to these questions at the end of the chapter.

1. What steps should you take if you want to check 100 computers running Windows 7 to see whether they are missing a specific software update?

2. What steps would you take to ensure that one group of computers running Windows 7 received an update but another group of computers waited 3 weeks before that update was deployed?

3. How would you remove a deployed update from a subset of computers running Windows 7 on your organization's network?

4. How can you ensure that users can complete their work and not be forcibly logged off after an update has installed that requires a restart?

Objective 7.2: Manage disks

In most real-world scenarios, you won't bother modifying the default volume configuration of a computer running the Windows 7 operating system. However you might modify the default volume configuration for reasons such as simplifying the backup process. For the exam, you'll need to know what modifications you can make to disks, including what steps you can take to make them perform better or be fault tolerant.

Exam need to know

- Managing disk volumes

  For example: How to shrink a volume to create additional space on a disk.

- Managing file system fragmentation

  For example: How to alter the defragmentation schedule.

- RAID

  For example: What versions of software RAID does Windows 7 support?

- Removable device policies

  For example: How do you block people from connecting their own USB thumb drives to their computers running Windows 7?

Managing disk volumes

You need to know how to create volumes and the type of volumes supported by Windows 7.

True or False? You can dual boot between Windows 7 and Windows XP only with a GPT disk.

Answer: *False.* Windows 7 supports two different disk partitioning systems: Master Boot Record (MBR) and Globally Unique Identifier Partition Table (GPT). The differences between them are as follows:

- When configured as a basic disk, GPT supports up to 128 partitions, but MBR supports only 4 partitions. When configured as a dynamic disk, both GPT and MBR support up to 2,000 volumes.
- A GPT partition can be up to 18 exabytes, although Windows file systems are limited to a maximum size of 256 terabytes.
- GPT has redundant partition tables.
- Windows XP 64-bit can read and write data from GPT disks, but can't boot from GPT disks.
- Windows XP 32-bit cannot read, write, or boot from GPT disks.

You can convert disks from MBR to GPT and from GPT to MBR as long as the disk is empty and contains no partitions.

MORE INFO To learn more about GPT, consult the following document: *http://msdn. microsoft.com/en-us/windows/hardware/gg463525.aspx.*

True or False? You can configure disk spanning across volumes hosted on basic disks.

Answer: *False.* There are two types of disks available in Windows 7: *basic disks* and *dynamic disks*. The differences between them are as follows:

- You can create new volumes, delete volumes, and extend or shrink existing volumes on basic disks.
- You can perform all basic disk functions on dynamic disks, as well as create spanned volumes and striped volumes. Extending a volume means consuming extra unpartitioned space on the same disk. Disk spanning involves extending a single volume over multiple disks.
- Dynamic disks are accessible only to the operating system instance that converted them to dynamic, making them problematic in multiboot scenarios.

MORE INFO To learn more about basic and dynamic disks, consult the following document: *http://msdn.microsoft.com/en-us/library/windows/desktop/ aa363785(v=vs.85).aspx.*

True or False? You can only create a simple volume on a basic disk.

Answer: *False.* You can create simple volumes on both basic and dynamic disks. Simple volumes, once called *partitions* and sometimes used interchangeably, can exist on a single disk. You can grow a simple volume if there is unpartitioned space available on the host disk. You can shrink a volume if there is available space without losing data. The amount of space you can shrink a volume depends on how much data is stored on the volume and the current level of file fragmentation.

You can create a simple volume using the Disk Management console by right-clicking the "unallocated" area of a disk when the Disk Management node of the Computer Management console is open and then clicking New Simple Volume. If you are using the DiskPart tool, you'll need to know whether you are working with a dynamic or a basic disk because the tool requires you to create partitions when working with basic disks and volumes when working with dynamic disks.

To shrink a volume using Disk Management, right-click the volume and click Shrink Volume. The Shrink dialog box opens and displays the maximum amount that you can shrink the volume. You can also shrink volumes when the volume or partition is selected in the DiskPart utility. The shrink querymax parameter displays how much free space is left, and the shrink parameter will perform the reduction.

> **MORE INFO** To learn more about managing simple volumes, consult the following TechNet document: *http://technet.microsoft.com/en-us/library/cc733060.aspx.*

True or False? You can't create and mount differencing virtual hard disks (VHDs) in Windows 7.

Answer: *True.* VHDs are a special type of file that can be mounted by the Windows 7 operating system as a hard disk. You can also configure the Enterprise and Ultimate editions of Windows 7 to boot from VHD. You can create two types of VHD files using the Windows 7 operating system: fixed size and dynamically expanding. When you create a *fixed size* VHD, all space is allocated to the VHD when the file is created. When you create a *dynamically expanding* VHD, the file can expand as needed to the maximum size, but this space is not allocated to the VHD file at creation. You can't create and mount a differencing VHD file, used by the Hyper-V role on Windows Server 2008 R2, by using the built-in Windows 7 SP1 operating system tools.

> **MORE INFO** To learn more about VHDs, consult the following document: *http:// msdn.microsoft.com/en-us/library/windows/desktop/dd323654(v=VS.85).aspx.*

True or False? You can create a spanned volume across VHD files.

Answer: *False. Spanned volumes* are volumes that are created across multiple dynamic disks. For example, a spanned volume might use 4 GB on the first disk, 3 GB on the second disk, and 5 GB on the third disk to make a spanned volume of 12 GB in size. You can create spanned volumes only across dynamic disks; you can't create spanned volumes across attached VHD files. The drawback of spanned volumes is that if one of the disks hosting the spanned volume fails, all data hosted on that volume is lost.

> **MORE INFO** To learn more about disk management, consult the following webpage: *http://technet.microsoft.com/en-us/library/cc771607.aspx.*

> **EXAM TIP** Remember which disk type supports spanned volumes.

Managing file system fragmentation

You need to know how to defragment a volume from the GUI and the command line and configure the disk defragmenter schedule.

True or False? You can configure separate defragmentation schedules for each volume.

Answer: *False*. File fragmentation occurs over time as computers write and delete files from storage devices. On traditional non–solid-state drive (SSD) hard disk drives, file fragmentation causes a decrease in disk performance because when reading a fragmented file, the computer must access different noncontiguous locations on the disk. Disk performance improves when you ensure that each file on the disk is stored contiguously. You can accomplish this by ensuring that traditional non-SSD drives are defragmented regularly. Because SSDs use a different method of performing disk read and write operations, there is less benefit in defragmenting files stored on this type of disk.

Windows 7 automatically performs a defragmentation operation on each volume at 1:00 A.M. each Wednesday. If the computer is powered off at the scheduled time, defragmentation begins after the next boot. You can configure the defragmentation schedule and determine which volumes will be defragmented by editing the properties of a disk, selecting the Tools menu, and then clicking Defragment Now. You can configure only a single defragmentation schedule for a computer. You can configure defragmentation to occur daily, weekly, or monthly.

> **MORE INFO** To learn more about disk defragmentation in Windows 7, consult the following webpage: *http://blogs.msdn.com/b/e7/archive/2009/01/25/disk-defragmentation-background-and-engineering-the-windows-7-improvements.aspx*.

True or False? You can use the defrag.exe command-line utility to consolidate free space prior to shrinking a volume.

Answer: *True*. You must run the defrag.exe utility from an elevated command prompt. The utility has the following syntax:

Defrag <volume> | /C | /E <volumes> [/A | /X | /T]

You can use these options in the following ways:

- **<volume>**   You can specify which volume the utility will defragment.
- **/C**   The utility defragments all volumes on the computer.
- **/E**   The utility defragments all volumes on the computer except the listed ones.
- **/A**   Provides a fragmentation analysis of the target volume.
- **/X**   Performs a free space consolidation. You should do this prior to attempting to shrink a volume.
- **/T**   Provides a report on an existing defrag.exe operation.
- **/H**   Forces the operation to run at normal rather than low priority.
- **/M**   Forces defragmentation of multiple volumes in parallel.
- **/U**   Displays progress of current defrag.exe operations on the screen.
- **/V**   Provides extensive defragmentation statistics.

MORE INFO To learn more about the defrag.exe utility, consult the following web-page: *http://technet.microsoft.com/en-us/magazine/ff458356.aspx.*

EXAM TIP To maximize the amount of space available when shrinking a volume, use defrag.exe to perform a free space consolidation prior to the shrink operation.

RAID

You need to know which redundant disk configurations are supported by the Windows 7 operating system.

True or False? You need a minimum of three volumes to create a striped volume.

Answer: *False.* You can create two types of RAID (Redundant Array of Inexpensive Disks) configurations using the Windows 7 operating system tools: RAID-0, known as a *striped* volume, or RAID-1, known as a *mirrored volume.* Striped volumes provide you with improvements in read and write speed, but if a disk hosting the mirror fails, all data on the striped volume is lost. Mirrored volumes provide no improvement in performance, but ensure that data remains available if a disk hosting a volume fails.

You create mirrored volumes using dynamic disks as long as you have space available on the target disk that is equal to or larger than the size of the volume you want to mirror. You can create striped volumes only on dynamic disks. You need a minimum of two volumes to create a mirrored volume or a striped volume.

You can't configure the operating system volume as a striped volume. You can configure a mirror of the volume that hosts the operating system as long as you have enough space on a separate disk. A striped volume can be hosted across two or more disks. The size of the striped volume is determined by the smallest available volume space on the constituent disks. For example, if you had a 100-GB disk, a 250-GB disk, and a 300-GB disk, using all three disks you could create a 300-GB striped volume because you are limited to a maximum of 100 GB from each drive. Using only the two larger disks, you can create a 500-GB striped volume.

MORE INFO To learn more about creating striped volumes, consult the following webpage: *http://technet.microsoft.com/en-us/library/cc732422.aspx.*

EXAM TIP Remember how many disks are required to create each type of RAID volume.

True or False? Windows 7 does not support software RAID-5 at the operating system level.

Answer: *True.* Windows 7 supports operating system RAID-0 and RAID-1, so you can create RAID-0 and RAID-1 volumes using the Diskpart utility or the Disk Management console. You cannot create RAID-5 volumes using either the Diskpart utility or the Disk Management node of the Computer Management console. The documentation for this feature can be contradictory, but when you try to accomplish this task, you'll find the option dimmed in the Computer Management console or it will lead to an error when using the Diskpart utility.

RAID-5 is disk striping with parity, and RAID-10 is a stripe of mirrored disks. RAID-5 requires a minimum of three disks, and RAID-10 needs a minimum of four. Although you could create RAID-5 arrays using the operating system in previous Windows client operating systems, you can't create RAID-5 volumes using the built-in Windows 7 operating system tools.

Windows 7 can be used with RAID-5 and RAID 10 if it is configured at the hardware level. So if you have a workstation that has a hardware RAID-5 array or a RAID-10 controller and array, you configure this hardware prior to installing the Windows 7 operating system. RAID-5 and RAID-10 do offer increased performance and are fault tolerant.

Removable device policies

You need to know how to control the use of removable storage devices in your organization.

True or False? You can allow administrators to use removable devices while blocking other users from using the same devices.

Answer: *True.* You can block the installation of removable devices, which include removable storage devices, by configuring policy settings located under the Computer Configuration\Policies\Administrative Templates\System\Device Installation\ Device Installation Restriction node in a standard Group Policy object (GPO). The policies that you can configure to block the installation of removable devices include the following:

- **Allow Administrators To Override Device Installation Restriction Policies** Members of the local Administrators group can bypass device restriction policies.

- **Allow Installation Of Devices That Match Any Of These Device IDs** Shows a list of Plug and Play (PnP) hardware IDs of devices that can be installed. Only used when the Prevent Installation Of Devices Not Described By Other Policy Settings policy is enabled. You can create a list of authorized devices while blocking all others.

- **Allow Installation Of Devices Using Drivers That Match These Device Setup Classes** Allows the installation of device drivers for devices that match the list of defined device class GUIDs.

- **Display A Custom Message Title When Installation Is Prevented By Policy** The message title presented to users when device installation is blocked.

- **Display A Custom Message When Installation Is Prevented By Policy** The message text presented to users when device installation is blocked.

- **Prevent Installation Of Devices Not Described By Other Policy Settings** You can block the installation of all devices except those listed in another policy.

- **Prevent Installation Of Devices That Match Any Of These Device IDs**   Shows a list of PnP hardware IDs and compatible IDs for devices that you want to block.

- **Prevent Installation Of Devices Using Drivers That Match These Device Setup Classes**   You can specify setup class GUIDs for device drivers that are blocked.

- **Prevent Installation Of Removable Devices**   You can block the installation of all removable devices. Any existing removable devices can't have their drivers updated. Takes precedence over other policies.

If your organization only wants administrators to use removable devices, you should enable the policy related to administrators. If you want to allow users to use specifically approved devices, you'll need to enable multiple policies.

> **MORE INFO**   To learn more about controlling access to external storage devices, consult the following webpage: *http://technet.microsoft.com/en-us/library/hh125922(WS.10).aspx*.

True or False? You can deny write access to devices not protected by BitLocker.

Answer: *True*. With BitLocker To Go, you can encrypt removable devices using the BitLocker Drive Encryption technology. With Group Policy, you can configure Windows 7 so that users can't write data to removable storage devices that are not protected by BitLocker To Go. This configuration is done using the Deny Write Access To Removable Drives Not Protected By BitLocker policy, which is located in the Computer Configuration\Administrative Templates\BitLocker Drive Encryption\ Removable Data Drives node of a GPO. You can also configure this policy to only allow data to be written to drives protected by BitLocker in the same organization. To use this policy, you also need to configure the Provide Unique Identifiers For Your Organization policy.

> **EXAM TIP**   You need to provide a unique organizational identifier if you want to only allow write access to BitLocker To Go–protected storage associated with your organization. BitLocker to Go is covered in more detail in Chapter 6, "Configuring Mobile Computing."

Can you answer these questions?

You can find the answers to these questions at the end of the chapter.

1. What kind of redundant volumes can you create using the default Windows 7 operating system tools?

2. What type of disks must you configure if you want to create a striped volume?

3. You have a 300-GB disk, a 500-GB disk, and a 600-GB disk. What is the maximum striped volume size you can create using these disks?

4. What steps do you need to take to ensure that users can write data only to removable devices from your organization?

Objective 7.3: Monitor systems

For the 70-680 exam, monitoring systems primarily involves being able to manage and maintain event logs, including configuring forwarding and filters, as well as being able to effectively leverage data collector set functionality.

Exam need to know

- Configuring event logging

  For example: How to configure maximum event log file sizes.

- Filtering event logs

  For example: How to create an event log filter.

- Event subscriptions

  For example: How to forward event logs to another computer.

- Data collector sets

  For example: How to create a data collector set.

- Generating a system diagnostics report

  For example: How to configure a schedule for the System Diagnostics data collector set.

Configuring event logging

You need to know how to configure the properties of the event log, including log size and location, and what to do when the maximum event log size is reached.

True or False? You can configure a computer to shut down if it can't write audit events to the Security event log.

Answer: *True.* All event logs have the same options, but you must configure these options on a log-by-log basis. For example, if you configure the Security log with a new maximum size, that new size applies only to the Security log, not the other logs. You can configure the following event log properties:

- **Log Path**   Defaults to the %SystemRoot%\System32\Winevt\Logs folder, but can be changed.
- **Maximum Event Log Size (KB)**   The default size is 20480 KB.

When maximum event log sized is reached:

- **Overwrite Events As Needed (Oldest Events First)**   This is the default option. When each log reaches the default 20 MB in size, the oldest events are replaced by newer events.
- **Archive The Log When Full, Do Not Overwrite Events**   This option creates archived logs that will have to be moved or deleted at some stage; otherwise, they will grow to consume the volume hosting them.

- **Do Not Overwrite Events (Clear Logs Manually)**   This option requires an administrator to clear event logs on a regular basis; otherwise, new events will not be recorded. If the Audit: Shut Down System Immediately If Unable To Log Security Audits Group Policy item is enabled, the system will shut down when it can't write new events to the Security log.

MORE INFO   To learn more about event logs, consult the following webpage: *http://technet.microsoft.com/en-us/library/cc722404.aspx.*

EXAM TIP   Remember that if you configure a log to overwrite events as needed, you'll overwrite existing events.

Filtering event logs

You need to know how to limit the visible items in a log to those that have specific properties.

True or False? Event log filters are persistent.

Answer: *False.* With filters you can limit the display of individual event logs on the basis of event time, event level, event source, event ID, keyword, user, or computer. You can create an event log filter by selecting the event log that you want to filter and then clicking Filter Current Log in the Actions pane. Event log filters are not persistent, and you must re-create them each time you restart the event viewers. To make a filter persistent, you must convert it into a Custom view, which is persistent and can be imported and exported to be used across multiple computers. Custom views also have the benefit that you can use them to find specific events across multiple logs.

MORE INFO   To learn more about event log filtering consult the following webpage: *http://technet.microsoft.com/en-us/magazine/gg131917.aspx.*

EXAM TIP   Remember the difference between an event log filter and a view.

Event subscriptions

You need to know about how event log items can be transmitted from one computer to another.

True or False? By using source-initiated subscriptions, you can add additional computers without reconfiguring the computer functioning as the event log collector.

Answer: *True.* Using event subscriptions and event forwarding, you can configure computers to consolidate event log items centrally rather than storing them separately on each computer where they are generated. Event subscriptions use HTTP or HTTPS to either send events from a source computer to a collector computer (known as *source-initiated subscriptions*) or have the collector computer retrieve certain event log items from source computers (*collector-initiated subscriptions*).

With source-initiated subscriptions, you can add additional source computers to the subscription as needed. You use source-initiated subscriptions when you have large numbers of source computers. You can configure these computers using Group Policy. Collector-initiated subscriptions are generally used in small environments.

True or False? You need to enable the Windows Remote Management (WinRM) and event collector services on all computers involved in event subscriptions.

Answer: *False.* You configure a source computer so a collector computer can retrieve events from it by running the winrm quickconfig command from an elevated command prompt. The computer account of the collector computer must be added to either the Event Log Readers or Administrators group on the source computer. It is necessary to add this account to the Administrators local group only if events in the Security log are being forwarded. You run the wecutil qc command on the collector computer to configure the event collector services. You run winrm quickconfig on the collector computer when you are using source-initiated subscriptions.

> *MORE INFO* To learn more about event subscriptions, consult the following web-page: *http://technet.microsoft.com/en-us/library/cc749183(WS.10).aspx.*

> *EXAM TIP* You don't have to configure the event collector service on the source computer.

Data collector sets

You need to know how to use and create data collector sets in Performance Monitor on computers running Windows 7.

True or False? Using data collector sets, you can collect performance information.

Answer: *True.* You can organize and record multiple data collection points. You can use Performance Monitor to view and analyze performance data, or you can create a report that summarizes the information gathered by the data collector set. Windows 7 includes the following data collector sets by default:

- **System Performance** You can gather and review information about system performance.
- **System Diagnostics** You can view and troubleshoot system reliability issues.

True or False? You can use data collector sets to trigger the execution of tasks after a particular threshold value is reached.

Answer: *True.* You can create one of the following types of custom data collector sets using the New Data Collector Set Wizard:

- **Performance Counter Data Collector** You can collect performance counter statistics over time for later analysis.
- **Event Trace Data Collector** You can collect information about system events and activities.

- **System Configuration Information** You can collect information about WMI management paths, registry keys, and the system state.
- **Performance Counter Alert** You can configure an alert that is triggered when a specific performance counter reaches a specific benchmark value. You can configure a task to run when this occurs.

You create data collector sets from the command line using the Logman command-line utility.

MORE INFO To learn more about data collector sets, consult the following webpage: *http://technet.microsoft.com/en-us/library/cc749337.aspx.*

EXAM TIP Remember that the System Diagnostics and System Performance data collector sets are included by default.

Generating a system diagnostics report

You need to know how to run the System Diagnostics data collector set and what it can tell you about a computer running Windows 7.

True or False? A user who is not a member of the local Administrators group can run a System Diagnostics report.

Answer: *False.* The System Diagnostics report is a special data collector set that is located under the Data Collector Sets\System node in Performance Monitor. The System Diagnostics report details the status of local hardware resources, system response times, and processes that are running on the local computer. It also provides detailed system information and configuration data as well as recommendations for ways in which you can improve the computer's performance. A user must be a member of the local Administrators group to run the System Diagnostics report.

EXAM TIP Remember what information can be provided by a System Diagnostics report.

Can you answer these questions?

You can find the answers to these questions at the end of the chapter.

1. You want to be able to find specific events on the basis of keyword each time you open the event viewer. These events can be in the System or the Security log. What tool should you use to accomplish this goal?
2. Which type of custom data collector set should you create if you want to retrieve information about registry keys and the system state?
3. Which command should you run on the source computer to configure it for event forwarding?
4. What method can you use to quickly find out about system response times and configuration data?

Objective 7.4: Configure performance settings

By configuring performance settings, you can improve the speed at which Windows 7 functions. There are often drawbacks to improving performance, from reduced battery life to increased chances of data loss in the event of a power failure.

Exam need to know

- Configuring page files

  For example: How to move the page file to a different disk.

- Configuring hard drive cache

  For example: How to disable write caching on a disk.

- Updated drivers

  For example: How to determine which tools you can use to update an existing device driver.

- Configuring networking performance

  For example: How to configure Background Intelligent Transfer Service (BITS).

- Configuring power plans

  For example: How to configure Windows 7 to use a different power plan.

- Configuring processor scheduling

  For example: How to set processor scheduling to favor background services.

- Configuring desktop environment

  For example: How to adjust visual effects for best performance.

- Configuring services and programs to resolve performance Issues

  For example: How to determine which processes are associated with a service.

- Mobile computing performance issues

  For example: How to describe the functionality of Windows Mobility Center.

- Configuring power

  For example: How to configure Windows 7 to issue a warning on a mobile computer when the battery is down to 5 percent of capacity.

Configuring page files

You need to know the options for managing page files on computers running Windows 7.

True or False? By default, Windows 7 automatically manages the size of the page file.

Answer: *True.* By default, the page file on computers running Windows 7 is managed by the operating system. The page file is stored in the root folder of the volume that hosts the Windows system files. The amount of physical RAM on the computer determines the size of the page file. For example:

- If the computer has less than 1 GB of physical RAM and has an x86 processor, the minimum page file size equals 1.5 times the amount of physical RAM.
- If the computer has more than 1 GB of RAM, the minimum is the amount of RAM plus 300 MB.
- The default maximum size is three times the amount of RAM.
- On computers that support Physical Address Extension (PAE), the maximum page file size is 16 GB.

You can configure the page file by opening the System item in Control Panel, clicking the Advanced tab, clicking the Settings button, clicking Advanced, and then clicking Change under Virtual Memory. You can then clear the Automatically Manage Paging File Size For All Drives check box to configure a custom size for the page file and to enable page files on each of the computer's volumes. A page file on a different volume can be custom size or system-managed size. Moving a paging file to a separate disk can improve performance. To remove a page file from a volume, choose No Paging File.

MORE INFO To learn more about Windows 7 page files, consult the following webpage: *http://technet.microsoft.com/en-us/magazine/ff382717.aspx*.

EXAM TIP Remember that you can improve performance by placing the page file on a disk separate from the one hosting the volume that hosts the operating system files.

Configuring hard drive cache

You know how to enable and disable write caching on a device.

True or False? Enabling write caching on storage devices improves performance.

Answer: *True*. Write caching is a technology that improves system performance by using RAM to store commands sent to data storage devices until the storage media can process them. The drawback of write caching is that it might lead to possible data loss during an equipment power outage. You enable or disable write caching by editing the storage device's properties in Device Manager. When you enable write caching on a device, you can also disable write-cache buffer flushing. If you do this, periodic data transfer commands are inhibited. Not all storage devices support this option.

True or False? Write caching is disabled on USB storage devices by default.

Answer: *True*. You can disable write caching on removable storage devices by configuring the Removal Policy. This policy is enabled by default in Windows 7, which is why you don't have to use the Safely Remove Hardware option when removing a USB storage device. If you enable write caching, you'll experience better performance on the device, but you'll have to use the Safely Remove Hardware option when removing the USB storage device.

Updated drivers

You need to know how to update existing device drivers on computers running the Windows 7 operating system.

True or False? You can only update drivers using Windows Update.

Answer: *False.* You can update device drivers by right-clicking a device within Device Manager and then clicking the Update Driver option. This process launches the Update Driver Software Wizard, with which you can check the local driver store as well as the Microsoft online driver repository for new drivers. You can also specify a local folder location if you have downloaded the updated drivers from the vendor's website.

You can configure the Turn Off Windows Update Device Driver Searching policy to prevent Windows 7 from checking Windows Update when a driver file is not found locally. This policy is located in the Computer Configuration\Administrative Templates\System\Internet Communication Management\Internet Communication Settings node of a standard GPO.

True or False? You can roll back to a previous version of a driver only if that version was previously installed on the computer.

Answer: *True.* With device driver rollback, you can restore a previously functioning driver if a new driver is found to be problematic. You can use driver rollback only if a previous driver has been installed. For example, you might have installed a driver released in January 2012 only to find it buggy. Even though you can then find a version of the same device driver released in August 2011, you can't roll back to that August 2011 version of the driver unless that version of the driver was installed for the device prior to you installing the January 2012 version.

You perform driver rollback through Device Manager by right-clicking the device, clicking Properties, clicking the Drivers tab, and then clicking Roll Back Driver. This option is available only if a previous driver version exists on the computer running Windows 7.

Configuring network performance

You need to know about technologies such as BranchCache and Background Intelligent Transfer Service (BITS).

True or False? A computer running Windows 7 can function as a server in Branch-Cache Hosted Cache mode.

Answer: *False.* BranchCache is a technology that allows computers running the Enterprise and Ultimate editions of Windows 7 to cache network file data from Branch-Cache-enabled sources on remote networks to be shared with other computers on the LAN. In Distributed Cache mode, each computer running Windows 7 hosts a part of the cache. In Hosted Cache mode, a computer on the branch office network running Windows Server 2008 R2 hosts the cache. You learned about BranchCache in more detail in Chapter 5, "Configuring Access to Resources."

True or False? You can use BITS to download large files without affecting other network applications.

Answer: *True.* You can use BITS, a file transfer service, to transfer files using idle network bandwidth. The advantage of BITS is that you can download very large files without adversely influencing the performance of other network applications. BITS transfers continue to function when users change their network connection or restart their computer. BITS transfers can also use other BITS clients on the local network as the source of files if they have recently accessed the same file. This is very useful for reducing traffic in situations such as software update deployment, meaning that software update files can be retrieved from BITS peers, not just from the WSUS server.

BITS usually runs automatically when used with services such as WSUS, but you can also manage BITS from Windows PowerShell with the BitsTransfer module. Once this module is imported, you can use the following cmdlets:

- **Add-BitsFile**   Adds files to an existing BITS transfer job.
- **Complete-BitsTransfer**   Completes a BITS transfer job.
- **Get-BitsTransfer**   Shows the current BITS transfer job.
- **Remove-BitsTransfer**   Stops the current BITS transfer job.
- **Resume-BitsTransfer**   Resumes a suspended BITS transfer job.
- **Set-BitsTransfer**   You can configure a BITS transfer job.
- **Start-BitsTransfer**   You can create and start a BITS transfer job.
- **Suspend-BitsTransfer**   You can pause a BITS transfer job.

You can configure the following BITS-related Group Policies:

- **Allow BITS Peercaching**   When enabled, client attempts to transfer files from other peers. Disabled by default.
- **Do Not Allow The Computer To Act As A BITS Peercaching Client**   When enabled, client downloads from source, not peers.

- **Do Not Allow The Computer To Act As A BITS Peercaching Server** Allows other peers to retrieve downloaded files from this computer.
- **Timeout For Inactive BITS Jobs** Number of days without a successful download action before a job is abandoned.
- **Limit The Maximum Network Bandwidth For BITS Background Transfers** You can specify limits. Not usually required because BITS manually manages bandwidth allocation.
- **Limit The Maximum Network Bandwidth Used For Peercaching** You can specify limits. The default is 8 Mbit/sec.
- **Limit the BITS Peercache Size** Maximum size of BITS file cache.
- **Limit The Age Of Items In The BITS Peercache** Maximum age of files in the BITS file cache.
- **Limit the Maximum BITS Job Download Time** Period during which an active download can run. The default is 90 minutes.
- **Limit The Maximum Number Of Files Allowed In A BITS Job** Maximum number of files in a single job.
- **Limit The Maximum Number Of BITS Jobs For This Computer** Maximum number of BITS jobs on a per-computer basis.
- **Limit The Maximum Number of BITS Jobs For Each User** Maximum number of BITS jobs on a per-user basis.
- **Limit The Maximum Number Of Ranges That Can Be Added To The File In A BITS Job** Ranges allow a portion of a file to be downloaded.
- **Set Up A Maintenance Schedule To Limit The Maximum Network Bandwidth Used for BITS Background Transfers** Restricts BITS bandwidth according to a schedule.
- **Set Up A Work Schedule To Limit The Maximum Network Bandwidth Used For BITS Background Transfers** Restricts BITS bandwidth according to a schedule.

MORE INFO To learn more about BITS, consult the following webpage: *http://technet.microsoft.com/en-us/magazine/ff382721.aspx*.

EXAM TIP Remember that BITS is managed from Windows PowerShell, not the BITSAdmin.exe tool.

Configuring power plans

You need to know how to modify the settings of existing power plans and how to create new power plans.

True or False? Computers running Windows 7 use the Balanced power plan by default.

Answer: *True*. A *power plan* is a collection of settings that determine how a computer running Windows 7 uses energy. By default, Windows 7 ships with the following three power plans:

- **Balanced** Provides full performance when required and saves energy when the computer is not being used. This is the default plan.
- **Power Saver** Limits system performance and reduces screen brightness on computers that support it. Allows mobile users to extend usage time when using a computer with a battery.
- **High Performance** Maximizes screen brightness on computers that support it. Increases computer performance at a cost of reducing the amount of time a mobile computer can be used with a battery.

You configure power plan settings using the Power Options Control Panel or the powercfg.exe command-line utility. You can configure basic and advanced settings for each power plan. The settings that are available depend on each computer's hardware configuration, with some computers not supporting the Dim The Display or Adjust Plan Brightness settings. When you configure power plan settings, you configure options for when the computer is running on battery power and when the computer is plugged into an external power supply. If the computer does not have an internal battery, only the Plugged In settings are available.

You can configure your own power plan based on an existing power plan. You can delete custom power plans only if the plan is not currently active. You can't delete any of the default power plans. Many OEMs configure their own power plans as a part of their default Windows 7 operating system image.

Users without local Administrator privileges can modify how the Power and Sleep buttons function. Users who can elevate privileges can also configure whether a password is required when the computer wakes from sleep. The difference between sleep, shutdown, and hibernation is as follows:

- **Sleep** The processor and majority of system devices are turned off. RAM remains active and maintains any open applications and documents. Appropriately configured devices, such as keyboards, mice, and network cards, can wake the computer from sleep. If the computer is not woken after a preconfigured amount of time, it shifts to the hibernate state.
- **Hybrid Sleep** Like sleep, the contents of RAM remain in RAM, but in a low-power state. The contents of RAM are also stored in a special file on the hard disk. Hybrid sleep is used only by computers that do not have internal batteries. .
- **Hibernate** All devices are powered off, and the contents of RAM are stored in a special file hosted on the operating system volume, which allows the computer to be restored to operation with applications and documents restored.

MORE INFO To learn more about power plans in Windows 7, consult the following webpage: *http://windows.microsoft.com/en-US/windows7/Power-plans-frequently-asked-questions.*

True or False? You can configure the power performance of a wireless adapter using advanced power plan settings.

Answer: *True.* Using advanced power plan settings, you can configure the following options:

- **Require A Password On Wakeup** Use this option to specify whether the user must enter a logon password when the computer wakes from sleep or hibernation.

- **Turn Off Hard Disk** You can configure the period of activity that triggers the hard disk to be switched off.

- **Desktop Background Settings** Use this option to specify whether animated desktops, including slide shows, are available.

- **Wireless Adapter Settings** You can specify power performance settings for wireless adapters. The Maximum Performance setting uses more energy than the Maximum Power Saving setting.

- **Sleep** You can configure the sleep and hibernation periods. It includes the option to specify whether timed events can be used to wake the computer.

- **USB Settings** Use this option to specify whether the selective suspend option is enabled for USB.

- **Power Buttons And Lid** You can configure what happens when the computer's lid is closed, what happens when the Sleep button is pressed, and what happens when the Power button is activated. Options include Do Nothing, Sleep, Hibernate, and Shut Down.

- **PCI Express** Use this option to specify whether Windows 7 can leverage the PCI Express Link State Power Management feature with idle devices. Can be set to Moderate Power Savings, Maximum Power Savings, or Off.

- **Processor Power Management** You can specify minimum and maximum processor states and whether a system cooling policy is enabled.

- **Display** Use this option to specify the periods that must elapse before the display is dimmed and switched off. You can also specify display brightness during normal and dim use.

- **Multimedia Settings** You can configure whether a computer is allowed to sleep when a remote computer is accessing media over the network. You can also optimize or reduce video playback quality as a method of minimizing power usage.

- **Battery** Use this option to specify the Reserve, Low, and Critical battery levels as a percentage and what actions to take when these levels are reached.

Power Management–related Group Policy items are located in the Computer Configuration\Administrative Templates\System\Power Management node. Through Group Policy, you can configure the additional options not available through the Advanced Power Settings GUI, including the following:

- Allow Applications To Prevent Automatic Sleep
- Allow Automatic Sleep With Open Network Files
- Turn On The Ability For Applications To Prevent Sleep Transition

True or False? You can use powercfg.exe to configure options that aren't available using GUI tools.

Answer: *True.* You can configure Windows 7 power settings from an elevated command prompt. With powercfg.exe, you can configure several power management settings that can't be configured through the power plan GUI, including specifying which devices can wake a computer from a sleep state.

> **MORE INFO** To learn more about powercfg.exe in Windows 7, consult the following webpage: *http://technet.microsoft.com/en-us/library/cc748940(WS.10).aspx.*

> **EXAM TIP** Remember the difference between sleep and hibernation.

Configuring processor scheduling

You need to know how to switch processor scheduling options between Programs and Background Services.

True or False? Windows 7 is configured by default to give better response time to background applications.

Answer: *False.* With processor scheduling, you can configure a computer running Windows 7 to prioritize one type of application over another. Processor scheduling is configured on the Advanced tab of the Performance Options dialog box, which is available through the Advanced tab of the System Properties dialog box. The options that you can configure include these:

- **Programs** This option gives active applications the best response time and a substantial share of available resources. It is the default setting on computers running the Windows 7 operating system.
- **Background Services** This option is suitable for computers running Windows 7 that are functioning in a server role, such as functioning as a file server, a print server, or hosting a small website.

Configuring desktop environment

You need to know how to configure visual effects settings to achieve the best mix between appearance and performance.

True or False? You can use visual effects performance options to disable edge smoothing for screen fonts.

Answer: *True.* On very fast computers, you will not notice a performance change, but on slower computers visual effects options can make a difference in how well a computer responds. The more visual effects settings that are enabled, the greater the decrease in overall performance. You can configure the visual settings of a computer running Windows 7 to increase performance. You configure these visual options on the Visual Effects tab of the Performance Options dialog box. You can access this dialog box by clicking the Settings button in the Performance area of the Advanced tab of the System Properties dialog box. You can choose one of the following options:

- **Let Windows Choose What's Best For My Computer** The operating system enables and disables appearance enhancements as necessary. This is the default option.

- **Adjust For Best Appearance** When this option is enabled, all appearance enhancements are enabled.

- **Adjust For Best Performance** When this option is enabled, all appearance enhancements are disabled.

- **Custom** When you choose Custom, you can enable or disable the following individual appearance elements:
  - Animate Controls And Elements Inside Windows
  - Animate Windows When Minimizing And Maximizing
  - Animations In The Taskbar And Start Menu
  - Fade Or Slide Menus Into View
  - Fade Or Slide ToolTips Into View
  - Fade Out Menu Items After Clicking
  - Show Shadows Under Mouse Pointer
  - Show Shadows Under Windows
  - Show Translucent Selection Rectangle
  - Show Windows Contents While Dragging
  - Slide Open Combo Boxes
  - Smooth Edges Of Screen Fonts
  - Smooth-Scroll List Boxes
  - Use Drop Shadows For Icon Labels On The Desktop
  - Use Visual Styles On Windows And Buttons

MORE INFO To learn more about disabling visual effects, consult the following webpage: *http://windows.microsoft.com/en-US/windows7/Optimize-Windows-7-for-better-performance.*

Configuring services and programs to resolve performance issues

You need to know how to alter the priority of a running process.

True or False? You can configure the priority of a service by configuring the priority of a process.

Answer: *True.* You can view which processes and services are consuming system resources by using the Resource Monitor. You can configure the priority of a process by opening the Task Manager, selecting the Processes tab, right-clicking the process, and then clicking Set Priority. You can configure one of the following priorities:

- Realtime
- High
- Above Normal
- Normal
- Below Normal
- Low

To determine which process or processes are used by a specific service, right-click the service on the Services tab of Task Manager and then click Go To Process. The processes related to the services on the Processes tab will display, so you can configure an appropriate priority. Selecting the Realtime option allocates almost all processor resources to a process and can have a negative impact on computer performance.

> **MORE INFO**   To learn more about Task Manager, consult the following webpage: *http://windows.microsoft.com/en-US/windows7/What-do-the-Task-Manager-memory-columns-mean.*

Mobile computing performance issues

Mobile computing performance issues means knowing the options in Windows Mobility Center.

True or False? You can use Windows Mobility Center to configure a computer in Presentation mode.

Answer: *True.* With Windows Mobility Center, you can configure items such as display brightness, volume, battery status, power plan, and wireless network status from a single Control Panel. By switching which power plan is in effect, reducing the display brightness, and disabling wireless, you can substantially increase the amount of time that the mobile computer can be used before the battery becomes completely drained. You can also use Windows Mobility Center to configure the computer to function in Presentation mode, which means that notifications do not appear on the screen. This is useful when you want to ensure that items such as instant messages don't appear on the screen during an important PowerPoint presentation.

> **MORE INFO**   To learn more about Windows Mobility Center, consult the following TechNet document: *http://windows.microsoft.com/en-US/windows7/Using-Windows-Mobility-Center.*

Configuring power

Configuring power means changing the power options for a device.

True or False? You can use the Power Management tab to block a specific device from being able to wake the computer from sleep.

Answer: *True*. You configure power options through the Power Management tab in each compatible device's properties dialog box in Device Manager. (Not all devices allow configuring of power options.) When you configure these power options, you can specify whether a specific device can wake the computer from a sleep state. For example, you can use this functionality to enable Wake On LAN, a feature that enables computers in a low-power state to be woken by network management services to install updates or new software. The options that you can configure on the Power Management tab include these:

- Allow The Computer To Turn Off This Device To Save Power
- Allow This Device To Wake The Computer

MORE INFO To learn more about device power options, consult the following web-page: *http://technet.microsoft.com/en-us/library/cc731895.aspx*.

True or False? You can generate a power efficiency diagnostics report using built-in tools.

Answer: *True*. You can create a power efficiency diagnostics report for a computer running Windows 7 by using the powercfg.exe utility with the energy parameter. This report will provide you with detailed information about how the computer uses energy and any issues that might exist, such as certain devices not properly entering hibernation or sleep modes.

MORE INFO To learn more about power efficiency diagnostic reports, consult the following webpage: *http://support.microsoft.com/kb/976034*.

EXAM TIP Remember that you configure power management options to determine whether a computer can be woken by a special Wake On LAN packet intercepted by a compatible network adapter.

Can you answer these questions?

You can find the answers to these questions at the end of the chapter.

1. What is the main drawback to enabling write caching?
2. Which technology should you use to support transfers of large files without interfering with network performance?
3. What tool can you use to lower the priority of a specific process?
4. What tool do you use to generate a power efficiency diagnostics report?

Answers

This section contains the answers to the "Can you answer these questions?" sections in this chapter.

Objective 7.1: Configure updates to Windows 7

1. You should use the Microsoft Baseline Security Analyzer to check whether 100 computers running Windows 7 are missing a specific update.
2. You can use WSUS groups to ensure that one group of computers running Windows 7 receives an update 3 weeks after another group of computers running Windows 7.
3. You can use WSUS to roll back a deployed update.
4. You can configure the No Auto-Restart With Logged On Users For Scheduled Automatic Updates Installation policy to ensure that users are not forcibly logged off to complete update installation.

Objective 7.2: Manage disks

1. You can create a mirrored volume, also known as a RAID-1 volume. You can't create a RAID-5 volume or a RAID-10 volume using the Windows 7 operating system tools.
2. You can only create striped volumes on dynamic disks.
3. You can create a 1000-GB striped volume if you use the 500-GB disk and the 600-GB disk only.
4. You need to configure the Deny Write Access To Removable Drives Not Protected By BitLocker policy and the Provide Unique Identifiers For Your Organization policy.

Objective 7.3: Monitor systems

1. You should create a Custom view because these views are both persistent and can be used to find events across multiple logs.
2. You create a System Configuration Information data collector set if you want to retrieve information about registry keys and the system state.
3. You should run the winrm quickconfig command to prepare the source computer for event forwarding.
4. You should run a Systems Diagnostic report.

Objective 7.4: Configure performance settings

1. Enabling write caching can lead to data loss if there is a power disruption.
2. BITS allows the transfer of large files by using idle network bandwidth, minimizing its impact on network performance.
3. With Task Manager, you can reduce the priority of a specific process.
4. The powercfg.exe command-line utility.

CHAPTER 8

Configuring Backup and Recovery Options

Because approximately 11 percent of the 70-680 exam focuses on the topic of configuring backup and recovery options, you need to have a good grasp of how to back up and recover computers running Microsoft Windows 7, including when to use functionality such as System Restore and Last Known Good Configuration (LKGC), and how to leverage previous versions of files stored using shadow copy.

This chapter covers the following objectives:

- Objective 8.1: Configure backup
- Objective 8.2: Configure system recovery options
- Objective 8.3: Configure file recovery options

Objective 8.1: Configure backup

Although up to 60 percent of organizational data is stored on client computers, most organizations don't have a coherent plan for ensuring that data on client computers is backed up. Windows 7 comes with a basic backup utility that you can use to schedule a regular backup and leave it to run. You don't have to constantly monitor the backup to determine whether there is enough available space on the backup device because when the utility is used with a local storage device, it automatically overwrites the oldest backup data with new backup data when the storage device reaches capacity.

Exam need to know

- Creating a system recovery disk

  For example: What steps do you need to take to create a recovery disk and in what situations would you use it?

- Backing up files, folders, or full system

  For example: Know what steps to take to back up user libraries.

- Scheduling backups

  For example: How to configure Windows 7 to back up a system image on a periodic basis.

Creating a system recovery disk

You need to know how to create and when to use a system repair disc.

EXAM TIP What the 70-680 exam objectives call a *system recovery disk* is called a *system repair disc* in the Windows 7 operating system user interface.

True or False? You can use the Windows 7 installation media to perform system repair tasks.

Answer: *True.* System repair discs give you the option of creating a bootable device that you can use to perform system recovery operations. You can also use the Windows 7 installation media to perform the same tasks.

You can create a system repair disc on any computer that is running Windows 7 and has a DVD or CD writer by performing the following steps:

1. Open the Backup And Restore item in the Control Panel.

2. In the left pane, click Create A System Repair Disc.

3. A routine runs, prompting you to insert a writable CD or DVD. Insert the writable optical media in the drive and allow the repair disc to be created.

If a failure occurs, and you don't have access to the installation media or a system repair disc, you can create a system repair disc on another computer running Windows 7 and use it with the computer that failed.

Unlike previous versions of Windows, Windows 7 automatically installs the Windows Recovery Environment (WinRE), which includes the startup repair tool. Windows 7 automatically opens WinRE if Windows 7 can't start, which allows the operating system to perform many repair tasks automatically without direct intervention. If the boot volume is damaged, you will need to access WinRE from the Windows 7 installation media or from a system repair disc.

Traditionally, a system repair disc is a bootable CD or DVD. It is possible to configure a bootable USB thumb device to function as a system repair disc, but you can't do this directly from the Backup And Restore Control Panel in Windows 7 SP1.

MORE INFO To learn more about creating a system repair disc, consult the following webpage: *http://windows.microsoft.com/en-US/windows7/Create-a-system-repair-disc.*

True or False? You can perform a Windows memory diagnostic from a system repair disc.

Answer: *True.* You can perform the following tasks from the system repair disc:

- **Startup Repair** You can fix certain problems, including replacing missing or damaged system files that might prevent Windows 7 from starting properly. Startup repair scans the computer looking for common problems, such as missing or damaged startup files, and attempts to repair them automatically.

- **System Restore** You can restore the computer's system files to an earlier point in time without affecting personal files such as documents, pictures, or email.

- **System Image Recovery** You can restore a system image to the disk. It is the most aggressive form of recovery because it will overwrite existing data on the volume. This method is the recovery method of last resort.

- **Windows Memory Diagnostic** You can perform tests against RAM to determine whether the RAM is faulty.

- **Command Prompt** You can open a command prompt to perform command-line tasks on the computer.

MORE INFO To learn more about system recovery options, consult the following webpage: *http://windows.microsoft.com/en-US/windows7/What-are-the-system-recovery-options-in-Windows-7.*

Backing up files, folders, or full system

You need to know the steps for backing up files, folders, or the full system either individually or collectively.

True or False? File and folder backups are stored as .zip files.

Answer: *True.* By using the Backup And Restore item in the Windows 7 Control Panel, you can perform the following types of backups:

- **System Image Backup** This backup is a block level backup of an entire volume that is stored in virtual hard disk (.vhd) format. This image is compacted to remove empty space. The backup can be stored on local media, including DVDs and removable hard disks, as well as on shared folders. If you are doing a regular system image backup to a local or removable hard disk, additional backups will be incremental at the block level. When you create a scheduled backup using the default settings, Windows 7 Backup And Restore creates a system image backup as well as the default Windows folders and local files stored in user libraries.

- **Data Files** Backup And Restore writes data file backups as compressed .zip files to the backup device. You can select individual files, folders, or libraries to back up. This type of backup is incremental by default, and Backup And Restore writes only files that have changed since the backup to the same location. Data file backup does not back up system files, program files, EFS-encrypted files, temporary files, user profile files, or files in the Recycle Bin.

True or False? You can't use Backup And Restore to restore items from another computer running Windows 7.

Answer: *False*. When you select an external volume as target for a backup, Windows 7 creates a folder that shares the name of the computer and saves backups in subfolders with the name Backup Set *<year-month-day> <time>*. For example, a backup that takes place on December 28, 2011 at 13:13:00 on a removable disk mounted as volume F: on a computer named Yarragon would be stored in the F:\Yarragon\Backup Set 2011-12-28 131300 folder. Automatically created folders with incremental names store changed files within subfolders, but the name of the parent backup set folder is not updated until another full backup is performed.

If you want to use the Backup And Restore Control Panel item to restore files from another computer, you'll need to use the Advanced Restore option and select Files From A Backup Made On A Different Computer.

> **MORE INFO**　To learn more about Backup And Restore, consult the following webpage: *http://windows.microsoft.com/en-AU/windows7/Back-up-and-restore-frequently-asked-questions*.

> **EXAM TIP**　Windows 7 Backup And Restore does not back up files stored on volumes formatted with the FAT file system.

Scheduling backups

You need to know how to configure and modify a backup schedule on a computer running Windows 7.

True or False? When you set up a backup using the default settings, a backup occurs once per day.

Answer: *False*. With Windows Backup you can configure "set and forget" backups. Backup And Restore is designed so that once you turn it on, it will continue to perform backups according to the schedule you specify. When the assigned storage device fills, older backups are removed to make space for newer backups, so backups occur continuously. If you want to ensure that Backup And Restore does not delete older backup data to make way for new backup data, perform a one-off backup to a separate location.

By default, Windows Backup backs up files weekly on Sunday at 7:00 P.M. You can change this schedule by opening the Backup And Restore item in the Control Panel, clicking Change Settings, and navigating through the Set Up Backup Wizard until you reach the Review Your Backup Settings page. Then click Change Schedule. You can choose how often you want to back up: Daily, Weekly, or Monthly.

- If you choose Daily, you need to specify a time starting on the hour. For example, you can choose to have a backup start at 2:00, but not at 2:15. Daily backup is the highest frequency backup option available using Backup And Restore.

- If you choose Weekly, you need to specify a day of the week and a time starting on the hour.
- If you choose Monthly, you need to specify which day of the month from 1 to 31, including the option of Last Day, and an hour to run the backup.

MORE INFO To learn more about scheduling backups, consult the following webpage: *http://windows.microsoft.com/en-AU/windows7/Back-up-and-restore-frequently-asked-questions.*

EXAM TIP Remember that you can't schedule backups to occur more often than once per day using Backup And Restore in Windows 7.

Can you answer these questions?

You can find the answers to these questions at the end of the chapter.

1. Which problems does startup repair attempt to automatically resolve?

2. You are responsible for managing a number of computers running Windows 7 and you have been performing system image backups to a removable hard disk drive. The primary disk drive on a computer running Windows 7 fails and you replace it. You don't have access to the Windows 7 installation media. What other method can you use to restore the computer?

3. You are planning a backup strategy for your organization. Your organization uses a standard hardware platform for all personal computers running Windows 7. You want to ensure that you can quickly recover a computer running Windows 7, including all its applications, personal files, and system settings, to another computer. Backups will be stored on external USB drives. What type of backup should you schedule on each computer to accomplish this goal?

4. What is the most frequent schedule you can configure for a system image backup using the Backup And Restore item in the Windows 7 Control Panel?

Objective 8.2: Configure system recovery options

The key to this exam objective is knowing when to use one recovery option instead of another. The main recovery options covered by this objective are system repair, System Restore, restoring a system image backup, driver rollback, and Last Known Good Configuration.

Exam need to know

- Configuring system restore points

  For example: How to configure Windows 7 restore point settings.

- Restore system settings

  For example: How to restore system settings without losing user data.
- Last Known Good Configuration

  For example: How to determine the situations in which to use Last Known Good Configuration.
- Complete restore

  For example: How to determine when it is necessary to restore from a system image backup.
- Driver rollback

  For example: How to know when you can roll a device driver back to a previous version.

Configuring system restore points

You need to know how to create a system restore point and allocate space to store restore point data.

True or False? You can manually create system restore points.

Answer: *True.* With System Restore, you can create a restore point that will return system files and settings to a specific earlier point in time without changing any personal files. Windows 7 automatically creates a restore point every day and also automatically creates a new restore point before you install a program, device driver, or system update. You can't manually configure a restore point schedule on a computer running Windows 7. You can force the creation of a restore point by clicking the Create button on the System Protection tab of the System Properties dialog box. You can also use the Checkpoint-Computer PowerShell cmdlet from an elevated PowerShell session to force the creation of a restore point.

You can configure the following settings by clicking the Configure button when the System volume is selected on the System Protection tab of the System Properties dialog box:

- **Restore System Settings And Previous Versions Of Files**   System Restore records system settings and file version information each time a restore point is created. This is the default setting.
- **Only Restore Previous Versions Of Files**   When you use this setting, only previous versions of a file's snapshot are taken automatically. You can't restore to a previous restore point.
- **Turn Off System Protection**   When this setting is enabled, restore points are disabled.
- **Max Usage**   You can specify the maximum amount of space to store system settings and previous versions of files for System Restore.
- **Delete**   You can delete all existing restore points.

MORE INFO To learn more about System Restore, consult the following webpage: *http://windows.microsoft.com/en-US/windows-vista/System-Restore-frequently-asked-questions.*

Restoring system settings

You need to know how to perform a system restore—restoring a computer's configuration to a specific previously existing restore point.

True or False? Performing a system restore deletes any user documents created since the restore point was created.

Answer: *False.* Performing a system restore only returns a computer's system files to an earlier point in time. Performing a system restore does not affect personal files, such as user-created documents, photographs, or email messages.

You can perform a system restore in two ways:

- By opening the System Restore utility from within Windows 7, either through the Control Panel or by running the rstrui.exe utility
- By accessing the System Restore item on the System Recovery Options menu, which you can access by booting off the Windows 7 installation media or a system repair disc

True or False? You can use System Restore to recover any damaged or deleted file.

Answer: *False.* You can only use System Restore to roll back system files and settings to an earlier point in time. You can't use System Restore to recover damaged or deleted user files. When you create a system restore point, it creates a new previous versions of files point, however you don't access previous versions of files through the System Restore functionality.

MORE INFO To learn more about System Restore, consult the following webpage: *http://windows.microsoft.com/en-US/windows7/What-is-System-Restore.*

EXAM TIP Remember to be clear about the difference between System Restore and system image recovery.

Last Known Good Configuration

You need to know when you use this recovery option instead of other system repair or restore options.

True or False? Last Known Good Configuration (LKGC) is updated after a successful logon.

Answer: *True.* You use LKGC if the operating system starts but then fails after the Starting Windows logo is displayed. LKGC reverses the most recent system, driver, and registry modifications. Windows 7 writes a new LKGC only after the computer successfully starts in Normal mode and a user performs a successful logon. If you use LKGC, you lose all configuration modifications that were made since a user last logged on successfully.

Starting in LKGC does not modify any user files on the computer, so a user doesn't lose any new documents or changes made to existing documents when re-starting using LKGC. Restarting in LKGC means that system changes made since the last successful logon will be lost. You have to reapply any changes, such as installing updates or installing drivers. When taking this action, keep in mind the configuration issue that required you to resort to LKGC in the first place.

True or False? You can access LKGC after the Starting Windows logo appears.

Answer: *False.* You should use LKGC if you make a change to the computer and the computer displays the Starting Windows logo after restarting, but you can't perform a successful logon. You should not use LKGC if the computer does not reach the stage of displaying the Starting Windows logo.

To access LKGC, perform the follow these steps:

1. Ensure that you remove all bootable media from the computer. Restart or power on the computer and then press F8 after the firmware POST process completes. If the Starting Windows logo appears, you need to restart because you have missed being able to enter LKGC.

2. On the Advanced Boot Options menu, choose Last Known Good Configuration.

MORE INFO To learn more about LKGC, consult the following webpage: *http://windows.microsoft.com/en-US/windows7/Using-Last-Known-Good-Configuration.*

EXAM TIP Remember when you should use LKGC as a recovery option.

Complete restore

You need to know what steps to take to perform a complete restore from a system image backup and when complete restore is appropriate.

True or False? You can perform a complete restore by booting from the Windows 7 installation media.

Answer: *True.* You perform a complete restore by choosing the System Image Recovery option from System Recovery Options. Performing a complete restore means you don't choose to restore individual items; the entire contents of the volume that you restore to are replaced by the contents of the system image. You can perform a complete restore by booting from the Windows 7 installation media or from a system repair disc. You can perform a system image restore only to a volume that is the same size or larger than the volume captured by the system image. You can create a system image that includes multiple drives and partitions.

To perform a complete restore, follow these steps:

1. Ensure that you have access to the device that hosts the system image.
2. Boot the computer using either the Windows 7 installation media or a system repair disc.
3. When prompted, specify your regional preferences. Click Next.
4. Click Repair Your Computer.
5. In the System Recovery Options dialog box, choose the Restore Your Computer Using A System Image That Was Created Earlier option. If your backup was stored on a DVD, insert the DVD at this point. Click Next.
6. On the Select A System Image Backup page, you can choose between the most recent image located on the media that hosts the system image or a previous image if you have more than one system image.
7. Choose whether you want to Format And Repartition Disks.
8. Click Next and then click Finish. When the restore completes, the computer restarts.

Because system image files are stored in .vhd format, it is possible, with careful preparation, to configure them as disks on virtual machines hosted on computers running Hyper-V. It is even possible, with special configuration, to configure a computer to use the Windows 7 boot to .vhd functionality to boot into a .vhd created through the system image backup process, although this scenario is unlikely to be canvassed in the 70-680 exam.

MORE INFO To learn more about restoring a system image, consult the following webpage: *http://windows.microsoft.com/en-US/windows7/What-is-a-system-image*.

EXAM TIP Remember that restoring a system image wipes out everything on the current volume and replaces it with the contents of the system image.

Driver rollback

You need to know in which situations you should roll back a driver to a previous version to resolve a configuration problem.

True or False? You can roll back to a previous version of a driver if you have the driver installation files available on removable storage media, and the driver was not installed on the computer previously.

Answer: *False*. You can use driver rollback to return to a previously installed device driver, which is useful when a device driver causes problems after you have updated it. You can use driver rollback only if a previous version of the device driver was installed on the computer at some time in the past. You perform driver rollback by editing the properties of a device in Device Manager. You learned about driver rollback in Chapter 7, "Monitoring and Maintaining Systems that Run Windows 7."

MORE INFO To learn more about rolling back a device driver, consult the following webpage: *http://technet.microsoft.com/en-us/library/cc732648.aspx*.

EXAM TIP If your computer doesn't start because a newly installed device driver won't let you log on, you can use LKGC to resolve the issue. If you can successfully log on, you have to use driver rollback to resolve the issue.

Can you answer these questions?

You can find the answers to these questions at the end of the chapter.

1. This morning, a malware infection compromised a computer running Windows 7. Despite your best attempts to remove the malware, you don't know whether the system is clean. The computer was configured to take daily system image backups, and you want to return the computer to a state in which you are sure that all system files and user data are free of the infection. You can lose up to 48 hours of data if you cannot meet this goal. What steps should you take to accomplish this?

2. You update several drivers on a laptop computer running Windows 7 in preparation for rolling these drivers out across your organization's fleet of laptops running Windows 7. You reboot to complete installation, and the system freezes at the logon screen. Which technology should you use to resolve this issue as quickly as possible?

3. The system files of a computer running Windows 7 appear to be corrupt, and you want to roll back these files to a previous point in time without altering any of the user data stored on the machine. Which system recovery option should you use to accomplish this goal?

4. You update the video driver of your computer running Windows 7. You restart the computer and log on. After a few minutes, you notice several display corruption issues. Which method should you use to resolve this issue?

Objective 8.3: Configure file recovery options

The most common form of recovery that IT professionals have to perform is that of deleted or corrupt files or folders. The frequency of this type of recovery vastly exceeds the frequency of system restore or system image recovery operations. Through previous versions of file functionality, Windows 7 provides users with a simple way of being able to recover recently deleted files and folders without requiring a restoration of files from backup.

Exam need to know

- Configuring file restore points
  For example: How to create a new restore point.
- Restoring damaged or deleted files by using shadow copies
  For example: How to restore a deleted file or folder.

- Restoring previous versions of files and folders

  For example: How to restore a previous version of a file.
- Restoring user profiles

  For example: How to fix a corrupt user profile.

Configuring file restore points

You need to know how to create restore points and how to allocate disk space to host restore point data.

True or False? You can directly force the creation of a restore point.

Answer: *True.* Previous versions of files are copies of files and folders as they exist at a particular point in time. Windows 7 creates previous versions of files at the same time that it creates system restore points. By default, Windows 7 allocates 5 percent of a volume's space to storing previous versions of files. You can modify this amount to allow a greater number of previous versions of files to be stored by clicking the Configure button on the System Protection tab of the System Properties dialog box. You can also reconfigure this amount by using the vssadmin.exe command-line utility. A volume can contain a maximum of 512 previous versions of the same file, though the number of previous versions is usually much lower and is dependent on the amount of disk space allocated to previous versions of files. The default is 64 shadow copies. You can change this number by editing the registry. By default, the system volume is configured to host previous versions' data. You have to enable this functionality on additional volumes.

Restore points aren't created according to a configurable schedule, but instead are created in response to specific events. You can force the creation of previous versions of a file's restore point by clicking the Create button on the System Protection tab of the System Properties dialog box. You can also use the Checkpoint-Computer PowerShell cmdlet from an elevated PowerShell session to force the creation of a restore point. You can use this cmdlet in a Task Scheduler task to automate the creation of checkpoints at specific times of the day.

> **MORE INFO** To learn more about volume shadow copies, consult the following webpage: *http://technet.microsoft.com/en-us/library/ee923636(WS.10).aspx.*

Restoring damaged and deleted files by using shadow copies

You need to know how to access the previous versions of files' functionality to recover files without needing to restore them directly from backup.

True or False? Previous version functionality isn't enabled by default on computers running Windows 7.

Answer: *False.* A *shadow copy* is a copy of a file as it existed at a previous version in time. Previous versions of files are copies of the files as they existed when a restore point is created or a backup is taken. By default, Windows 7 does this once per day, although if you store files on volumes other than the default system volume, you might need to enable this functionality. You can enable it on the System Protection tab of the System Properties dialog box. Although a user might modify a file several times throughout the day, only the version of the file as it exists when the restore point is created is available through previous file versions.

True or False? You can recover damaged files using previous versions of files.

Answer: *True.* You can use Windows 7's previous versions of the files' functionality to restore previous copies of files stored on the local file system. You can use this process to recover damaged files without having to recover those files from backup. Instead of restoring to the original location, you can copy previous versions of files to an alternate location. Users might need to recover several different versions of the same file to find a version that meets their recovery needs.

You can restore previous versions of files by following these steps:

1. Right-click the file that you want to restore and click Restore Previous Versions.

2. On the Previous Versions tab, you'll see a list of previous versions of the file. If you are also using backup, you'll see previous versions of the files that are available through restoring from backup. This works best if you are using locally attached storage or a removable device attached to the computer to store backup files.

3. If you choose Restore, the previous version of the file will overwrite the current version of the file. If you choose Copy, you can copy the previous version of the file to an alternate location, which doesn't overwrite the current version of the file. You can also open the file directly by clicking Open. (This option is not available if the previous version is stored on a backup instead of as a shadow copy.) If you are restoring a version that is contained within a backup, the Restore Files Wizard will be triggered, and you'll need to make the backup location available.

Previous versions are not available in the following situations:

- The file has not been modified. Previous versions of files are available only for those files that have been altered or deleted.

- A restore point or backup has not been made since the file was altered.

- System protection is not enabled for the volume hosting the files. You need to enable system protection on each volume that hosts files if you want to use previous versions of files' functionality.

You can control how previous versions of files function through Group Policy settings located in the \Administrative Templates\Windows Components\Windows Explorer\Previous Versions node in both the Computer Configuration and User Configuration areas of a Group Policy object (GPO). These policies are primarily used to restrict users from performing restoration using the previous versions' functionality. The functionality that you can block through these policies is as follows:

- **Prevent Restoring Previous Versions From Backups** You can disable the Restore button on the Previous Versions tab for files available through backup.
- **Prevent Restoring Local Previous Versions** You can disable the Restore button for files available locally.
- **Prevent Restoring Remote Previous Versions** You can disable the Restore button for files and folders hosted on file shares.
- **Hide Previous Versions Lists for Local Files** You can hide the list of previous versions available for local files.
- **Hide Previous Versions List For Remote Files** You can hide the list of previous versions available for files hosted on file shares.
- **Hide Previous Versions Of Files On Backup Location** You can hide the list of previous versions of files stored on backups.

MORE INFO To learn more about restoring previous versions of files, consult the following webpage: *http://windows.microsoft.com/en-US/windows7/Previous-versions-of-files-frequently-asked-questions.*

EXAM TIP If the hard disk hosting the files fails, all the previous versions of files hosted on that hard disk are also lost. Previous versions of files written to backup are not lost, however.

Restoring previous versions of files and folders

You need to know how to recover previous versions of files and folders that have either been changed or deleted.

True or False? You can restore a previous version of a file or folder that has been deleted.

Answer: *True.* As you learned earlier, previous versions of files are copies of files and folders as they existed when a restore point is created or a backup is taken. You can use the Windows 7 previous versions of files' functionality to restore deleted files and folders just as you can use it to restore undamaged versions of files that have become corrupt. Restoring deleted items is a little different from restoring previous versions of files that already exist. To restore a deleted item, right-click the parent folder, which can be the volume if the file or folder is in the volume's root directory. Then click the Restore Previous Versions item. You can then restore deleted items or folders to their original location or copy them to new locations, just as you would when using the restore previous versions' functionality normally.

EXAM TIP Remember that previous versions of files are available only if the file has been modified or deleted.

Restore user profiles

You need to know how to recover corrupt user profiles.

True or False? All user profile data is stored in the ntuser.dat file.

Answer: *False.* User profiles are collections of settings, including those for desktop background, pointer preferences, sound settings, and screen savers. User profiles are updated when users log off from the computer. User profiles are stored in the following way by Windows 7:

- A folder hierarchy under the C:\Users folder stores user-specific startup applications, shortcut links, and desktop icons.

- A registry hive stores user-specific desktop settings, application, settings, persistent network connections, printer settings, mapped network drives, and so on. The ntuser.dat file, which is stored in the user's profile folder, is mapped to the HKEY_CURRENT_USER area of the registry when the user logs on.

Sometimes Windows 7 might not load a profile correctly. Prior to taking extreme action such as creating a new profile, restart the computer and attempt to log on again. If this doesn't work, you'll need to repair the user profile by re-creating it.

True or False? You copy the ntuser.dat file when repairing a user profile.

Answer: *False.* You can repair an existing profile for a computer that is a member of a domain or locally by following these steps to re-create it:

1. Log on to the computer running Windows 7 with a user account that has local Administrator rights. Use this account to create a new user account.

2. Navigate to the \Users folder. On the View tab of the Folder Options dialog box, ensure that the Show Hidden Files, Folders, and Drives option is selected. Clear the Hide Protected Operating System Files check box.

3. Open the folder associated with the old user account that has the corrupted profile. Select all file and folders in this folder, except the following:

   - Ntuser.dat
   - Ntuser.dat.log
   - Ntuser.ini

4. Copy the files from this old user account folder to the folder associated with the newly created user account.

5. You can log on to the computer using the newly created account, which should have the profile data from the original account.

6. If the account is a member of a domain, but you aren't using a roaming user profile, follow these steps:

   a. Log on to the computer locally and copy the files listed in step 3 to a temporary directory.

   b. Delete the profile of the domain account.

    c. Log on to the computer again with the domain account to re-create the profile.

    d. Log off and log back in with the account that has local administrator privileges. Copy the files and folders back from the temporary directory to the newly created administrator account.

MORE INFO To learn more about repairing corrupted user profiles, consult the following webpage: *http://windows.microsoft.com/en-US/windows7/fix-a-corrupted-user-profile.*

Can you answer these questions?

You can find the answers to these questions at the end of the chapter.

1. Several days ago, a user of a stand-alone computer running Windows 7 deleted a folder containing several files. The user's computer is running Windows 7 Enterprise Edition in the default configuration. This folder had been stored on his computer for a number of months, and the user regularly edited the files it contained. After he deleted the files, he then emptied the Recycle Bin. This morning, he realized that he wanted to keep one of those files, but did not keep any backups. What option could you suggest to the user to restore the files?

2. What PowerShell cmdlet can you use to force the creation of a restore point that can be used with previous versions of files?

3. Which files should you not copy when attempting to create a new profile based on an existing profile?

4. You notice that only a week's worth of previous files are stored on a computer running Windows 7. How can you increase this so that more than 2 weeks' worth of previous files are available on the computer running Windows 7?

Answers

This section contains the answers to the "Can you answer these questions?" sections in this chapter.

Objective 8.1: Configure backup

1. Startup repair tries to fix startup problems and replace damaged or missing system files.

2. Create a system repair disc using another computer running Windows 7. Use this disc to boot and perform a restore using the existing system image backups.

3. Schedule a system image backup, which enables you to perform a system restore on another computer because they have the same hardware platform.

4. You can configure a once-per-day schedule for system image backups.

Objective 8.2: Configure system recovery options

1. Restart using the installation media or a system repair disc. Perform a system image recovery. This process will remove all existing files on the computer and replace them with files that you know are safe.

2. With LKGC, you can return to the configuration as quickly as possible.

3. Use System Restore to restore system files to an earlier point in time without changing personal files.

4. You should use driver rollback. Because you logged on successfully, using LKGC does not work.

Objective 8.3: Configure file recovery options

1. The user should be able to use previous versions of files to restore the files. When Windows 7 computers are in the default configuration, previous versions of files are created on a regular basis. It is possible to recover previous versions of files for some time after they were deleted, depending on the amount of space dedicated to storing previous versions data.

2. Checkpoint-Computer can be used from an elevated command prompt to force the creation of a restore point to be used with previous versions of files.

3. You should not copy the ntuser.dat, ntuser.dat.log, or ntuser.ini files when attempting to create a new profile based on an existing profile.

4. You can increase the amount of space allocated on each volume to storing previous files data to increase the retention period for previous files.

Index

Symbols

32-bit version of Windows 7
  hardware requirements, 2–3
  Windows Easy Transfer restrictions
    for, 16
64-bit version of Windows 7
  hardware requirements, 2–3
  signed drivers used on, 44
802.1x authentication, 67

A

accelerators, IE, 60
Account Logon policies, 140
Account Management policies, 140
Account Policies, 108
accounts. *See* groups; users
activation
  resetting, 22
  skipping at installation, 4
Active Directory
  for DirectAccess, 131
  for TPM backup, 127
add-ons, IE, 59–60
administrators, 113
  CMAK configured by, 138
  devices uninstalled by, 43
  elevating privileges to, 115–116
  event logs cleared by, 164
  event subscriptions used by, 165
  LoadState tool used by, 17
  offline file availability configured
    by, 134
  prompt behavior for, configuring, 109–
    110
  removable device policies for, 161
  scanning for updates with MBSA, 155
  ScanState tool used by, 17
  Software Restriction Policies not apply-
    ing to, 52
  System Diagnostics reports run by, 166
  UAC configured separately for, 109–110

updates installed by, 149, 152
updates uninstalled by, 154
upgrades to Windows 7 by, 11
user account password reset by, 112
user profiles repaired by, 192
VPN client access configured by, 141
Windows Update configured by, 148,
  151
WSUS groups created by, 150
Advanced Audit Policy Configuration, 108
Aero user interface, disabling, 48
answer files, 27
  applying to system image, 27
  automating image capture, 23
  creating, 27
  deploying system images, 30
anycast address, 75
APIPA address, 66–67, 72
Application Compatibility Toolkit, 50
Application Control Policies. *See* AppLocker
  Policies
applications
  adding to system image, 25–26
  adding updates to system image, 27, 36
  allowing or denying with Windows
    Firewall or WFAS, 84–86
  compatibility of, 47–51
    compatibility mode, 47–49
    Internet Explorer, 50
    Program Compatibility Assistant, 48
    shims, deploying, 49
  installed in Windows XP mode, launch-
    ing from Start menu, 48–49
  processes, priority of, 175–176
  removing from system image, 26
  restrictions for, configuring, 51–56
AppLocker Policies, 53–55, 108
Arp utility, 71
Audit mode
  AppLocker rules for, 55
  booting in, 22
audit policies, advanced, 140–141

About the Author

 Orin Thomas, MCITP, MCT, Microsoft MVP, is an author, consultant, and contributing editor at Windows IT Pro magazine. His first job was supporting Windows 3.11 clients and he's certified on each Windows client operating system since Windows NT 4 Workstation. He regularly speaks at events in Australia and around the world including TechED and Microsoft Management Summit. Orin founded and runs the Melbourne System Center Users Group, and has authored more than 20 books for Microsoft Press including books on Windows Server, Windows Client, Exchange Server, and SQL Server. You can follow him on Twitter at *http://twitter.com/orinthomas*.

What do you think of this book?

We want to hear from you!
To participate in a brief online survey, please visit:

microsoft.com/learning/booksurvey

Tell us how well this book meets your needs—what works effectively, and what we can do better. Your feedback will help us continually improve our books and learning resources for you.

Thank you in advance for your input!